ALSO BY RYAN HANLEY

Beyond Slavery and Abolition: Black British Writing, c. 1770–1830
(Cambridge University Press, 2018)

Britain's History and Memory of Transatlantic Slavery: Local Nuances of a "National Sin," edited with Katie Donington and Jessica Moody
(Liverpool University Press, 2015)

Robert
Wedderburn

BLACK LIVES

———

Yale University Press's Black Lives series seeks to tell the fullest range of stories about notable and overlooked Black figures who profoundly shaped world history. Each book is intended to add a chapter to our larger understanding of the breadth of Black people's experiences as these have unfolded through time. Using a variety of approaches, the books in this series trace the indelible contributions that individuals of African descent have made to their worlds, exploring how their lives embodied and shaped the changing conditions of modernity and challenged definitions of race and practices of racism in their societies.

ADVISORY BOARD

David Blight Henry Louis Gates, Jr. Jacqueline Goldsby
Yale University Harvard University Yale University

Robert Wedderburn

BRITISH INSURRECTIONARY, JAMAICAN ABOLITIONIST

Ryan Hanley

Black Lives

Yale University Press | New Haven and London

The Black Lives series is supported with a gift
from the Germanacos Foundation.
Published with assistance from the Annie Burr Lewis Fund.

Copyright © 2025 by Ryan Hanley.
All rights reserved.
This book may not be reproduced, in whole or in part,
including illustrations, in any form (beyond that copying permitted
by Sections 107 and 108 of the U.S. Copyright Law and except by
reviewers for the public press), without written permission
from the publishers.

Yale University Press books may be purchased in quantity for
educational, business, or promotional use. For information,
please email sales.press@yale.edu (U.S. office) or
sales@yaleup.co.uk (U.K. office).

Set in Freight Text Pro type by Integrated Publishing Solutions
Printed in the United States of America.

Library of Congress Control Number: 2024939341
ISBN 978-0-300-27235-2 (hardcover : alk. paper)

A catalogue record for this book is available from the British Library.

This paper meets the requirements of ANSI/NISO Z39.48-1992
(Permanence of Paper).

10 9 8 7 6 5 4 3 2 1

To Alex, Hannah, Hester, and Richard—in solidarity

CONTENTS

CAST OF CHARACTERS ix
A NOTE ON NAMES xiii

PROLOGUE. My Mother Was a Slave 1

PART I. TESTIMONY

CHAPTER 1. A Troublesome Woman 19
CHAPTER 2. Obeah Witch 38
CHAPTER 3. The Skull Affixed to Temple Bar 55

PART II. ILLEGITIMACY

CHAPTER 4. There Is a Day Coming 73
CHAPTER 5. The Press Is My Engine of Destruction 90
CHAPTER 6. Notorious Firebrand 110

PART III. DESTITUTION

CHAPTER 7. Inside 131
CHAPTER 8. Outside 144
CHAPTER 9. Outsider 161

EPILOGUE. Legacy 181

NOTES 195
ACKNOWLEDGMENTS 215
INDEX 217

CAST OF CHARACTERS

Robert Wedderburn	abolitionist, ultraradical, insurrectionist, author, lecturer, debater, tailor, reputed brothel-keeper, and our protagonist
Amy	(also known as Talkee Amy) Robert's grandmother; market trader, smuggler's agent, and reputed obeah woman
Henry Brougham	(later styled Lord Henry, first Baron Brougham and Vaux) lord chancellor, abolitionist, and advocate for parliamentary reform
George Cannon	(also known as Erasmus Perkins) London radical, author, publisher, pornographer, and Robert's lawyer
Richard Carlile	London radical, journalist, author, atheist, and prisoner at Dorchester Gaol
Andrew Colvile	Slaveholder and colonialist; Robert's paternal half-brother, the legitimate son and heir to James Wedderburn, Sr.
William Davidson	London radical, British-Jamaican insurrectionist, Cato Street conspirator, and would-be

CAST OF CHARACTERS

	assassin, the illegitimate son to a White Jamaican father and free Black mother
Basilia Douglas	Rosanna's onetime "mistress," a distant relation of the Duke of Queensbury
Charles James Sholto Douglas	Customs and excise officer for Kingston, Jamaica, and Rosanna's onetime "master"
William Dugdale	London radical and publisher of obscenity
George Edwards	London radical, government spy, and agent provocateur
Thomas Evans	London radical and de facto leader of the Spencean Philanthropists
Charles Jennison	London radical, Spencean Philanthropist, and co-editor, with Robert, of *The Forlorn Hope*
Anne Knight	(née Thompson) chambermaid and wife to Joseph
Joseph Knight	enslaved footman to John Wedderburn, Jr., litigant in legal freedom case, and husband to Anne
Mary Ann Middleton	London sex worker and Robert's tenant
John (Jack) Mitford	London pornographer and Robert's business partner
Robert Owen	socialist, industrialist, philanthropist, and cotton factory owner
Joseph Payne	Amy's "master," a Kingston smuggler
Phibbah	enslaved woman, nominated "wife" to Thomas Thistlewood in his will

CAST OF CHARACTERS

Rosanna	Robert's mother, an enslaved servant and cook
Thomas Spence	London radical, would-be revolutionary, land reformer, and Robert's mentor
Arthur Thistlewood	London radical, insurrectionist, Cato Street conspirator, would-be assassin, and illegitimate nephew to Thomas Thistlewood
Thomas Thistlewood	slaveholder, serial rapist, sadist, and diarist
Elizabeth Wedderburn	(née Ryan) Robert's first wife, an impoverished Londoner and later a workhouse inmate
James Wedderburn, Jr.	Robert's elder brother, Rosanna and James's son, a formerly enslaved millwright on the Wedderburn estate
James Wedderburn, Sr.	(later styled James Wedderburn-Colvile) Robert's father, a slaveholder, and surgeon to the enslaved
John Wedderburn, Jr.	(later styled Sir John Wedderburn) Robert's uncle, a slaveholder, surgeon to the enslaved, plantation owner, and Joseph Knight's "master"
John Wedderburn, Sr.	Robert's grandfather, a Jacobite insurrectionist executed for treason in 1746
Mary Wedderburn	(née Durham) Robert's second wife, an impoverished Londoner and paper flower seller

A NOTE ON NAMES

NAMES ARE DIFFICULT for a historian of slavery, illegitimacy, and the shadowy criminal underworld of ultra-radicalism. Some of the most important actors in Robert Wedderburn's life are known only by their first names, while others are mentioned in the records only by their surnames, requiring tentative identification. Some surnames were imposed upon enslaved people as a marker of a slaveholder's claim to property in their persons and the persons of their children and descendants, a practice which I naturally do not wish to endorse. At the same time, some of Robert's contacts and family members shared either given names or surnames—or both—with other important people in his life. Then there are pseudonyms, code names, noms de plume, anonymous authorship, collaborative authorship, and amanuenses (scribes), all of which were essential parts of the political world in which Robert operated. I have taken an intuitive rather than completely systematic approach to the use of names in this book, but as a general rule I refer to the most frequently mentioned and important individuals by their first names.

Robert
Wedderburn

PROLOGUE

My Mother Was a Slave

EVENTUALLY, Robert Wedderburn had to be asked to leave. The public debate at the City of London Tavern on August 21, 1817, had been called to discuss a potential solution to an increasingly pressing problem: what could be done to relieve Britain's distressed poor? Wages were in free fall in the imperial metropolis. In the great manufacturing centers in Glasgow, Manchester, Birmingham, Sheffield, and especially in London, the streets seemed to be overflowing with homeless veterans and starving orphans. It had been this way since the end of the war: the widely celebrated victory over Napoleonic France, just a few years prior, had come at a steep economic, as well as human, cost. The poor, as always, bore the brunt of both.

The hearts of the well-off bled for them. One of the gentlemanly committees set up to deal with the "pauper problem," the Association for the Relief of the Manufacturing and Labouring Poor, exasperated by their lack of progress, had approached the famous philanthropist and cotton factory owner Robert Owen for help. Owen was widely celebrated for the way he looked after his workers at the village of New Lanark in Scotland, supplying them with quality food and housing, limiting working hours, and taking a special interest in the moral education and welfare of the children. The results spoke for themselves: every gentleman who visited New Lanark remarked on the happiness, sobriety, and good manners of the workers and their families—and with a happy and thus efficient workforce, the financial returns were fantastic. Perhaps, reasoned the Association, Owen was the man to clear Britain's streets of its indigent subjects.

Amid much public anticipation, Owen presented his preliminary report and plan in early April 1817. There were three immediate causes for the miseries of the poor, he contended. First, new technology was rendering many workers in traditional trades obsolete. After all, "mechanical power was much cheaper than human labour." Second, now that the war was over, there was far less need for manpower. Britain's empire had become so vast that, at least in peacetime, there was not enough demand anywhere to support the fruits of all that labor. As Owen put it, "the revenues of the world were inadequate to purchase that which a power so enormous in its effects did produce."

Of course, Owen knew all about the products of imperial labor. He had been importing cotton grown by enslaved laborers for decades, and two years previously he had worked with the slaveholder and member of Parliament Edward Lascelles to lobby for a reduction in the import taxes. Celebrated even today as "the father of British socialism" for his progressive views on labor conditions, Owen was a far more conventional industrialist when it came to his connections to global racial capitalism. He was equally conventional in his moral assessment of the effects of poverty. Indeed, he argued that the third and largest challenge facing the poor in Britain was not only that they were "left in gross ignorance" but that they were "permitted to be trained up in habits of vice, and in the commission of crimes" and "perpetually surrounded with temptations which cannot fail to produce all those effects." The modern city was not only destroying their bodies and minds; it was also destroying their souls.[1]

Owen's plan to rescue the poor was, in effect, to round them up and send them to work on plantations. He proposed constructing hundreds of small settlements of about twelve hundred people each in the British countryside, combining large farms, factories, dormitories, and schools. The urban unemployed would be whisked away and engaged in wholesome, highly disciplined labor in the country, rendering them economically productive and removing them from the temptations of the big cities. Children would be educated on-site, to prevent the contagion of vice being passed from one generation to another. Discipline in both labor and morality would be maintained by paid "superintendents." Profits would accrue to the landholder, whether that was the local parish, a district, or the national government. Private landlords were also encouraged to try the experiment. In early nineteenth-century England, "doing well by doing good" combined two of the most important national virtues. In some detail, Owen calculated that the average cost for this plan would only be around £4 per worker—and, he added, that outlay could be recovered easily enough by simply withholding wages until each worker's debt was paid. The plan proved controversial, to say the least, and many of London's reformist and radical leaders showed up to speak against it when it was presented for the public debate on August 21st.

Robert Wedderburn was the most outspoken and impolite of them all. He interrupted Owen's introductory lecture several times, shouting loudly from the back of the packed room. When Owen's ally Mr. Barber stood to speak in support of the plan, Robert had himself lifted onto his friends' shoulders and tried to shout him down. With some difficulty, Robert was eventually pushed out of the room so the speeches could continue, but "even there," as one journalist reported, "he made so much noise, as to disturb the Meeting considerably." He got back inside, forced his way to the front of the room, and continued to make a nuisance of himself until he was finally allowed to say his piece. He climbed up onto the speakers' table and addressed the crowd. The journalist's account continues: "He begged to be heard for only 10 minutes. To get rid of him in some way this was agreed to. He then said that his name was Robert Wedderburn, that he was the son of James Wedderburn, Esq., of Jamaica, by Rosanna, his slave. He described, in strong terms, the horrors of slavery, and contended that the present plan would be a refined species of slavery, It would destroy the independent spirit of freemen."[2]

For some of the more respectable reformers in the room, Robert cut quite an alarming figure. He was a broad-shouldered man with a "lusty" physique, about five feet five inches tall. He was most frequently described by White reporters and officials as being "a man of colour" and sometimes as having a "very dark" complexion. Although he was a skilled artisan—a journeyman tailor—with his own business, he was struggling to make ends meet in the postwar recession, and on this particular evening his own outfit was a little the worse for wear. "When on the table," the *Suffolk Chronicle* reported, "he was without shoes, and his stockings, if such they might be called, but ill-concealed his brawney legs and feet." Robert had picked up a couple of noticeable scars: one across the bridge of his nose and another on the left side of his forehead—souvenirs perhaps, from a street brawl back in October 1809.[3]

But scars from fighting were not unusual sights in London political meetings, and neither for that matter were men of color. Robert was just one of thousands of Black men, many of them survivors of slavery in the Americas, who had settled in London following service in the British military. It was his style of address, more than his appearance, that made him remarkable. Having limited literacy and no spare cash to waste on fripperies like notepaper, Robert made it a point of honor that he always spoke on the spur of the moment and very much from the heart. At Owen's meeting, such was his intensity that he "considerably alarmed several of the Ladies who sat near, and the impression was that the man was insane."[4]

As someone who had always resisted the allure of "respectability" that drew in many of his radical associates, he would have been thrilled to hear he'd made such an impression. Born into slavery in Jamaica around 1762 and emancipated at a very young age, Robert was proud to have inherited his "rebellious and violent temper" from Rosanna, his enslaved mother. He was raised in Kingston by his grandmother, an enslaved market trader and reputed obeah woman known as Talkee Amy, who further reinforced in him a disdain for established authority. These two women, Rosanna and Amy, were his greatest intellectual and moral influences, and he reiterated his debt to them throughout his writing and debating career, right into his seventies. After migrating to London around the age of sixteen, he spent some time with a good Christian family, but he soon went off the rails, living among "a set of abandoned reprobates" for several years. He fell for a cockney girl named Elizabeth Ryan, and they married in 1781. They started a family together while Robert learned his trade and served a couple of stints in the Royal Navy, but they separated by 1795. In 1816 he was married again, to a woman named Mary, and they raised four children, scraping by on his meager wages and what the children could make selling paper flowers on the street. Robert lived an exceedingly difficult life in the capital, dogged by poverty and the constant threat of criminal prosecution. Despite these challenges, it was clear that he possessed a rare intellect, and he had somehow managed to publish a short theological pamphlet around the turn of the nineteenth century.[5]

By the time of Owen's meeting at the City of London Tavern, Robert had conjoined his lifelong hatred for slavery—and the "respectable" White supremacist British establishment it supported—to an abiding concern for the rights of the poor in Britain. Since around 1813, he had followed the ideas of Thomas Spence, a reformer who advocated for common ownership of the land and the overthrow of all landlords. This kind of talk was of course deeply disturbing to the authorities, and much of what we know about Robert's political activities during this period comes to us through Home Office informers, paid to infiltrate and keep tabs on London's increasingly brazen revolutionary factions. By the beginning of 1817, Robert had been singled out by these spies as an especially dangerous and subversive figure. One of them had noted on January 15th that Robert had been spotted at the Cock tavern on Grafton Street—a far rougher pub than the City of London—where he had opened a radical debate "in his usual inflammatory stile," giving "additional proof of his infidelity" by proclaiming that "we were all born in the same way and must all perish alike, we were but animals."[6]

This kind of radical language, tinged with skepticism of both Christian doctrine and the established social hierarchy, marked Robert out as occupying the more extreme fringes of Britain's working-class reform movement. His intervention at Owen's meeting in August, however, seems to have elevated him to wider notice than before—both among radicals and with the government spies. Robert's short speech that night was widely reported in the major London newspapers, with the *Morning Post* describing this "Gentleman of colour" as one of the two speakers "who attracted most notice, and were most successful in exciting the risibility of the crowd" against Owen's glorified work-camps idea. The famous

PROLOGUE

Figure 1. Detail from George Cruikshank, "A Peep into the City of London Tavern [. . .] Or, a Sample of the Co-Operation to be expected in one of Mr. Owen's Projected Paradises," monochrome engraving, 1817. Robert is depicted with a clenched fist, haranguing Owen while a lady nearby flinches from him.
© The Trustees of the British Museum

satirist George Cruikshank later immortalized the meeting in an engraving, depicting Robert prominently—and with more than a hint of racist caricature—as he stepped up onto the table and declared, "I understand slavery well!—my mother was a slave" (fig. 1). If before this meeting only a handful of the radicals present had heard of Robert Wedderburn, the firebrand son of an enslaved woman from Jamaica, they all certainly knew about him now.[7]

| 7 |

This moment represented a waypoint in Robert's life. Behind him lay the horrors of the plantation; ahead lay a turbulent career as one of the most charismatic and distinctively radical political voices of the nineteenth century. In so many ways, his life and work challenge what we think we know about the character of British abolitionism. When we think of the leaders of the antislavery movement, we generally conjure images of serious, reputable, well-connected men and women, collecting signatures for petitions to Parliament and evangelizing about slavery as a "national sin." Up to the mid-twentieth century, the dominant story told by historians was one in which elite, White, well-to-do evangelicals inspired a national moral awakening and led a grand, democratic victory over the slaveholders to secure freedom on behalf of the enslaved. This interpretation has long fallen out of favor with most academics, but it continues to enable a great deal of complaisant self-congratulation in populist accounts of British history—handily obscuring the nation's much longer role in slavery itself in the process.[8]

Partly because they give the lie to this kind of narrative, enslaved and formerly enslaved people like Robert have only been properly acknowledged as key actors in the British antislavery movement more recently. Since the 1970s, historians and literary critics alike have worked to accord Black writing its proper place in both antislavery and British history more generally. But even as we reevaluated the abolitionist achievements of those born into the brutalizing system of slavery, politeness—that cardinal British virtue—continued to wield great influence over whose stories we tended to focus on. For most, Olaudah Equiano (known in his daily life as Gustavus Vassa) remains the archetypical Black British abolitionist: steadfast, enterprising, devoutly Christian—a reformer with unshakeable moral purpose, but above all a self-consciously respectable intellectual. Indeed, it was these qualities that allowed him to be taken seriously by establishment liberals at the time, despite his association with several prominent radicals. Such has been the impact of Equiano and his powerful account of slavery, *The Interesting Narrative*, that we still tend to read *all* Black British writers of this period in comparison to him and his very effective way of expressing his political views.[9]

Yet while he shared many of the same values as Equiano, Robert presented himself very differently. He emphatically did not care what establishment figures—liberal or conservative—thought of him. In fact, he derived great joy from deliberately alienating those who were invested in the idea of social respectability. He denounced slaveholders and all their enablers, whether in Parliament, the Church, or the ranks of the landed elite, without fear—and indeed without much thought to the consequences. Unlike almost all his abolitionist peers, he did not see freedom as something that should be bestowed on the enslaved. He believed it had to be taken. He was among the first and only British political figures of the nineteenth century to publicly call for enslaved people in the Caribbean to rise up and claim their liberty, by force of arms if that was what it took. At the same time, he was no less outspoken an advocate for the poor in Britain, whose struggles he saw as part of the same grand contest against those in power.

Historians have long been fascinated by the question of how—or even whether—the apparently socially conservative abolition movement found support among rowdy, urban working-class populations, especially during periods of sharp economic deprivation. By following Robert's eventful life, from the plantations of the Caribbean to the back-alley pubs and brothels of London, we can glimpse a different side to the intertwined stories of how slavery was abolished and how political rights were won for working people in Britain.[10]

Robert's work not only encapsulates a neglected aspect of

popular politics in imperial Britain but also gives a flavor of the distinctively working-class, transgressive humor that allowed it to spread, even in an era of government suppression. He often used his mastery of Christian scripture to mock the hypocrisy of the powerful. At a boisterous, packed meeting in October 1819, for example, he denounced the government and clergy's joint efforts to quell rising discontent among the poor: "they tell us to be quiet like that *bloody spooney Jesus Christ* who like a *Bloody Fool* tells us when we get a slap on one side of the Face turn gently round and ask them to smack the other—But I like jolly old Peter give me a Rusty Sword." Many in the audience, including the spies that the Home Office had sent to inform on him, were shocked by the blasphemous language. Others, though, recalling that the apostle Peter cut off the ear of one of the men sent to arrest Jesus, laughed at his audacity. It is this quality—his characteristic ability to leaven rage with wit, to mix horror and optimism, and to link "over there" to "right here" in his politics—that makes him such a compelling and important figure in the history of slavery and abolition.[11]

Robert's ability to reconcile apparently opposite demands was a product of both the churning political and social currents of his day and his own complex character. As we will see, his ambiguous feelings about family and kinship suffused many of his seemingly contradictory impulses, reflecting the fact that different members of his family were responsible for enslaving his body and for liberating his mind. As an adult, his political views were shaped as much by the callous condescension of the British class system as by the invigorating prospect of solidarity between Black and White laborers across the Atlantic. He lived precariously on the margins of London society, always under the shadow of destitution and abandonment, and yet he is rightly remembered by historians as the "linchpin" of British working-class antislavery thought, linking the intellectual worlds of disreputable, impoverished radicals and evangelical abolitionists. Yet, for all his significance, he remained in many ways an outsider, even in the ultraradical world he helped build. As we will see, his marginal status as a man of color in nineteenth-century London acted as a potent catalyst for his eventual descent into extreme poverty and violent criminality.[12]

Robert was a man in equal parts inspiring and troubling, optimistic and cynical, radical and reactionary. He was resigned to being a product of his time, but he also aspired to become an architect of a better future. This is a biography of a unique and significant, if underappreciated, Black British leader, and it is also a story about the roiling and sometimes contradictory world that both made and broke him.

His speech at the City of London Tavern was the first time, as far as we know, that Robert spoke publicly about his enslaved mother or the issue of colonial slavery. He was not the only working-class radical to invoke the specter of enslavement as a possible fate for the British working classes: by this time, "let's die like men, and not be sold like slaves" had become one of the unofficial mottos of the reform movement. (In fact, it was soon to become the *official* motto on the masthead of one radical periodical, *The Medusa*.) Most of the time, when reformers talked about "slavery," they were trafficking in metaphor, usually to prove a point about the treatment of the poor or to note the powerlessness they faced in an unreformed political system that denied them the vote. Robert, however, had a different perspective, for he had lived through the real thing.[13]

There is good reason to think that his mother might have been on Robert's mind more than usual that summer. Enslaved mothers had frequently been in the news at the time. There had been a well-publicized libel case against the abolitionist organization the African Institution, surrounding its accusation that an aide to the governor of Antigua had "severely cart-whipped a negro woman of his own, who was pregnant." In July, during a debate over a proposed Slave Registry Bill, the House of Commons had heard shocking accounts from Dominica of "the beating of a female slave in a state of pregnancy so cruelly that her arm was broken." There was nothing new about this sort of report. As far back as 1790, a parliamentary select committee had heard about pregnant women being chained naked to stakes in the ground and whipped, including the chilling detail that "when they were so far advanced in pregnancy, that the size of the belly prevented them from being stretched flat upon the ground, ... a hole has been sometimes dug to receive the belly." Robert knew this practice. As a young child, he had witnessed this very outrage committed on his mother's body, "at the time when she was far advanced in pregnancy." It was a core trauma for him; it changed his life.[14]

Robert's public disclosure at Owen's meeting marked the beginning of the most important phase of his career, when he began to draw on his own family's experiences of enslavement in Jamaica in his political work. He began now to argue, in extraordinarily powerful terms, not only for the immediate and total abolition of colonial slavery by any means necessary but for a broader awakening, a recognition of the rot at the heart of the British Empire. Whereas many of his radical peers in London focused on the superficial similarities between their situation and that of the enslaved in the West Indies, Robert saw that they were two structurally connected forms of exploitation: two parts of a global machine designed to keep men like him, and women like his mother and grandmother, under the heel of the immoral and hypocritical landed elite, the landlords and slaveholders.

After Owen's meeting, Robert seemed to be overtaken by the need to bear witness to the atrocities he had seen inflicted on his family and to attest to the way that same global system of exploitation continued to haunt him and those he loved. Six weeks later,

PROLOGUE

he commenced publication of *The "Forlorn Hope," or a Call to the Supine*, a new weekly periodical he co-edited with his friend and fellow reformer Charles Jennison. In its pages, Robert again attacked Owen for "making the people out fools," and, in another article, he more firmly connected his family's experiences under slavery to the corruption of the British government. "Why," he demanded, "are my relations held as slaves, who never forfeited their right of protection by a committal of crimes?" The very injustice and tyranny of slavery, he believed, invalidated the British government's claim to legitimacy and called for disobedience and violent retribution. If we would celebrate the Christian who slaughtered his enslaver for his freedom, he wrote, "how should I feel if my relatives, who are slaves to the Christians, should perform similar deeds? Furthermore, should the receivers and stealers of Africans become rich, and buy one of those seats in the House of Commons, which is sold at noon-day, ought they to be called the representative of a free people? ought they to be obeyed, when there is an opportunity to oppose with success?"

A few weeks later, Robert wrote again about his family origins. Just as he had at Owen's meeting, he now introduced himself squarely in relation to his mother and the injustice of colonial slavery:

> Be it known to the world, that, I Robert Wedderburn, son of James Wedderburn, esq. of Inveresk, near Musselborough, by Rosannah his slave, whom he sold to James Charles Shalto Douglas, esq. in the parish of St. Mary, in the island of Jamaica, while pregnant with the said Wedderburn, who was not held as a slave, (a provision being made in the agreement, that the child when born should be free.) This Wedderburn, doth charge all potentates, governors, and governments of every description with felony, who does wickedly violate the sacred rights of man—by force of arms, or otherwise, seizing the persons of

men and dragging them from their native country, and selling their stolen persons and generations.[15]

From here, Robert moved impatiently through his family background, his account tripping over itself grammatically in its desire to set each sordid detail straight. His condemnation of the global injustice of slavery itself, his bold accusation of "governments of every description" of "felony" for their part in it—these emerged directly from his reflections on what had happened to the brilliant, difficult, troublesome women who raised him. "Oh, ye Africans and relatives now in bondage to the Christians, because you are innocent and poor," he wrote, "receive this the only tribute the offspring of an African can give."[16]

Outrage at how his mother and grandmother were treated by men claiming the "legitimate" authority of ownership was a topic he returned to again and again throughout the rest of his life. In his 1817 speeches and periodicals; in a series of public lectures and debates in 1819; in his trials for seditious blasphemy in 1820; in an exposé of his father's misdeeds published in a national newspaper in 1823; in an antislavery memoir of their lives published in 1824; and in his final text, published in 1831, four years before his death—in all of these settings, he wrote of his mother's and grandmother's experiences and their responses to the impossible "predicament" of enslavement.[17]

It was not only disgust at the violence he had witnessed against his family that motivated Robert, nor was he solely concerned with the connections between the exploitation of the powerless in Britain and Jamaica—though these were both key facets of his worldview. What was most important for his political work was bearing witness—not just to the atrocities themselves but also to the possibility that those with seemingly no power at all could bloody the noses of the men in charge. If there was any common impulse to all of his antislavery work, it was to testify to the strength and to celebrate the defiance of his "afflicted countrymen and relatives still in bondage." He began with his first models for rebellion. He needed people to know about Rosanna and Amy.

PART I

Testimony

CHAPTER 1

A Troublesome Woman

There was often something pornographic about how violence against enslaved women was represented by the British press. The cheapest sort of print culture—the sort people like Robert could afford—was especially exploitative. Take, for example, the illustration accompanying the fourpenny pamphlet *Barbarity to a Female Slave! Authentic Particulars of the Inhuman Cruelty of Jacobus Overeem to America, his Female Slave* (1818), published by John Fairburn a year after Wedderburn disrupted the meeting with Owen (fig. 2). In this illustration, America, the woman who had been tortured, is depicted naked and spread-eagled, facedown and chained to four stakes in the ground. No hole has been dug; her pregnant belly pushes her exposed backside up, toward the leering figure of the overseer, who is clad in a white suit and smoking a long pipe. She looks over her shoulder and directly up at him. Absurdly, she is wearing what looks like a string of pearls around her neck. Two bare-chested, hypermasculine Black men stand over her, miserably undertaking the whipping that has been ordered. The colors are watery, but lurid; the ground is a livid shade of peach, and the blue-green brushstrokes

Figure 2. Details from "INHUMAN CRUELTY to an INNOCENT FEMALE SLAVE, while in a State of Pregnancy," hand-colored engraving on paper, in *Barbarity to a Female Slave! Authentic Particulars of the Inhuman Cruelty of Jacobus Overeem to America, his Female Slave* (London: John Fairburn, [1818])

delineating the bushes and trees in the background splash haphazardly over a crowd of enslaved onlookers, painting them decisively out of the theater of action. The sheer cheapness of the artwork, the lack of care in its production, and the framing of the scene all make this an especially sleazy representation of the horrors of slavery, even in a genre now infamous for its eroticization of violence. We can only guess what Fairburn expected his customers would want to *do* with such an image once they'd bought it.[1]

Robert would not have liked this engraving. While he knew from experience that the scene itself was all too real, he would not have believed what it was trying to say about the woman in the picture. America is not a person in this image, not really; she is just a vector for suffering, a means to provoke the gratifying thrill of sympathy—and perhaps a guilty sort of sexual titillation—in a near-exclusively White readership. The image substitutes one species of dehumanization for another. As Marisa Fuentes explains in her brilliant study of enslaved women in the colonial archive, *Dispossessed Lives*, scenes like this one are "spectacular and sexualized by the male witnesses, in part because the violence exceeds our ability to reach the enslaved female subjects beyond their terror." Viewers of Fairburn's engraving were never invited to see America as a real person with real suffering, only as a spectacle of violence and horror. Yet for so many enslaved women, such depictions are the only trace of them that remains in the historical record—aside, perhaps, from an enslaver's ledger, a record of sale, or a note of legal punishment. As Saidiya Hartman once put it, "how does one recuperate lives entangled with and impossible to differentiate from the terrible utterances that condemned them to death, the account books that identified them as units of value, the invoices that claimed them as property, and the banal chronicles that stripped them of human features?"[2]

The best response may not be to see this as a "problem" that can be solved but as a core part of the story itself. Black feminist scholars, including Fuentes, Hartman, Jennifer Morgan, and Stephanie Smallwood have in recent years undertaken the crucial work of confronting the limits of the traditional archive, considering if and how it might be possible to glimpse the complex personhood of enslaved women in the records that colonialists and abolitionists have bequeathed to us—records that document the denial of that same personhood. If we as historians must depend on sources that are profoundly hostile to enslaved women, we should at least recognize the sly and perverse nature of that hostility. At the same time, we also know that, even amid enslavement, Black women made their own records. These might not wear the same mantle of state legitimation that colonial archives do, but they can offer us far less mediated connections to their lived experiences. Several historians have explored how family stories—of survival, of everyday life, and of resistance—were passed down orally through generations of enslaved people and their descendants, forming an essential counternarrative to hostile "official" records of slavery. These insurgent narratives were kept alive and recorded for posterity by children as honoring acts—acts of love.[3]

We might understand Robert's invocation of his mother in the same way, as an insurgent narrative of love and survival, as much as a record of her pain. He began to write about his mother in earnest in his periodical *The Axe Laid to the Root*, around November 1817. Although he dealt with an ostensibly similar form of outrageous violence, his account was fundamentally different in character from the two-dimensional image of Black female victimhood provided by hack publishers like Fairburn. "My heart glows with revenge, and I cannot forgive," he wrote. "O Boswell, ought not your colour and countrymen to be visited with wrath, for flogging my mother before my face, at the time when she was far advanced in pregnancy. What was her crime? did not you give her leave to visit her aged mother; (she did not acquaint her mistress at her departure,) this was her fault. But it originated in your crime in holding her as a slave—could not you wait till she returned, but travel 15 miles to punish her on that visit." Notice that Robert made no attempt to apologize for his mother's "fault" in breaking the rules. Indeed, Rosanna appears here not as the inarticulate, violated victim we see in Fairburn's illustration, but as a person who makes decisions—decisions that embroil her unjustly in a complex negotiation over the limits of her freedom. The very messiness of Robert's account, with its syntax splintering in the middle, hints at the possibility of another kind of narrative—one with the potential to move beyond making a spectacle of enslaved women's suffering for sympathetic metropolitan readers.[4]

Taken together, Robert's writings about his family form a kind of radical counter-archive: a sort of rebuke to both colonialist and abolitionist records. Beginning with *The Axe Laid to the Root*, but developed most fully in his narrative *The Horrors of Slavery* (1824), he reconstructed an alternative history not just of himself but of the women who raised and protected him in the midst of their own enslavement. The difference between these counter-archival accounts and most other forms of historical record-keeping about enslaved women's lives in the eighteenth-century Caribbean is that the women being represented here had actually played a part in putting together the archive itself. *The Horrors of Slavery* was not an autobiography, though it is still, even now, often mistaken for one. It actually contains very little information about Robert himself, because most of the events it describes took place before he was even born. Even though many of the basic facts in Robert's accounts can be verified against colonial records in terms of detail, they are nevertheless, at least in part, transcriptions—or rather *translations*—of stories he was told by Rosanna and Amy. The consistency with which he was able to repeat certain events and details from their lives when he was not himself a witness indicates that these were shared family stories, reinforced in his memory by repeated retellings from the women who raised him.[5]

Robert's radical counter-archive is our starting point in an exploration of Rosanna's and Amy's experiences in Jamaica during the 1760s and 1770s. Robert's writing gets us one step closer to hearing these enslaved women's stories from their own perspective. We should not get too carried away, though: what we know of Rosanna's and Amy's experiences still comes to us secondhand, through a male interlocutor. Just like more traditional archives, Robert's accounts are themselves a form of knowledge production, an attempt to fix memory and lived experiences in a particular shape, to ascribe actions a particular meaning, and they were produced for quite specific, historically defined purposes. Nevertheless, what Robert wrote down provides us with a rare opportunity to begin not with silence or isolated moments of violence but with presence, defiance, individuality, and the arc of each woman's life.

Robert's mother and grandmother appear in his accounts as anything but passive. But neither are they shown to be heroic leaders of collective armed resistance or assassins poisoning slaveowners, though such women certainly did exist. Rosanna and Amy appear as complex, unafraid, and frankly rather difficult women, who never conceded an iota of their personhood to the predicament of their enslavement. Sometimes they were willing to compromise to attain their goals, though more often—in Robert's accounts at least—they were willfully obstructive of slaveholders' desires, even to the point of confrontation. Their stubbornness and obstinacy, and the stories they told about themselves, were inspirational sources of strength to their young charge throughout his life, allowing him to imagine himself as an heir to their rebellious tempers.[6]

Robert was quite clear about his motivations for recording what happened to his mother and grandmother from their perspective. As he wrote at the beginning of *The Horrors of Slavery*, "I deem it an act of justice to myself, to my children, and to the memory of my mother, to say what I am, and who were the authors of my existence."[7]

There were many types of work undertaken by enslaved people on a Jamaican estate, and some jobs were better than others. On sugar plantations—by far the commonest type of plantation on the island—the vast majority worked in the cane fields. The strongest men and women were assigned to the First Gang, tasked with digging out cane holes or harvesting the tough canes with machetes. It was backbreaking work. By their mid-thirties, most had been demoted to the Second Gang, lifting and carrying the cut canes or else working in the dreaded sugar mill or the boiling house, where grisly accidents were commonplace. The Third Gang was reserved for those with the least physical strength to be exploited: the injured and disabled, the elderly, and the children, who were in charge of clearing weeds and keeping the work site tidy. Enslaved people also undertook highly skilled work such as carpentry, animal husbandry, and haberdashery, work that permitted marginally better living conditions. There was also a great demand for "inside work." West India planters were used to ostentatious luxury, and most maintained an extensive domestic staff to support their lifestyle and status. This kind of job was ostensibly more desirable: enslaved domestic servants generally lived in the house, received better food, and performed work that was physically less harmful, at least most of the time. Nonetheless, there could be other dangers, especially for enslaved women, which made domestic work just as dreadful as toiling in the cane fields.

When Robert's parents first met in the late 1750s, Rosanna was working for Basilia Douglas at the Grange estate in Hanover parish, in northwest Jamaica. A "distant relation of the Duke of Queensbury," Lady Douglas was not herself a major member of the British landed gentry, but her wealth and access to power (via her husband, Charles, the customs officer for Kingston and a member of the island's parliament, the colonial assembly) meant that she was very much a member of the plantocratic social elite. Rosanna was a lady in waiting, a relatively senior position among the household staff at the Grange, and Robert tells us she "had received an education which perfectly qualified her to conduct a household in the most agreeable manner." Rosanna's day-to-day routine would have consisted of chores such as laundry, cleaning, and cooking, as well as assisting Lady Douglas at her toilette, for example, helping her to dress in the mornings and styling her hair.[8]

There was an aspect of emotional labor to this kind of work. Women in Rosanna's position were often educated from early childhood to take care of the lady of the house, and part of their role could be to provide companionship and conversation for White women. The delegation of caring and emotional labor to the enslaved meant that women like Lady Douglas were required to place a great degree of trust in women like Rosanna. For instance, enslaved maids were often involved in caring for and even wet-nursing their mistresses' children. The Jamaican slaveholder and historian Edward Long fulminated against this practice, describing it as a "shameful and savage custom" that "Creole ladies . . . disdaining to suckle their own helpless offspring! they give them up to a Negroe or Mulatto wet nurse, without reflecting that her blood may be corrupted, or considering the influence which the milk may have with respect to the disposition, as well as health, of their little ones." Such racist and misogynist pomposity could only poorly obscure the profound unease that many slaveholders felt over the depth of trust placed in enslaved women by their White "Creole" mistresses.[9]

Lady Douglas demonstrated her affection for Rosanna by agreeing to stand as godmother for Robert when he was baptized, and, as he put it, "as long as she lived, never deserted me." It is difficult to gauge how Rosanna felt about Lady Douglas, but as we will see, there was a time when she at the very least saw her as capable of providing a refuge from the sexual violence of subsequent male enslavers. This bond of trust, a "tense and tender tie" of empire, forged in the intimacies of the colonial home, meant greater chances of survival for Rosanna. As Lady Douglas's maid, she would also have enjoyed a slightly broader degree of latitude in her movement through the house and in deciding her own work schedule, compared to other enslaved domestic laborers. Rosanna would also have been well informed on Jamaican current affairs and politics through her close proximity to Charles and his frequent high-status visitors to the Grange estate. In 1758, one of these visitors, Dr. James Wedderburn, noticed Rosanna as she served the tea. He soon made an offer to purchase her from Lady Douglas.[10]

James and his elder brother John had settled in the neighboring parish of Westmoreland in the late 1740s. They were likely known to the Douglases through their work in the area as physicians and "man-midwifes" to the enslaved. Eighteenth-century medicine was a grim business in the most skilled of hands, and these two brothers had taken up their practice in Jamaica with neither qualifications nor experience. Not that this mattered much to planters; as Robert put it bitterly in 1824, his father "turned an honest penny by drugging and physicing the poor blacks, where those that were cured, he had the credit for, and those he killed, the fault was laid to their own obstinacy." By the time he came into contact with Rosanna, James was already well known as a serial rapist of enslaved women, though of course no one called it that until Robert wrote about it decades later. "My father ranged through the whole of his household for his own lewd purposes"; he kept "a *Seraglio of Black Slaves,* miserable objects of an abandoned lust, guided by avarice." This was the situation into which James sought to bring Rosanna. His motives seemed self-explanatory.[11]

However, the position of confidence that Rosanna had carved out for herself with Lady Douglas presented an impediment to James's "brutal lust": "His character was well known; and therefore he was obliged to go *covertly* and *falsely* to work. In Jamaica, slaves that are esteemed by their owners have generally the power of refusal, whether they will be sold to a particular planter, or not; and my father was aware, that if *he* offered to purchase her, he would meet with a refusal." It is extremely difficult to verify this claim by recourse to the traditional archive. On the one hand, enslaved people had no legislative protections regarding to whom they could and could not be sold. As long as Lady Douglas and James both agreed to the sale, Rosanna would have no legal basis to challenge it. On the other hand, Rosanna had lived with and served Lady Douglas for a long time, and there was clearly some kind of bond between them. It was entirely possible that Rosanna's strong objection to being sold, especially on the grounds that her chastity might be threatened, would be respected. In this instance, Robert's account suggests that Rosanna was able to leverage her personal accomplishments, professional skills, and intimate connections with her mistress in an attempt to protect herself from the threat of sexual violence.[12]

Nevertheless, James was "determined to have possession of her," and he employed one of his contacts, Dr. Cruikshank, to negotiate the purchase of Rosanna from Lady Douglas, pretending to act on behalf of another client. Only after the sale was finalized around 1759 did Rosanna discover that she would be taken to James's "seraglio" in Westmoreland. This underhandedness, as much as the subsequent violence itself, stuck with Rosanna, and it became the originating narrative in a shared family history that she passed down to Robert and his siblings—the beginnings of their counter-archive. As Robert recalled in 1824, "I have often heard my mother express her indignation at this base and treacherous conduct of my father—a treachery the more base, as it was so calm and premeditated."[13]

What kind of life awaited Rosanna at James's house? The sexual exploitation of enslaved women was endemic in eighteenth-century Jamaica, and clearly rape was a prime motivating factor in James's desire to purchase her. But Robert's narrative suggests that his father was also looking for something more than sex from Rosanna. It was not uncommon for West Indian planters to take on an enslaved "mistress," who would be favored over others in exchange for a facsimile of sexual consent, the performance of emotional reciprocity, and domestic companionship. Some enslaved women were willing to enter into these grotesque pastiches of "relationships" on the understanding that they would retain a small degree of autonomy over their bodies and gain certain allowances for themselves and any children they might bear, including the prospect of eventual manumission. Light-skinned "mulatto" women, especially those like Rosanna trained in domestic service and companionship roles, were especially valued as sexual and emotional partners by White planters. Given what Robert described as Rosanna's "chaste and virtuous" character, James might have seen her as a potentially good candidate for this kind of arrangement.[14]

James certainly knew how this type of relationship worked. He was the physician and midwife for the nearby Egypt plantation, owned by his friend Thomas Thistlewood, a notorious sadist and sexual predator. Alongside his assaults on multiple enslaved women, Thistlewood maintained a quasi-consensual relationship with a favorite named Phibbah for over thirty-four years. His diaries—chillingly detached logs detailing hundreds of sexual assaults and degrading tortures, alongside notes about the weather and business appointments—reveal that Phibbah did retain some personal autonomy as a result of this arrangement. She was occasionally able to withhold sexual consent from him and felt confident in doing so in no uncertain terms. On August 31, 1759, for example, Thistlewood noted in his diary with some vexation that "Phibbah got away, very sawcy and impudent." These occasional refusals notwithstanding, he clearly felt that his deep affection for this woman was reciprocated. In his will, Thistlewood named Phibbah as his "wife," and he always acknowledged their son, Mulatto John, seeing to it that he was freed. As the doctor for Thistlewood's plantation, James played an important role in this perverse family setup. On April 29, 1760, the day Mulatto John was born, Thistlewood returned home from buying flowers for Phibbah to find he had received a letter "from Dr. James Wedderburn, with a purge, ingredients for a poultice, and some salve" to help with the symptoms of his raging syphilis. That evening, James even made a house call at the Egypt plantation to check up on mother, father, and baby.[15]

Perhaps seeing Thistlewood and Phibbah together gave James the idea to procure a well-educated and light-skinned enslaved woman to serve as his "wife." There were, in the event, some important parallels between the sordid family arrangement at Egypt and the one eventually wrought between James, Rosanna, and their sons. But if James was hoping that Rosanna would warm to him once he got her under his roof, he was sorely mistaken. The sneaky way he had contrived to take her from the relative stability of Lady Douglas's household, as much as his bad reputation, turned her permanently against him. No matter how much he wished for her to perform consent or affection—to play along as his willing concubine—she was determined to make his life as difficult as she possibly could.

Reader, she fought him.

Rosanna was initially placed in charge of "the direction and management" of James's house. This new situation meant that, even as he sought to prey upon her, James was now dependent on Rosanna complying with his demands for emotional support, or at least adhering to a basic standard of personal agreeableness, if he wanted a pleasant home life. On the contrary, Rosanna seems to have been unwilling to hide her disgust with James. From the beginning she was extremely uncooperative. In fact, she caused such constant trouble that even James's White, Scottish children, who had never even met her, heard all about her unruly disposition decades after she had left the estate. Robert's half-brother Andrew Colvile recalled in March 1824 that "this woman had so violent a temper that she was continually quarrelling with the other servants, and occasioning a disturbance in the house." Robert responded to this in his characteristic style: "yes, and I glory in her *rebellious* disposition, and which I have inherited from her."[16]

Robert suggested that the other enslaved women in James's house, "all objects of his lusts," resented Rosanna for being placed in such a senior position and possibly for creating such a fractious atmosphere. Despite her struggle, in such an environment Rosanna could not protect herself for long, and she was pregnant by April 1759. Yet far from making her resigned to her situation this development appears to have hardened her resistance to James's advances, and his resolve to extract affection from her appears to have faltered slightly at this point. Perhaps he was scared of pushing her too far. It was rare, but enslaved domestic servants had been known to poison slaveholders. In February 1816, the novelist and planter Matthew "Monk" Lewis witnessed the trial of a fifteen-year-old girl who admitted to "having infused corrosive sublimate" in her master's bedtime brandy; she then stood by and calmly watched him die writhing in agony. She was, of course, found guilty and executed for murder. Maybe for her it was worth it. "I am told," Lewis remarked, "that when she went down the steps of the courthouse, she was seen to laugh." There was only so far enslaved women could be pushed—and men like James could not forget who brought them their food and drink.[17]

Even though she was now pregnant with James's child, it was

clear that Rosanna was not going to suddenly begin behaving herself. It was not long before he had to bring in another servant—a woman named Esther Trotter, described as a "free female mulatto" in her christening record—to take over as the head domestic servant. Robert later related that Trotter looked down on Rosanna for her enslaved status, ordering her around and constantly insulting her. This aspect of social hierarchy was part of life in colonial Jamaica. Yet the two women were to be bound in blood. Both Rosanna and Esther bore James's illegitimate children. Esther's were sent back to Scotland, to be raised under the name of Graham at Wedderburn's estate in Inveresk, near Edinburgh. Rosanna's were to remain in Jamaica, for the time being at least.[18]

In January 1760, Robert's older brother, James Jr., was born. His christening record is an elliptical, fragmentary piece of evidence, one of only two places in the surviving official colonial record that Rosanna's name appears. It reads, simply, "James Wedderburn son of Rosanna a mulatto woman the property of James Wedderburn by James Wedderburn born Jan: bap: July 20." Rosanna's name here appeared almost fenced in by the threefold repetition of "James Wedderburn." It is a dry, bureaucratic record, but the depravity of James's actions bleeds through the paper, the church recorder stretching conventional language to accommodate it. First, Rosanna's status as an enslaved woman is so circumscribed by the legal power James holds over her that she must legally be identified as "the property of James Wedderburn." Then, to make sense of the document, we need to pause, shift our emphasis, and elongate that little word "by," to make sure we are using it in the correct sense, meaning "fathered by." The child is identified first as Rosanna's because, for obvious reasons, enslaved status was passed down through the mother. James's claim to ownership over Rosanna thus devolved to his own son. As Robert put it, "amongst his own slaves my father was a perfect parish bull; and his pleasure was the greater, because he at the same time increased his profits." In January 1760, like many planters before him, James did not just gain a son; he gained a slave.[19]

James Wedderburn, property of James Wedderburn, *by* James Wedderburn. The sheer prominence of the name in this brief record raises several questions. Considering how much she despised him and resisted coming into his power, did Rosanna consent to naming her son after her rapist? Or was James so intent on coming to some kind of terms with her that he suggested that the child should take his name? Was it chosen as a mark of his affection? Perhaps he hoped that his firstborn son would take after him, a chip off the old block?

On the other hand, perhaps this record is further evidence of Rosanna causing trouble for James. As several scholars have established, both baptism and naming ceremonies were especially important in the eighteenth-century Black Atlantic for many reasons, and baptism in particular was often believed to strengthen claims for manumission. If Rosanna's son was christened into the Anglican Church with the name James Wedderburn, she might reason that he stood a better chance in any future suit for freedom. It was not uncommon for slaveholders to manumit their mixed-race children or to buy their freedom from a subsequent owner. Emancipated mixed-race children of slaveholders could carve out comparatively good lives for themselves, and many were sent from Jamaica to Britain to be educated. This was a significantly different future than a lifetime working on the plantation, one which Rosanna might well have dreamt for her son. Even if his freedom was not her primary goal, ensuring that James's paternity was properly recorded could strengthen any claim she might be able to make on him in the future for help in raising the child.[20]

Nevertheless, any hope that James may have held for a quasi-consensual relationship with Rosanna was doomed to disappointment. When she found herself pregnant a second time, in 1761, she became depressed and refused to work. Her quarrels with Trotter and the other servants became more severe. Again, Robert's retrospective account of the trouble she caused at James's house suggests that she had told him all about her rebellious actions, which became part of Robert and Rosanna's shared family history: "Insulted on one hand, and degraded on the other, was it likely that my poor mother could practise the Christian virtue of humility, when her Christian master provoked her to wrath? She shortly afterwards became again pregnant; and I have not the least doubt but that from her rebellious and violent temper during that period, that I have inherited the same disposition—the same desire to see justice overtake the oppressors of my countrymen." The situation was becoming intolerable. Eventually, "the animosity in [James's] house had grown to such an extent" that Rosanna fled, seeking asylum with James's older brother John, who lived nearby. It was now clear that she would rather die than return to James's power. Seeing that she could not be convinced to come back, James finally relented and agreed to sell Rosanna, then five months pregnant with Robert, back to the Douglases at the Grange estate.[21]

Again and again throughout his adult life, Robert told the same story about his own narrow escape from a life of slavery. It was often how he introduced himself. The story went like this: when James sold Rosanna back to the Douglases, "one of the stipulations of the bargain was, that the child which she then bore should be FREE from the moment of its birth. I was that child." However, as Nadine Hunt discovered, this claim conflicts with the account provided by the colonial record, which suggests that Robert was in fact emancipated by purchase along with his brother James on June 5, 1764, when he was about two years of age. This was, by Robert's accounting, around two and a half years *after* Rosanna had been sold back to the Douglases.

Rosanna was once again likely a key actor here. She had made herself so difficult that James appeared to have wanted to get rid of her by any means. He had involved himself, or rather tried to involve himself, with a woman who continued to refuse him and who had now positioned herself to make claims on him for the support she required to raise and care for his children. There are a few explanations for the deal that was reached. Perhaps James held enough affection for Robert and James Jr. to see to it that they did not grow up in slavery. Perhaps Charles, who purchased Rosanna on his wife's behalf, did not want to add two young boys to his household charges. But it is equally possible that Rosanna negotiated with James to secure freedom for her sons. If he wanted to be free of this woman and "her troublesome temper," this may have been her price. If this was indeed the case, then it was not outright resistance, nor total compliance, but sheer obstinacy—being a "troublesome" woman—that had secured Rosanna her desired outcome.[22]

Rosanna must have been relieved to return to Lady Douglas's service, but the battle of wills with James had taken its toll on her physical and mental health. In 1762, when Robert was only around four months old, he had to be weaned to save both mother and child, and he was delivered to his maternal grandmother, Amy, to be raised in Kingston. Although Rosanna never fully recovered her health, she also never made herself easier to live with for any slaveholder. The next few years were marked by constant movement from one purchaser to the next, all within an extended network of Scottish expats. When Lady Douglas died around 1766, Rosanna was sold to a Dr. Campbell. She was soon pregnant, reputedly by Campbell. When he and his wife began to mistreat her, Rosanna informed them that she planned to starve herself to death, alarming them both enough to agree to sell her on once more. This was becoming a pattern for her. Once again, she had negotiated her own escape from an impossible situation by being willing to introduce emotional distress and dissonance into a slaveholder's household. It was not a gallant spectacle of resistance, but it got her out.

Her last known purchaser was one Dr. Boswell—probably the attorney Charles Boswell who would go on to become a magistrate for the county of Middlesex by 1779.[23] Having recovered her health a little and now heavily pregnant, Rosanna asked Boswell for permission to visit Amy and Robert near Kingston. Permission was granted, and she duly set out on the fifteen-mile journey to see her mother and son. But she had committed a transgression: Boswell's wife—wives tended to dislike enslaved mistresses—was furious that she had not been informed that her maid would be absent for the day. The lady of the house remonstrated with her husband; the punishment for this oversight could not wait. In the end, Boswell followed Rosanna out on the road toward where Amy and Robert lived. When he arrived, he ordered the pregnant woman to be tied at the hands and feet and stretched out on the ground, just like in the Fairburn engraving. With Robert, still just a little boy, standing by, holding on to his elderly grandmother's hand, Boswell flogged her with a cowskin whip.

That was in the late 1760s. Witnessing this outrage was one of Robert's first and most painful memories. In 1817, when he was about fifty-five years old, his anguish and rage were still palpable: "O Boswell, ought not your colour and countrymen to be visited with wrath, for flogging my mother before my face. . . . how can I forgive you?" At sixty-nine, it still haunted him. "My mother was also stretched on the ground, and actually flogged before me, while she was in a state of pregnancy," he wrote from a jail cell in 1831.[24]

Yet despite her own struggle against the horrors of slavery, Rosanna had also managed the extraordinary feat of protecting her sons from its worst excesses. Whether it was by leveraging James's emotional attachment, by making herself unbearable for him to live with, or simply by getting him to acknowledge his sons as his own, she had seen James Jr. and Robert freed—and at an age before they could remember ever being enslaved. And though many challenges lay ahead for these two boys and their siblings in colonial Jamaica, their future was far more hopeful as a result of Rosanna's stubborn defiance. Robert was living near Kingston now, under the care of his elderly grandmother, a reputed "witch" and smuggler's agent. He eventually crossed the Atlantic to carve out a life on the mean streets of London. His elder brother's path lay a little closer to home. Though he was free, James Jr., their father's namesake, remained on the Wedderburn estate into adulthood, working as a millwright. But one of the many benefits of freedom was that it was entirely within his power to choose a new name to bestow on his own child. On July 21, 1797, with his wife still in childbed, James Jr. took their son to be baptized at the Westmoreland Anglican chapel. He called him Robert.[25]

CHAPTER 2

Obeah Witch

Nothing discomfited men like James Wedderburn more than a Black woman with a voice. Controlling speech—who was allowed to speak to whom, and how and when they were allowed to do it—was an integral aspect of maintaining the racialized social order in any slave society. Transgressive speech was feared by slaveholders for good reason. Insurrections in the Caribbean almost always began with whispers, murmurs, and rumors. As we will see, "conspiracies" were the great terror of the Jamaican colonial elite throughout the 1760s. But these two extremes—speech as a tool of planter oppression and speech as a facilitator of resistance—only tell part of the story about language and enslaved life in the Caribbean. There were other ways to negotiate power dynamics through speech. For most enslaved people, and especially enslaved women, choosing their words carefully around enslavers was an important survival skill. In other cases, talking out of turn, being deliberately "sawcy" or "impudent," concealing what had been said, or even hurling insults were among the most common ways to register a challenge to an unequal social relationship. This is not, in itself, quite the same thing as resistance to enslavement, but it undermined the fiction that slaveholders commanded respect beyond their capacity to enforce it through violence.[1]

As he grew up, Robert learned the power that lay in the gray areas between permitted and unpermitted speech from his grandmother, Amy. He recalled her as a formidable woman who said what she pleased and was unafraid of White planters, including his father. Indeed, her loquacity was so renowned that it had become part of her identity: "no woman was perhaps better known in Kingston than my grandmother, by the name of *'Talkee Amy,'* signifying a chattering old woman." His characterization was more affectionate than dismissive: in fact, Robert deeply respected the words of older enslaved women. When, in 1817, he penned some advice to his "dear countrymen" in Jamaica on how they should run the island once they had overthrown the plantocracy, he suggested that women over the age of fifty should sit as councilors and arbitrate local disputes. "Do not despise the judgement of old women," he wrote, "for they are generally clear in their perceptions."[2]

Like Robert, many of the enslaved people he addressed were raised by grandmothers, either biological or surrogate. The Antiguan planter Alexander Willcock described the "grass gang," where young children, from the age of "six or seven years" were "put under the charge of a careful old woman, and pick grass merely to keep them employed," an arrangement that enabled their mothers to work long hours in the fields. Relying on elderly enslaved people to take up the indispensable labor of childcare was one way that slaveholders could continue to exploit them economically. But it also had the effect of elevating older women to positions of both fondness and respect in enslaved societies. One element of caregiving is protection; it denotes strength. Writing of the antebellum period, Brenda Stevenson notes that "aged grandmothers, as powerful anchors of extended, multigenerational families, continued to provide material, spiritual, and emotional support to younger members of their families across decades." Old women were sources of stability and inspiration to many enslaved people and their children, including Robert. Slaveholders, meanwhile, tended to underestimate or forget about them and so were often shocked when they spoke up for themselves or on others' behalf.[3]

James, who must have thought he had washed his hands of Robert when he sold his mother and agreed to manumit their sons, had not counted on the audacity of one particular "chattering old woman." Shortly after the time of Rosanna's flogging, with a very young Robert in tow, Amy crossed the island and surprised James at his home in Westmoreland, demanding financial support to help raise his son. The memory of the encounter stuck with Robert: "I never saw my dear father but once in the island of Jamaica, when I went with my grandmother to know if he meant to do any thing for me, his son. Giving her some abusive language, my grandmother called him a mean Scotch rascal, thus to desert his own flesh and blood; and declared, that as she had kept me hitherto, so she would yet, without his paltry assistance."[4]

A *mean Scotch rascal!* Though it might seem like a minor altercation, to Robert it was a transcendent moment. His grandmother, an elderly woman, herself enslaved, had marched right up to a White planter and demanded that he honor his duty to his Black son. What was more, she had insulted him to his face and gotten away with it. Aside from trading in a bit of "abusive language" of his own, James hadn't dared try to punish her. In a society founded on the unchallengeable authority of White men, it was to Robert as though the world had been turned upside-down. Even though Amy could not convince James to do the right thing with such a confrontational approach, she did have the satisfaction of getting the better of him, just for a moment. Robert was an intelligent child. He was watching closely.

Amy took an immense risk by trading insults with James, but she was in a stronger position to get away with it than most enslaved women. She was well regarded within the enslaved community, as she ran a stall in Kingston's huge Sunday or "negro market," which was attended by up to ten thousand people each weekend. The Sunday market was a central feature of the Jamaican economy in the eighteenth century, an important space where White surveillance was far less pervasive than on the plantations. White Kingstonians generally traveled around the city by carriage, and they disliked the hustle and bustle of the marketplace, where men and women loudly hawked a wide variety of wares and victuals to both free and enslaved customers. Writing of the Sunday market in Antigua in 1788, the planter John Luffman complained that the "noise occasioned by the jabber of the negroes, and the squalling and cries of the children basking in the sun, exceeds any thing I ever heard in a London market." He seemed a little scared of the market, where "rum grog is swilled in large quantities": "some [of the traders] dance, others play at dice.... It is not uncommon for them, when intoxicated, to turn out to fight." Because of the types of work they undertook, enslaved people in towns and cities generally had greater latitude for directing their own day-to-day movements than those on plantations anyway, but the markets in particular "belonged to enslaved and free people of color, not to whites."[5]

The Kingston market was at the center of Amy's world. As well as trading on her own account, she sold a number of goods for her "master," Joseph Payne, including "cheese, checks, chintz, milk, gingerbread, &c.," and she also sold goods for other merchants as an agent, receiving a commission for her troubles. As

Winnifred Brown-Glaude has demonstrated, enslaved "higglers" or market women like Amy were important figures among Kingston's diverse populace, representing for some White planters an alarming intrusion into the traditionally male world of free commerce. Certainly, some enslaved higgler women were able to use their skill in trading commodities to leverage forms of economic and social independence for themselves, unavailable to many in rural Jamaica. Although some free people of color attached a kind of "rough" or unfeminine stereotype to them, these women nevertheless commanded widespread respect, not least because they had a hand in controlling access to food and other goods. In itself, the fact that higglers held on to planters' cash and conducted business on their behalf put them in a comparatively empowered position, especially considering that the market was a Black-led space notorious for harboring runaways. In June 1779, William Harris discovered the consequences of pushing an old woman too far when he had to place an advertisement in the *Royal Gazette of Jamaica:* "PRISCILLA, a Market-Woman, well-known in Kingston; is elderly, and has absconded with money that she has received for provisions &c. she has sold." Independent trade at the Kingston Sunday market could therefore open avenues to renegotiate the limitations imposed on enslaved women by their urban merchant slaveholders.[6]

However, for Amy, it was not legitimate commerce but Kingston's thriving black market in smuggled and contraband goods that gave her the greatest leeway and personal agency. Amy's "master" was a smuggler, and she sold illicit goods for him. Despite being a young child at the time, Robert remembered that "though a slave, such was the confidence that the merchants of Kingston had in her honesty, that she could be trusted to any amount; in fact, she was the regular agent for selling smuggled goods." The smuggling of contraband between Jamaica and the Spanish West

Indies had long been tolerated, especially in port towns such as Kingston. Historically, this kind of trade, though technically illegal, had been carried on as an open secret during peacetime. In truth, it accounted for a significant portion of the entire economy of the British Caribbean. But during the second half of the eighteenth century, and especially during and after the Seven Years' War, colonial officials began to take the issue more seriously. In 1762, the Jamaican colonial assembly passed an act that forbade smuggling and mandated the death penalty for convicted smugglers—a move so "sanguinary" and out of line with custom that it caused something of a stir at the Board of Trade back in Britain. In Kingston, the man in charge of cracking down on smuggling was Charles James Sholto Douglas, Rosanna's onetime owner, but Robert never mentioned Amy running into trouble with him. What is clear, however, is that the ever-greater levels of trust that Payne was required to place in her helped to secure Amy's position as a highly valued and even respected individual within his household.[7]

Even the contraband smuggling, serious though it may have been, was not the worst of the dirt Amy had on her enslaver. Toward the end of his life in 1831, when Amy was long dead, Robert made the extraordinary claim that she was involved, along with Payne and his wife, in smuggling enslaved people off the island. Her role was to hide the runaways who had been "seduced to leave the country," most likely concealing them around the market. Although Robert noted that Payne had chosen to liberate about five enslaved people from his own household, this alleged operation was not a philanthropic or abolitionist exercise; it was more likely a service paid for by the enslaved themselves, closer to human trafficking than the Underground Railroad. The ship itself was largely crewed by enslaved rather than free people, and Amy herself remained under Payne's claim of ownership over her up to and indeed beyond his death. If Robert's claims were true, Amy's position in the smuggling ring not only spoke to the trust that the Paynes and their associates placed in her—their lives literally depended upon her discretion—but also to the enormous amount of power she could wield against them if she so chose. "Talkee" Amy's greatest source of leverage may well have been in knowing the value of keeping her mouth shut.[8]

No matter how discreet the business partners, illegally transporting goods and especially people is an inherently dangerous occupation. Most smugglers are bound to get caught sooner or later. Payne's number came up during an expedition around 1773, when he was apprehended by the Spanish while running mahogany from Kingston into the Bay of Honduras. The Honduran authorities were a little more lenient than the Jamaicans, and Payne was sentenced to a year of hard labor at the Castillo de San Fernando de Omoa, near San Fernando. He never made it back; according to Robert, he died on the return voyage "and was tossed overboard to make food for fishes." It is difficult to see how the inevitable misfortune of being caught smuggling could be blamed on Amy, who never left Kingston, but she was flogged almost to death for it nonetheless by Payne's nephew, who inherited his estate. "Now," Robert later wrote, "what aggravated the affair was, that my grandmother had brought up this young villain from eight years of age, and, till now, he had treated her as a mother."[9]

Once again, the child Robert could not be protected from witnessing this violence, and it left almost as much of an impression as seeing his mother flogged while pregnant. If nothing else, the assault on Amy consolidated in his mind that unrestrained "legitimate" authority—the legal right to wield unlimited power over another person—was incompatible with natural or moral justice. For the rest of his life, whenever he encountered men who exercised arbitrary power over others based on a claim to "legitimate" force—judges, magistrates, officers of the peace, or landlords—what he saw was a slaveholder, standing over the bloodied body of his aged grandmother. What could possibly motivate such a cruel and illogical use of violence against an old woman? The answer speaks to a deep-seated, almost primal fear that coursed through White Jamaican society throughout the second half of the eighteenth century: a fear of witches.

"Talkee" Amy was reputed to be a practitioner of obeah. A "creole" religion, combining aspects of both West African and Christian practices, obeah was understood by many enslaved people as a means of communication between the physical and spiritual planes as well as a way to influence people and the natural world. In 1799, the former planter Benjamin Moseley, for example, noted the widespread belief that "Obi-women" were able to control the weather and that they could "sell foul winds for inconstant mariners; dreams and phantasies for jealousy; vexation, and pains in the heart, for perfidious love," and so on. Obeah men and obeah women acted as priests and oracles, as officiants at naming ceremonies and funerals, and, most importantly, as healers and medical practitioners. As such, they represented an alternative kind of authority to that of the White plantocracy, beyond their surveillance or understanding. This was a problem: as Vincent Brown suggests, "Jamaican masters could not abide sources of authority they did not wholly control."[10]

Communicating with the dead, as much as with the living, lay at the core of obeah practices. Obeah involved communion with spirits—of deities, ancestors, or the recently deceased. Sensationalized accounts that feature in both published slaveholder memoirs and fictional depictions tended to fixate on the material elements of obeah rituals, such as the use of "blood, feathers, parrot's beaks, dog's teeth, alligator's teeth, broken bottles, grave-dirt, rum, and egg-shells." British audiences were thrilled by the exotic and, to them, faintly sinister accoutrements of West Indian creole religions, particularly "country fetishes." But those on the ground in Jamaica knew that different forms of speech—chanting, singing, and speaking in tongues—were equally definitive components of these subversive forms of spiritual expression. In this context, the name "Talkee Amy" might not signify a harmless "chattering old woman" but instead an interlocutor between worlds, whose powers and influence were unknown and—in the minds of both enslaved people and slaveholders—potentially dangerous.[11]

Many people in Jamaica were afraid of obeah practitioners, and perhaps they were right to be. White commentators were profoundly unsettled by these practices because they enabled some enslaved people to gain significant levels of influence over others. Belief in the power of obeah was seen as a major factor in violently resisting enslavement, notably during Tacky's War of 1760–1761, when over a thousand enslaved people fought colonial authorities for control of the island. During the campaign, Tacky, one of the leaders of the enslaved forces, consulted closely with obeah practitioners, who claimed that the spirits they called upon would protect insurgent Africans from the musket balls of the colonial forces. During Tacky's War, the practice of obeah was outlawed by the Jamaican colonial assembly, adapting the language of older English legislation designed to curtail the belief in witchcraft. Note the difference: as the historian Diana Paton puts it, whereas "the main purpose of the English Act was to suppress *belief* in witchcraft, the makers of Jamaican antiobeah legislation were far more concerned with *suppressing obeah itself*—even while they purported not to believe in its power."[12]

Whether they believed in it or not, planters still lived in fear of obeah. Beyond the specter of collective uprisings, White colonialists were obsessed with connecting the practice to poisoning attempts. Indeed, any unexplained death might be deemed the result of poisoning inspired or enabled by an obeah practitioner. As the historian Sasha Turner Bryson notes, this was partly a way to put to rest any lingering doubts that there might be something to the claims that obeah men and women had supernatural abilities: "Obeah was a convenient explanatory device for mysterious catastrophes, and poison was the logical materialization of something they otherwise disparaged as fraud." It is also important to recognize that obeah techniques could be "remarkably violent and dangerous—and not only for whites." Some obeah rites involved the application of violence against enslaved people found to be under the influence of malevolent spirits, and, in extreme cases, some practices could lead to deaths. It is little surprise, then, that obeah women as well as men commanded respect—and some degree of awe—among many enslaved people in eighteenth-century Jamaica.[13]

What was perhaps just as important, enslaved people recognized that, after obeah was outlawed in 1760, *accusing* another enslaved person of practicing obeah could have a major impact on the social dynamics and labor hierarchy of a household or plantation. As we have seen in the fractious dynamic between Rosanna and Esther Trotter in the Wedderburn house, relationships between women of color in colonial Jamaica were, like relationships between anyone else, susceptible to resentments, jealousies, and betrayals, as well as solidarity and friendship. This, at least, was how Robert explained why Amy was punished for "bewitching" Payne's ship and causing it to be captured. He blamed "a malicious woman-slave" for Amy's punishment, claiming that this unnamed rival falsely accused his grandmother in order "to curry favour" with the new head of the Payne household. Robert took this as a personal and deliberate attack, and he noted after the story of Amy's flogging that this woman lost her only child soon afterward: "plainly," he stated, a little coldly, "a judgment of God."[14]

Robert's account implies that this bereaved mother was less worried about God than she was about Amy's powers as an obeah woman. When the child died, she came straight to Amy to "beg pardon... for the injury she had done her, and to solicit my grandmother to assist her in the burial of her child." She also made a public recantation and "confession of her guilt" at the market in Kingston. This contrite response, and especially the request to help with the burial of the child, is consonant with the suggestion that she sincerely believed Amy to be an obeah practitioner. It was not unheard of for enslaved people whose children had died suddenly to explain the death as the action of a malicious spirit, or even the result of harmful obeah. It is quite possible, given the partial and carefully framed nature of Robert's account, that this woman believed her own loss was brought about by supernatural means and wished to make amends with Amy for protection from further harm. Unsurprisingly, given their role as intermediaries between the worlds of the living and the dead, "*Obia-Women*" were observed leading funeral rites for enslaved people in Jamaica well into the 1780s, long after the practices had been banned.[15]

In his several accounts of his grandmother's flogging, Robert remained absolutely consistent that there was no such thing as supernatural influence. Indeed, he never used the word "obeah" or any of its derivatives. Neatly reversing the spirit of the 1760 obeah law, he characterized White anxieties over these practices as a superstitious belief in "the doctrine of witchcraft."[16] In 1817, for instance, he demanded of his British readers, "repent, ye Christians, for flogging my aged grandmother before my face, when she was accused of witchcraft by a silly European."[17] When he himself stood convicted of seditious blasphemy in 1820 (a charge in many ways not dissimilar from the one facing those accused of practicing obeah in Jamaica), he explained to the courtroom exactly why he did not believe in the existence of "witches," even those mentioned in the Bible: "His impression on this subject arose from the circumstance of seeing his aged grandmother, a poor black slave in the island of Jamaica, several times most cruelly flogged by order of her master, a white man and a christian, for being a WITCH; now as he, when a child, had frequently picked her pocket of sixpences and shillings, he was well convinced she could not possess the qualities and powers attributed to witches, or she must have detected his petty depredations."[18]

It was typical of his character to protest his innocence of one crime by admitting to another. His invocation of the tender relationship between his younger self and his "aged grandmother" was rather a clever expression of the idea that one can commit a crime and still be innocent—a canny strategy, considering he was speaking at his own sentencing hearing at the time. The "everybody does it" sensibility of Robert's subversively sentimental little tale reflected his settled belief that all expressions of legal authority were fundamentally based on moral hypocrisy. This seems to have been the biggest lesson he took from his time in Jamaica, raised by an old lady whose punishment as a "witch" was legally justifiable only on the basis that witchcraft was not real and so witches were charlatans.

The whole affair with the smuggling ship was seared into the family's collective memory. Witnessing Amy being flogged seems to have been the point at which Robert could no longer bear to remain in the strange legal limbo of his childhood. As a child he had been manumitted, but because of his father's refusal to acknowledge him publicly he remained under the care and parental control of enslaved women. In spite of Amy's latitude of movement and formidable personality, the flogging was a stark reminder that she remained at the sometimes violent whim of the man who claimed to possess her body and life. As Robert approached adulthood—a legally ill-defined term in the eighteenth century and especially so for the enslaved and their children—he understandably sought to remove himself from the site of his trauma. Early in 1776, at the age of thirteen or fourteen and "possessing an inclination to rove," he struck out on his own.[19]

The exact chronology of Robert's teenage years is mysterious. By his own admission, he moved in circles with limited respect for Jamaican legal authority, and he led an itinerant lifestyle; in any event, he left no imprint in the traditional colonial record after his manumission. In his later published writings and speeches, he remained circumspect when it came to specific times, dates, and places he had visited as a free agent in Jamaica. As an elderly man, he recalled having "travelled as a jobbing millwright, throughout the different parts of Jamaica: though only a lad . . . being reared in Kingston, and having also lived eighteen months in Spanish Town, and the like period in Port-Royal." He mentioned that he stayed in regular contact throughout this period with his matrilineal family, including Rosanna and Amy, his brothers, and his sister-in-law, who worked as a nurse to the minister of St. Peter's church in Port-Royal. In the towns, he was disgusted to witness Methodist missionaries "preach up passive obedience to the poor black slaves" while exhorting them to make cash donations; he was convinced that the missionaries were embezzling the money. At some point, he appeared to have gained inside knowledge of maroon societies, including their food preservation techniques, though whether he came by this knowledge from personal observation or was told about it secondhand is not clear.[20]

Equally mysterious is how and why he migrated to Britain, leaving behind his large and close-knit family. He always maintained that he made the journey across the Atlantic in 1778 and arrived in 1779, and toward the end of his life he revealed that he had worked his passage aboard the Royal Navy storeship the *Nabob* as a gunner's mate. The *Nabob* did indeed make a voyage from Jamaica to Britain, departing Port-Royal in November 1778 and arriving in Portsmouth in late January 1779, before the crew were discharged in Woolwich near London in March. However, Robert's name did not appear anywhere on the ship's muster. The two gunner's mates on board, Robert Morty and Thomas Heifer, had been part of the crew since it first departed Britain in October 1777.[21]

There are three possible explanations for this inconsistency between Robert's archive and the Royal Navy's. First, Robert might have simply gotten his dates mixed up, though he remained quite consistent about 1778 being his year of departure, and the *Nabob* did not make any other transatlantic voyages that year. The second explanation is more dramatic. A number of shipping reports mention that another Royal Navy ship in the same convoy with the *Nabob*, the *Cupid*, foundered off the coast of Newfoundland in bad weather during the voyage and that nine of the crew perished. It is possible that Robert enlisted and served aboard the doomed *Cupid* and was among those rescued by the *Nabob* before coming to Britain. Yet it would be odd that Robert—not one to pass up an opportunity to tell a dramatic story—never mentioned being plucked from the stormy ocean just in the nick of time. Moreover, his name did not appear among the "supernumerary" crew on the *Nabob's* muster roll or pay records.[22]

A final possibility is that Robert enlisted using a false name. Regardless of the reality of his legal status, he was always paranoid about being arrested or re-enslaved, and the precarity of his freedom was a constant worry. In 1824 he alluded to being afraid of criminal prosecution by planters in Jamaica, "for such is their hatred of any one having black blood in his veins, and who dares to think and act as a free man, that they would most certainly have trumped up some charge against me, and hung me." If his oblique allusions to associating with maroons were true, that would be enough in itself to cast a major shadow of suspicion over him. At the very least, his family ties to the "troublesome" women Rosanna and Amy, as much as his connections to Kingston's insurgent Black underground, would have left him easily singled out as a potential troublemaker.[23]

Under such intense scrutiny, trouble is easy to come by. In White supremacist colonial Jamaica, men of color could seldom count on a fair hearing. His young age was another factor. A spy who attended one of his debates in London in 1820 recorded a story he told about these years: "He [Robert] began his discourse about Blacks in Jamaica and said that a black who had a chapel at Kingston who preached to the slaves that all men [who] were Christians ought to be free they pulled down his Chapel and put him in prison and sent to know whether he was free[;] his master did set him free at sixteen then they said that it was not lawful to be set free before twenty." When he left Jamaica, Robert was just sixteen or seventeen years old. If he did believe this could be used as a pretext for re-enslavement, then he might well have felt it expedient to leave the colony as discreetly as possible.[24]

It will likely never be possible to answer the many questions that remain over Robert's teenage years traveling around Jamaica. His experiences as a marginal and somewhat shadowy figure within the colony hint at a world beyond the reach of plantocratic surveillance and thus beyond the reach of the traditional historical archive. In that sense, the functional invisibility of this world to historians is an indication of its subversive strength, rather than its fragility. As Robert always took pains to note, women played a far more central role in this world than colonial authorities were willing to countenance. Robert's grandmother Amy was his introduction into parallel structures of power and authority in Jamaican society, especially into the side that was criminalized and considered illegitimate. Robert learned from his time with Amy that, in a society that winked at injustices committed by the powerful, legally questionable activities could pave a way to a more dignified and self-directed life. He carried this lesson with him into adulthood in England. Along with his mother, Robert's grandmother remained in his mind a powerful source of inspiration and wisdom. But at the age of sixteen, he saw that it was time for him to make his own way in the world. In 1778, Robert entered service in the Royal Navy and set sail for the imperial metropolis, leaving behind the two women who had provided his first education in radicalism.

The stories passed down to Robert about his powerful grandmother and his indignant, sometimes bellicose mother taught him that insubordination and a disrespect for traditional authority figures was his birthright. The very recent memory of insurrection in Jamaica provides an important context for explaining how these women were able to achieve so much simply by making themselves difficult. Enslaved smuggling agents, obeah practitioners, and domestic servants with access to planters' intimate lives represented a significant weak spot in the colonial regime. In the aftermath of Tacky's War, when conspiracies and insurrections were uncovered all over the island, people like James Wedderburn, Charles James Sholto Douglas, and Joseph Payne were forced to double down on the level of trust they placed in women like Amy and Rosanna. This narrowing down of planters' choices had the effect of opening up new, though subtle, negotiating positions for the enslaved, yet at the same time, as Amy discovered when she was flogged under accusation of witchcraft, it could also frighten slaveholders into hasty and unwarranted repressive actions.

As a child, Robert watched as these tensions played out, remembering especially the injustices that his mother and grandmother underwent, and—perhaps—imagining the possibility of another uprising in which justice could finally overtake the planters. Indeed, he ended his 1824 account by promising a future publication that would examine "the treatment of the blacks in the West-Indies, and the prospect of a general rebellion and massacre there, from my own experience." As we will see in the next chapters, the justice of violent retribution for the horrors of slavery was to become one of his core beliefs as he left the care of these difficult, inspiring women and commenced his own insurrectionary career in the imperial metropolis.[25]

CHAPTER 3

The Skull Affixed to Temple Bar

ONE OF ROBERT'S earliest memories of London—or so he claimed—was staring up at a skull fixed to a spike and wondering if it had once belonged to his grandfather. Temple Bar was one of the traditional gates marking the entrance to the City of London from Westminster, but it also had a more gruesome ceremonial function as the spot where the severed heads of traitors were displayed following their executions. Exposed to the elements, the flesh of the heads soon rotted away, but the skulls remained in place for decades—a grimly persistent reminder of the wages of disloyalty to the Crown. Nineteenth-century legend had it that looking up at this spectacle every day could do strange things to the relatives of the victims. In January 1766, a man was arrested after he was spotted in the street quite methodically firing musket ball after musket ball up into the rotting heads. Upon cross-examination, it was found—much to the alarm of the magistrates—"that the man is a near relation to one of the unhappy sufferers." It was an appropriately visceral place for Robert, when writing his radical counter-history, to locate his own arrival in the land of his paternal family.[1]

He was right enough to wonder if his grandfather's head had ended up on one of those spikes. They were reserved for Scottish Jacobites, and that is just what his grandfather had been. Sir John Wedderburn had been a staunch defender of the cause, active in the uprising against Hanoverian forces in 1745, and he was indeed executed and beheaded for high treason. Sir John was bound by family tradition to take up the standard of Bonnie Prince Charlie; the family had always been supporters of the exiled Catholic monarch James II and his dynasty's claim to the British throne. Sir John's father—Robert's great-grandfather—had been a leading figure in the previous major Scots Jacobite uprising, back in 1715. A generation before, the Wedderburns had fought under James's banner after the Revolution of 1688. All this fighting for the losing side had seen the family fortunes severely diminished, and when Sir John met his grisly end in 1746, his branch of the ancient clan Wedderburn had lost everything but their name. In a roundabout way, that was why Robert ended up in London.

Sir John was captured after the battle of Culloden in April 1745, when the Jacobite forces were finally crushed by the Hanoverians. His eldest son, John, had accompanied him to the battlefield. Both had fled for their lives, losing sight of each other in the carnage. They never saw one another again. John the younger, only seventeen at the time, managed to escape and eventually smuggled himself to Jamaica, where the family had established networks with other Scottish sugar planters. Sir John was captured by the English and carted off to London, where he was tried in November 1746. His second son, James, who at fifteen was deemed too young to take up arms, rode down to attend the trial and keep him company in his cell. The outcome of the trial was a foregone conclusion; the jury had been handpicked by the judge for unshakeable loyalty to the Crown, and the prevailing mood in London was that exemplary punishments were required to stamp out the threat posed by these "rebellious Scots" once and for all. Sir John was found guilty and sentenced to be hanged, then beheaded, quartered, and his body parts dispersed. James was both traumatized and indignant; Sir John had seen to it that he was raised with "a just sence of what our Country has suffered in Generall and I in Particular." For the rest of his life, whenever business called him back to London, James would travel miles out of his way to avoid going near Kennington Common, the scene of the execution and dismemberment.[2]

Three decades after the young James had fled to join his brother in Jamaica, his illegitimate son crossed the Atlantic in the opposite direction. By then, Robert too was aware of his grandfather's grim fate. Robert admired Sir John, describing him as "a staunch Jacobite" who "exerted himself strenuously in the cause of the Pretender, . . . aiding to restore the exiled family to the throne of England." In 1824 he wrote about encountering the skull over Temple Bar but lamented that he "could never yet fully ascertain whether it was my dear grandfather's skull, or not." Robert appreciated Sir John's rebelliousness, and perhaps he even shared with James and John the sense that he had been martyred for his principles. But unlike his slaveholding father and uncle, Robert was not a welcome inheritor of this side of the family's story.[3]

This is literally true: in the compendious two-volume work of genealogy *The Wedderburn Book*, printed by private subscription for the family in 1898, Robert is listed under a section titled "Families and Persons Named Wedderburn, not Shewn to be connected to the . . . Family." As we have seen, Robert's attempt to evidence the precise nature of his connection to his paternal family was not an affectionate gesture, and there was clearly no love lost between him and the White members of his clan. As he was soon to discover, neither his father nor his White half-brother Andrew was willing to publicly admit to any relation, much less embrace him as family. Robert mentioned Sir John's part in the 1745 uprising, and the painful memory of his execution, partly to needle Andrew during a public quarrel between them that broke out in March 1824. Indeed, he was likely deploying some poetic license when he mentioned seeing the skull on Temple Bar when he arrived in England in 1779. The last of the Jacobite skulls that had been affixed there had in fact fallen down, to the sound of much shrieking, during a storm seven years earlier. But that was merely a detail. Robert's real purpose in mentioning Sir John—other than to irritate his White half-brother—was clear enough. He meant to situate himself as a born rebel, the inheritor of a pedigree of radical agitation stretching back generations, on either side. Disappointed in all others, this was the birthright he could claim for himself from his father's family. And he had every intention of using it against them.[4]

Robert was not the first enslaved person to cause enormous and very public trouble in Britain for the family. Indeed, when he arrived in early 1779, the Wedderburns were still dealing with the fallout from sustaining one of the most important legal defeats in the history of British slavery: the case of Joseph Knight.

Robert never met the men at the heart of this historic case, though it centrally involved his paternal family. But Rosanna certainly could have. When she had fled James's house in Westmoreland and stayed at John's estate around 1762, she may well have been sharing the house with a young African-born house servant named Joseph. John had bought Joseph from one John Knight, the captain of the slave ship *Phoenix*, and had taken a shine to him. Joseph was kept out of the fields and trained as a personal servant. When he was baptized, he took on the surname of the ship's captain, the first person to claim the right of ownership over him—thus becoming legally known as Joseph Knight.[5]

In 1768, John returned to Scotland to permanently settle down and reintegrate the family into the propertied classes. He married—much to his social advantage—Margaret Ogilvy, and he purchased Ballindean House, a grand country estate in Perthshire. Compared to his conduct with the enslaved people he had left behind on the Jamaica estates, John treated Joseph very well. A gentleman's manservant played a similar role to a ladies' maid, including providing an intimate kind of friendly companionship. John saw to it that Joseph was educated in Christianity, taught to read and write, and baptized. This pseudo-paternal relationship closely resembled the forms of support that many Scottish (and English) planters extended to their illegitimate children borne by enslaved or free women of color. Indeed, it was not dissimilar to the relationship that Robert claimed had been shared between Rosanna and Lady Douglas. It might have been an affectionate relationship, up to a point. But the simple fact remained: Joseph was still enslaved by John.

Or perhaps that fact was not so simple, after all. On July 3, 1772, Joseph happened to pick up a copy of the *Edinburgh Advertiser*, where he read a report from London. A historic judgment relating to the legal rights of enslaved people in England had been passed in the case of *Somerset v. Stewart*. The *Edinburgh Advertiser* carried a verbatim report of the rather oblique judgment of the presiding judge, Lord Chief Justice Mansfield. It read that the "state of slavery is of such a nature, that it is incapable of being now introduced by courts of justice upon mere reasoning or inferences from any principles natural or political; it must take its case from *positive law*. . . . no master ever was allowed here to take a slave by force to be sold abroad, because he had deserted from his service, or for any reason whatsoever." Like many people, Joseph thought that this ruling meant that enslaved people in Britain— including himself—were now legally free. Technically speaking, he was wrong. The ruling only affirmed that enslaved people in England could not be arrested and forced to leave the country against their will if they chose to leave their masters' service. Moreover, the case was tried in an *English* court; it was by no means clear that the ruling applied in Scotland.[6]

Around this time, Joseph asked John about obtaining his freedom, and he later claimed that John then promised to free him in seven years, take him to Jamaica, and set him up with "a House & Some Ground where he might live comfortably all the days of his Life." For a while, the question was academic. Joseph had a decent life in Scotland and no particular desire to leave John's house. In fact, he had a strong reason to stay: he had fallen in love with the chambermaid. By the time Joseph had read about the Somerset case in July 1772, Anne Thompson was already pregnant. As an unmarried couple, they had rather limited options, and this was not a secret that would keep in the closed atmosphere of a house like Ballindean. As was conventional when female servants "fell pregnant," Anne was dismissed from the household staff. In the usual run of things, pregnant women would be discharged to the care of their husbands. A hasty wedding could be arranged if necessary. But John was attached to Joseph, and he personally disliked Anne, having, as his lawyers later put it, "no good opinion of any of that Ladies Virtues." He was unwilling to allow Joseph to start a family with her, especially if that meant losing his closest servant. To his credit, he did provide some money to support Anne through the pregnancy, including enough to rent out a room in nearby Dundee.[7]

Tragically, their child died while Anne was living alone in the city and Joseph was still working at Ballindean. Seeing an opportunity to break up the couple and keep his enslaved manservant close at hand, John abruptly cut off financial support for Anne after the child's funeral was settled. His plan backfired; the couple wanted to be together, and they got married in secret on March 9, 1773. Joseph now gave John an ultimatum: rehire Anne and let them stay in one of the empty cottages on the estate, or he would leave forever. What Joseph was asking for would not have been uncommon; indeed, in many great houses, multiple generations of staff lived and served in the same great house, allowing domestic stability for both sets of family. It was one of many traditions of codependency between servants and masters in the British country house. But John had spent a long time in Jamaica; he was not used to being challenged by servants, especially not Black servants. He refused Joseph's request.[8]

This was the final straw for Joseph. Recalling the court ruling he had read about the previous year, he left the house to start a new life with Anne in Dundee, where, as he later stated in court, he wanted to "apply himself to some honest and lawful industry for his own and his family's support." John, incensed, had him arrested and brought back to Ballindean on November 15, 1773. There, a group of local justices of the peace, handpicked by John, met to pass judgment on whether Joseph was free or enslaved. In his petition to them, John painted himself as a generous, perhaps overindulgent benefactor under siege from an ungrateful slave. "Your petitioner not only maintains him in Cloaths but also allowed him some money for his private uses to induce him to be an honest Servant," he wrote, though he was hasty to add that "the Petitioner never gave him any Manumission or promised to release him from his Slavery ... and humbly presumes that the Law will not disappoint him of his Service during Life." In the event, the "hearing" was a kangaroo court. Not only were the three assembled justices of the peace all "closely connected through marriage with Wedderburn or each other," but every single one of them had a financial or familial interest in West Indian slavery. One of them employed John and James's younger brother Peter as an overseer on his plantation. Of course they believed that the rights of a slaveholder should be upheld in metropolitan Britain. Unsurprisingly, they sided with John and reaffirmed his right to hold Joseph in perpetual slavery. He was to continue working at Ballindean without pay.[9]

However, John had equipped Joseph with the tools of resistance when he had him educated and baptized. Joseph knew enough about Scottish law to know he could get the case referred to the next most senior court, the sheriff's court at Perth, which he duly did in December 1773. Now he was seeking not only his freedom but compensation for the wages he was owed and restitution for "Damages, Exp[ense]s According to Justice." The language Joseph's lawyer used at the hearing on January 5, 1774, must have been profoundly troubling to John, whose fortune was still tied up in West Indian slavery. The sheriff-depute appeared to agree with Joseph's case that he "denies that he has done anything which by the Laws of any Country could bring him into a state of slavery and he knows of no natural right which any man can have to deprive him of his freedom," and, even more alarming, that "the Law of nature gives him a right to assert his invaded liberty whenever he finds an opportunity by Law or even by Force." Now John had gotten himself into a tricky situation. The sheriff-depute at Perth had not only ruled in Joseph's favor but declared that he had done so explicitly because "the State of Slavery is not recognised by the Laws of this Kingdom and is inconsistent with the principles thereof." The ruling did not order John to pay damages or compensation for lost wages, but it was a clear enough judgment on his right to ownership over Joseph.[10]

Moreover, this looked worryingly like a legal precedent under which any enslaved person in Scotland could now abscond, leaving slaveholders with no legal recourse to have them arrested and returned to service. In attempting to settle what had started out as a private dispute with Joseph, John was now facing no less than the de facto abolition of slavery within his home country. For the sake of his brother-planters, he had little choice but to escalate the case, taking it to the Court of Session in Edinburgh, Scotland's supreme civil court, in February 1776. In the face of growing public awareness of the case, John was keen to keep the spotlight away from the broader issue of slavery as much as possible and to focus instead on the specifics of this particular case. His counsel acknowledged that "he should not be surprised if the popular clamour should rather be against him" on the issue but also noted that John had never intended to *treat* Joseph as though he was enslaved, even if that was the basis of his claim to have him returned to service. It was "almost unfair even to quote the word Slavery against him, and . . . there is no sort of necessity for entering into a Discussion of that Question in the present cause." But the genie could not be put back into the bottle. Whether he liked it or not, the whole case hinged on the question of whether or not John was entitled to assert the right of ownership over Joseph and claim his labor, without paying wages, as his slaveholder. The court would have to decide if that claim—the claim of one man to hold another in slavery—was lawful or not.[11]

It was a huge, complicated legal question, and the litigation dragged on for two more years. Some of the finest legal minds in Britain were deeply interested and actively participated in the case. For instance, Henry Dundas, who went on to become one of the most influential British politicians of his generation, advocated for Joseph, "giving a particularly brilliant speech" before the court. In England, the famous Dr. Samuel Johnson followed the case closely by correspondence with his friend and biographer James Boswell, even composing a written pleading against John's claim to send to Joseph's lawyers. In the end, on January 15, 1778, the twelve presiding judges voted eight to four in Joseph's favor, giving a wide range of legal opinions on the status of slavery in general and this case in particular. The upshot was that the highest court in Scotland had issued a serious repudiation to any slaveholders who thought they could wield the same powers in Scotland as they had in the West Indies.[12]

For Joseph, the immediate consequence was that he was now finally at liberty to join Anne and their new child, who had been born while the proceedings were still underway. The family receded into the comparative comfort of obscurity—at least as far as written state records are concerned. For John, an unwelcome new aspect had accrued to his precious reputation. Not only had he lost a "slave" and a trusted personal servant, but he had to live and die with the knowledge of having personally sustained one of the most significant legal blows against slavery ever recorded in the history of his nation. For the largely proslavery landed elite with whom he was so desperate to re-ingratiate himself, this was the kind of quiet ignominy that people avoided talking about at parties. He was one of history's losers, and surely a deserving one. In the end, this defeat was his most enduring legacy.

Robert disembarked the storeship *Nabob* at the Woolwich docks after the *Somerset v. Stewart* ruling, and thus he emerged into a country where enslaved people could not be legally detained against their will. Thanks to his uncle's defeat, this legal protection now extended to Scotland, too. As we have seen, Robert was not himself enslaved, and so he had no need for the protection of the new ruling. Yet this also meant that he had no freedom papers to present if he had been arrested, as he had feared his father meant to do. The legal ramifications of the *Knight v. Wedderburn* case could only have been reassuring for him, and given his fears of re-enslavement in Jamaica, an awareness of this new situation might have encouraged him to put down roots in Britain.

Life in London has never been easy for young immigrants with no money. In 1779, Robert was lucky enough to find a situation with a "family professing religion," perhaps working as a servant or beginning his apprenticeship as a tailor. But this respectable lifestyle was not to last. He soon fell in, as he later put it, with "a set of abandoned reprobates; he there became a profligate, and so continued for the space of seven years." He was being self-critical here—though perhaps not undeservedly so. Still, amid all the revels, a family life beckoned. Among his wild crew was an English woman named Elizabeth Ryan, about ten years Robert's senior. At the age of twenty-nine, she was old enough to be defined as a "spinster" by the church clerk when she and the then nineteen-year-old Robert married, on November 5, 1781. At this stage in his life, Robert was still illiterate, and he marked the wedding register in the traditional way, by making a little X where his signature would normally go. The clerk helpfully annotated it: "the mark of Robt. Wedderburn."[13]

The date of their wedding is an important one in the history of English insurrectionism. Of course, it was Guy Fawkes Night, commemorating the foiled "gunpowder treason": an attempt to blow up the Houses of Parliament in 1605. The Fifth of November also commemorated the landing of William of Orange in England in 1688, marking the beginning of the dethroning of the Stuart dynasty for whom Robert's grandfather had fought and died. In England, it was celebrated more generally as a victory over Jacobite forces, further entrenching the populist anti-Catholic emphasis of the anniversary. The politics of the Fifth of November commemorations were, broadly speaking, a state-approved celebration of Protestant English nationalism. But in truth, the politics of the night were unimportant for most working-class people. For England's poor, it was more an opportunity to let off some steam, an occasion noted for gleeful, drunken misrule. As the historian David Cressey puts it, "The Fifth of November provided an annual occasion for the contest between rowdiness and discipline, a ritualized challenge to hierarchical power, in which the events of 1605 were largely forgotten. . . . Now the historical anniversary served as a pretext for violence, a cover for challenges to the established order." Respectable newspapers complained about the conduct of the working classes around this time of year, especially their wanton and often dangerous use of fireworks. It was an oddly fitting day for a wedding between two "abandoned reprobates" like Robert and Elizabeth.[14]

The wedding reception must have been quite a scene, but the party could not last forever. On July 18, 1782, Robert was pressed into service in the Royal Navy, fighting what was rapidly becoming clear as a lost cause against another group of rebels in the North American colonies. He was forced to leave his wife and friends behind in London and once again cross the Atlantic, serving as an ordinary seaman aboard the HMS *Polyphemus*. But Robert did not much care for taking orders, and when he witnessed the bloody whipping of the cook and cook's mate for the crime of "taking an extra drop of grog," he knew he had to get out.[15] The pay book for the *Polyphemus* tells the story of his short stint of service in economical language:

Entry?	18th July 1782.
Prest or not?	Prest.
Name?	Robt. Wedderburne.
Quality?	Ordinary Seaman.
Discharged, Discharged Dead, or Ran?	Ran.
Whither?	Barbadoes.[16]

This simple record reflects something more than itself: a struggle between the annihilating bureaucracy of the colonialist state and one person's bid for self-determination, rendered in a handful of words—an interrogation, almost, between unequal antagonists, frozen in the archive.

Robert was on the run in the Caribbean again. As soon as the *Polyphemus* stopped to resupply at Barbados—the British gateway to the Americas—he deserted his post, disappearing into the crowd at Bridgetown. By his own design, the paper trail of his brief time revisiting the Caribbean stops there, but what is clear is that he did not wish to hang around in the slave society of Barbados any longer than necessary. He had a wife in London to get home to. It is possible that Robert made his way back to Britain aboard a privateer. Several years later, during a debate about the necessity for British revolutionaries to learn how to handle weaponry, he said, "I served on board a privateer, my station was in the Top there I learnt to handle small arms."[17]

By whatever means, at the close of the American Revolutionary War, Robert once more recrossed the Atlantic and returned to Britain, keen to settle down with Elizabeth. By the winter of 1784, she was pregnant, and on July 24th the following year she gave birth to twins, a boy and a girl. Three days later, the twins were baptized and named Robert and Elizabeth, after their parents. This little detail—naming the children after themselves—speaks to the hopefulness with which this young family began the next chapter in its history. Though they did not have any money, it is clear that they invested their own hopes for the future in their firstborn children—the next generation of Roberts and Elizabeths. Perhaps it was with this sense of hopefulness, or perhaps it was in the awareness of newly heightened necessity, that Robert decided to make the journey up to Scotland to call on his father and ask him, one more time, to do right by his son.[18]

Inveresk Lodge is a lovely building set in acres of picturesque and carefully manicured gardens, which are today maintained by the

National Trust for Scotland. Its relatively modest size, at least in comparison to the vast palaces built by other British slaveholders, reflects James's fairly modest fortune. John, the eldest, had received the family inheritance and made the most advantageous marriage. James, very much the second son, managed to regain his own respectable, if comparatively lesser, footing in Scottish high society partly through money from the plantations and partly through the wealth of his new wife, Isabella Blackburn, herself heiress to a significant West Indies fortune. Clawing his way back up the social ladder had come at the cost of James's surname, which he had changed to Wedderburn-Colvile in order to inherit an additional estate in Fife. His legitimate (White) children, incidentally, dropped the "Wedderburn" in favor of the more prestigious name Colvile. Thus while Robert and Elizabeth, living in near-poverty in London, joyfully bestowed their names on their infant twin babies as a symbol of their love, Robert's paternal family's pursuit of property and, above all, their desire to secure the legitimate inheritance of wealth led them to cast their vaunted clan moniker by the wayside. Ironically, by the time of James's death, only the children he refused to acknowledge as "legitimate" still publicly bore the name of clan Wedderburn.[19]

For Robert, though, approaching Inveresk Lodge, the grueling, multiday stagecoach journey must have been a bitter reminder that he was owed much more than a name. He surely knew that he was unlikely to be welcomed with open arms, but he might have at least hoped for a little charity. In the event, the exchange was brief and quietly brutal. When he was in his sixties, Robert reflected on his encounter with his father that day in 1785 or 1786—only their second, after Talkee Amy had called James a "mean Scotch rascal" in Jamaica some ten years earlier. Robert was still stirred to rage by the cruelty with which his father dismissed him. "I visited my father, who had the inhumanity to threaten to send me to gaol if I troubled him.... nor did he deny me to be his son, but called me a *lazy fellow*, and said he would do nothing for me." To add insult to injury, Robert had to leave via the servants' entrance, where James's cook gave him a draft of weak beer and the footman tossed him a cracked sixpence to set him up for the 350-mile journey back to London. Obviously, it wasn't enough, and Robert was forced to apply to the City Council at Edinburgh for a traveler's pass so he wouldn't get picked up for vagrancy along the way.[20]

Could Robert reasonably have expected any more than this from his father, despite his obviously illegitimate status? In some senses, yes, he could. Many Jamaican planters were perfectly happy to provide for their "mixed-race" children during the late eighteenth century, though this tended to be a quiet arrangement that took place alongside the normal process of inheritance. Some individuals bucked this trend, such as Henry Redhead-Yorke, the son of a formerly enslaved woman named Sarah Bullock and a White colonial administrator in Barbuda. Yorke was not only recognized by his father but brought home to Britain, educated at Cambridge, and raised with the expectation of becoming part of the family enterprises. This, however, was an exceptional circumstance. Much more often, illegitimate children were incorporated into the emotional structures of the family while being sidelined when it came to the inheritance. It was too late for a comfortable childhood, but Robert might have reasonably hoped for a little financial help on the strength of his blood relation. No such luck. James made it clear that he wanted nothing to do with, and would do nothing for, his son by the rebellious woman who had made his life so difficult back in Jamaica.[21]

It was a crushing rejection, and Robert never really got over it. What he had never truly appreciated until that day was how profoundly and instinctively the landed elite understood the difference between blood kinship and "legitimate" inheritance. He had, clearly overoptimistically, imagined himself to have some kind of claim to his father's regard, or even just his charity, because he was his son. But in the event, James did not care much about his sons; he was only concerned for his heirs. That old question of legitimacy, again. Now, Robert saw it for what it was. Legitimacy was a weapon, used by the powerful to maintain their position over the powerless. It was a trick of sophistry to disinherit and consign to destitution unwanted sons while the chosen heirs, raised in luxury, were set up to become captains of industry and leaders of empire. It was the justification for keeping his mother in slavery; for beating his wise and revered grandmother; for discarding even his name, the one written claim he'd ever had to their compassion, all in the grasping pursuit of ever more power and land and status. Even parentage did not matter, at all; Robert would *never* have legitimacy. If he was to have justice, instead, then it would have to come through some other means. This had been a hard lesson to learn, but Robert had a long walk back to London ahead of him to mull it over.

PART II

Illegitimacy

CHAPTER 4

There Is a Day Coming

Disappointed expectations and the disconnection between blood ties and the rights of property profoundly influenced Robert's political outlook. Life for the poor in early nineteenth-century London was hard, and it could be cruel, too. Impoverishment led inexorably to criminalization and judgment, not only from the state but by individuals with means and authority, especially landlords and business owners. Robert could never abide the finger-wagging moral condescension of those who had inherited comfortable lives, who never had to make hard choices between following the rules and carving out a space for their own dignity. And he was not alone. Historians call this period "the century of illegitimacy" for good reason. The radical world that Robert helped to build in London during the 1810s was filled with the bastard scions of ne'er-do-well fathers who had forgotten about them.[1]

Little wonder, then, that it was also the crucible for a host of new ways of thinking about the social inequalities sustained by the inheritance of capital and their effects on the political legitimacy of the nation's rulers and lawmakers. The plebeian political movements of this period were intellectually diverse, but they were united in questioning the legitimacy of what they saw as a failing political class and the corrupt networks of authority and influence that boiled down, ultimately, to inherited privilege. "Rotten boroughs"—parliamentary constituencies with only a handful of people in them eligible to vote—were one of the clearest symptoms of the "old corruption" at the heart of government, where political power came about as a side effect of owning land and having money. In this period, property ownership was a precondition for the franchise, leaving the vast majority of the population out of the democratic process altogether. In practice, this meant that most political rights were more an accident of birth than a universal condition of citizenship, inspiring many radicals to question the legitimacy of the state itself. Robert had seen how both personal and legal ideas around legitimacy were used against the powerless in Jamaica, and he knew how easily such "tyranny" could make its way back to the imperial metropolis. Over the next ten years in London, his education in the real meaning of "legitimate authority" was completed by living through grinding poverty and the glaring injustices of the nineteenth-century British class system.

"Slavery" was how some described it: the condition of the majority of the British population with no legitimate claim to representation. With debates over the abolition of the slave trade going on simultaneously, this touched a nerve. As we have seen with John and James Wedderburn, the money from West Indian slaveholding enabled a rapid kind of social mobility among the very wealthy in Britain, from the ranks of enterprising businessmen to the landed gentry. The progressive infiltration of both creole and absentee slave-owners into the old school of the British aristocracy during the early nineteenth century, and their almost universally conservative, loyalist political alignment, were deployed by many radicals as evidence of the corrupted roots of the "legitimate" British establishment. When Edward Lascelles, the slave-owning Earl of Harewood, gave a speech at a loyalist dinner in April 1818, he decried the radical press as reducing ordinary Britons' ability to become "better subjects." The radical journalist William Hone responded with scorn, claiming that these sentiments were "worthy of a trafficker in blood. They are the *legitimate* growth of a West India climate, and may be pursued with impunity on a plantation of slaves; but we still hope there remains amongst us . . . sufficient public spirit to resist their adoption in this country."[2]

There is another side to this story. Rebellious enslaved people in the West Indies played a bigger part in the British radical imagination during this time than has been acknowledged by many historians. The Haitian Revolution that began in 1791, opening up the previously unthinkable concept of a government run by those who had been enslaved, played a crucial part in the way that both plebeian and elite political thinkers in Britain rethought concepts of political legitimacy during this period. As we will see, this is most certainly true of Robert, who saw in the Haitian Revolution a model for justice and freedom in both his birthplace of Jamaica and his adopted home of Britain. However, for him—just as for most of London's impoverished working-class radicals—the revolution would have to wait until more pressing needs could be met. The stalking horse of radicalization in early nineteenth-century Britain, as is so often the case, was hunger.[3]

When Robert returned to Elizabeth and the twins from Scotland empty-handed, around 1786, the family entered a short-lived period of relative stability lasting into the early 1790s. There can be little doubt that they were extremely poor during this time, since Robert was at this point a relatively inexperienced journeyman tailor and Elizabeth had two young children to care for, likely preventing her from working full-time. But the macroeconomic outlook was reasonably steady in the late 1780s, with the British economy recovering surprisingly quickly after the end of the American Revolutionary War. This appears to have protected Robert and Elizabeth from extreme deprivation, for a while at least. The same could not be said for the many hundreds of formerly enslaved Black soldiers who migrated to London in the 1780s following service for Loyalist forces in the Revolutionary War. With no access to parish relief (which was reserved for those born within the district of a particular church or those who had been settled there for a number of years), these veterans were left to fend entirely for themselves on the streets of London.

Much has been written about the terrible hardships endured by many of London's migrant Black community in the 1780s and about the efforts of the charitable Society for the Relief of the Black Poor to alleviate these needs. The initial distributions of food, medical care, and cash relief rapidly evolved into a plan for a more permanent solution: to transport the former Loyalist soldiers back to Africa by creating a new settlement in Sierra Leone. The motivations behind this plan are still hotly contested by historians, with some arguing that it was a genuinely philanthropic plan and others agreeing with the African-born abolitionist Ottobah Cugoano's appraisal in 1787 that "they were to be hurried away at all events, come of them after what would." But focusing on attempts to transport Black people out of London can obscure just how important these years were for the establishment of a permanent, resident Black British community.[4]

The late 1780s saw transformations in London's human geography, with certain regions, such as the area around St. Giles and Seven Dials, becoming popularly associated with working-class Black people. Indeed, Robert casually mentioned hearing a Methodist preacher while passing by the Seven Dials one Sunday during his early years in London, suggesting that he, too, was drawn to the neighborhood. He might even have attended one of the weekly dances Black Londoners organized for five shillings a head, much to the alarm of certain sectors of the White community. Robert liked a drink now and again; it is eminently plausible that he stopped into one of the pubs noted for their "mixed" clientele, such as the Yorkshire Stingo or the White Raven on the Mile-End Road. Pubs like these were not just watering holes but also important spaces for political discussion and even centers of resistance. This much was clear when about one hundred Black men came together to prevent one of their number, John Pegg, from being arrested by the sheriff's officers at the White Raven in September 1786.[5]

This was also a period of political awakening for Robert. In 1787, the London Committee of the Society for Effecting the Abolition of the Slave Trade was formed. Over the next seven years, the committee spearheaded a nationwide campaign, including publishing testimony, parliamentary activism, and large-scale public meetings. Robert attended two of these public meetings during this period. He was agnostic about their methods, and he particularly objected to the "base practice, of exhibiting pictures of the different modes of punishing slaves." Such images undoubtedly brought back painful memories for him, but as we have seen, he also objected to their misleading emphasis on helplessness and degradation. This was the period when well-meaning middle-class supporters of abolition wore Josiah Wedgwood's "Am I Not a Man and a Brother?" cameo—depicting a kneeling, supplicant enslaved African in chains—as a fashion accessory. As the abolitionist Thomas Clarkson fondly recalled, "some had them inlaid in gold on the lid of their snuff-boxes. Of the ladies, several wore them in bracelets, and others had them fitted up in ornamental manner as pins for their hair." It is easy to see why a man of Robert's temperament was put off the White-led British abolition movement, even while his hatred of slavery remained fiercely personal.[6]

Given that he went on to become a leader of working-class radicalism in the late 1810s, when he was well into his fifties, we might expect to find a younger Robert engaging with zeal in the vital and optimistic reformist scene of the early 1790s. His absence from the ranks of the London radicals who had been inspired by the outbreak of the French and Haitian revolutions during this period is likely the result of more immediately pressing concerns. The briefly sunny economic conditions of the mid- to late 1780s had given way to falling wages again in the early 1790s—indeed, not an inconsequential factor in the rise of radicalism in Britain's manufacturing centers during these years. Robert and Elizabeth had always eked out a precarious existence on the margins, but this fluctuation hit them hard. Like many poor people, they had moved around a lot, but even though the house they had been renting at Holywell Lane in Shoreditch for the past nine months cost only one pound per month, they were still struggling to make ends meet. When their third child, Maria, was born on March 4, 1790, their shaky finances began to tip over the edge. The marriage came under severe strain in the early 1790s, and they began to quarrel. On May 16, 1795, Robert left Elizabeth and the children for good.[7]

It turned out that they had been keeping each other afloat. Living together as man and wife, they had some claim to "honest poverty," a condition much romanticized at the time and since, chiefly by people unburdened by the prospect of living in it. Once separated, they found they could not survive London and were now subject to the discipline of both the labor market and the police. Robert and Elizabeth both fell quickly into homelessness. On October 3rd, Robert was picked up as "a Rogue and a Vagabond," living on the streets. He was brought in for questioning before one of the justices of the peace at Middlesex, where he confirmed that he was not begging but actually had work as a journeyman tailor. The wages were simply not enough for him to house himself. In these circumstances, Robert said, he hoped he did not need to be taken into custody. By that time, Elizabeth had been taken into the workhouse at Saint Leonard Shoreditch, and she was also examined to confirm Robert's account of their separation. Her testimony did not help him. On November 5th, Robert was imprisoned for fourteen days for vagrancy. Elizabeth was returned to the workhouse. It was their fourteenth wedding anniversary.[8]

This was a wake-up call for Robert. Although he still had many hard times ahead of him, after his release he did go on to regain his financial footing to avoid more charges for vagrancy. Elizabeth, however, never made it back. As far as we know, she never saw Robert again after that day, and she spent the rest of her life in and out of the Shoreditch workhouse. Eighteen months after her examination in the Middlesex Court of Session, she appeared before the Churchwardens of St Botolph Without, Aldgate, "being poor and unable to provide for herself," to apply for parish relief. Twenty-four years later in January 1819, now in her sixties, she was picked up by the Churchwardens and Overseers of the Poor in St. Giles in the Fields as a vagrant and sent back to Shoreditch. When she was examined, she described herself as the "widow of Robert Weatherburn." They had by then been estranged so long that she probably didn't know if he was alive or dead. In any case, it was a prudent way to identify herself; a widow attracted far less moral judgment from the authorities than an abandoned wife.[9] We do not know to whom the care of the children devolved after their separation, but Robert's occasional stints of work at sea would make it difficult for him to look after them.

One senses that Robert and Elizabeth's relationship was occasionally a turbulent one, marred by his impressments and the absences they caused. Their status as a "mixed" family may have led to additional trouble in finding work and in finding an all-important place within a supportive community of neighbors and friends. Almost all Black men who recorded their experiences of life in late eighteenth-century Britain recounted some form of discrimination, and this could extend to the White women who loved them and, of course, to their children. But, as we take our leave of Elizabeth, an elderly woman sent from one workhouse to another, we should not be naïve about who had depended more on the other in their marriage. Poor women almost always worked, but most women's wages were so low that families were usually dependent on the father having full-time work just to scrape by. When Robert was taken in on the vagabondage charge, Elizabeth told the overseers the truth: he had "unlawfully run away" and left her utterly "without support." With no husband, she faced almost insurmountable odds against recovering any semblance of economic stability, much less a claim to respectable "honest poverty." Eighteenth-century gender norms heaped brutal social liabilities upon "spinsters" and "abandoned women," especially those like Elizabeth who were approaching the end of their childbearing years. Single again at forty-four, she would have likely struggled to find another partner willing to get married and settle down.

We cannot know precisely how Robert and Elizabeth's marriage broke down—whether it was a mutual decision, or if he had more literally "run away," as in the generic wording of her deposition to the Overseers of the Poor. Whether their separation was amicable or acrimonious, Robert must have known that he was to all intents and purposes abandoning his wife to fend for herself and their children. He knew how hard it was out there. Throughout his life, he raged at the way women like his mother were used and then cast aside by men; yet he too could act callously toward the women he loved. Elizabeth's sad fate does not place him in the same category as his rapist father, but it does raise the troubling prospect that even his most deeply held principles were subject to the bitter realities of living on the margins in nineteenth-century London.

Robert managed to scrape together enough money after his short stint in the house of correction to find somewhere to live. Over the next few years, he slowly got himself back on his feet, but he never lived in a situation that could be described as economically stable, much less comfortable. The economic bad news rumbled on into the early 1800s. When Robert began campaigning for working people to trust their own consciences and reject the authority of corrupt ministers, he did so from the parlous situation of the precariously housed, and on an empty stomach.

By about 1801, he had married again, this time a widow named Mary Durham. They were to stay together for at least the next two decades, and the union produced no fewer than three siblings for Mary's existing daughter, Mary-Ann. They put down roots in Soho and St. Giles, where "mixed" families like theirs were more common and less likely to attract stares. While they managed to stay within the area, they were still forced to move constantly between tiny accommodations, usually accessed from filthy courtyards with little to no sewage runoff. In 1809, they were living in Green's Court, off Peter Street; by 1816 they were at 9 Smith's Court, off Great Windmill Street, about three minutes' walk away; and by 1822, when Robert was in jail, Mary and the children had moved on to the barely more salubrious accommodations at number 9 New Compton Street, some nine minutes' walk northeast from there. These are just a few snapshots in time, provided mainly by the parish records and Robert's court appearances. They were almost certainly not the only addresses they lived at during this period.[10]

Money was a constant worry, and it was never clear when more would be coming in. The most immediate concern for people like Robert and Mary was feeding themselves and their children. The cost of bread reached record highs during this period, the worst since 1795, resulting in food riots around the country. The food crisis of these years was compounded for the family by the fact that Robert was struggling to find work. Journeyman tailors generally got paid through commissions, and in lean times there was simply less work to go around. Mary, meanwhile, was one of the many thousands of people who worked on the streets of London selling fripperies to passersby for next to nothing. In many cases, poor women sold the net bags that people used to boil their vegetables, hence the appellation "cabbage-net sellers" to describe such street hawkers. For her part, Mary sold artificial flowers made of wire and paper. When she went into childbirth around 1801, the family lost even this meager stream of income.[11]

Pride is of little use to those whose children are facing starvation. Robert still held some residual hope that his name might be worth something to one of his wealthier relatives. The merchant company of Wedderburn and Company had an office in London at 35 Leadenhall Street, and business was reasonably good. Robert sought out his half-brother, Andrew Colvile, their father's eldest White son and heir to the family's fortune. He explained his situation, the distress he and his family found themselves in, and appealed to Andrew's better nature "for some pecuniary assistance." He needn't have bothered. Andrew was no more sympathetic than James had been; he would not even acknowledge that they were related. Nevertheless, something about Robert's visit clearly gave him pause, and he wrote to James at Inveresk to seek out more information. James replied that there was nothing to tell, except that a very difficult enslaved woman on his estate had named her children Wedderburn as a joke, and now one of those children, just like his mother, was deliberately causing trouble. James neglected to mention that he had paid to manumit Robert and his elder brother James in 1764. But he did note Robert's previous visit to Inveresk in the mid-1780s and said that he had sent him packing. This was good enough for Andrew. He gave Robert nothing at all— a sixpence and small beer less than even their father's household had been willing to part with. As far as Andrew was concerned, that was the end of the matter. He had business to conduct, importing rum made from sugar grown on the Wedderburn estates in Jamaica, where his other half-brother James still worked. But he had not heard the last of Robert.[12]

Robert would pull through as he had before, but not emotionally unscathed. The hardness of his decades in London and his father's family's near-total disregard for him, almost as much as what he had witnessed in Jamaica, precipitated a crisis of faith. In his twenties, he had dallied with Methodism, a nonconforming denomination of Christianity with wide appeal to the impoverished masses in Britain. However, he was dismayed to find that the Methodist preachers tried to dissuade him from ever questioning or "examining their doctrines." No demand could be more antithetical to Robert's fiercely independent intellect, or indeed his motivation for seeking religion. He had seen Methodist preachers abuse their power and require unquestioning loyalty before, among the enslaved in Jamaica. It disgusted him. He felt that "such was the influence of the errors they taught, that they darkened his understanding." Rejecting the authoritarian streak of the preachers he encountered in London, Robert began to turn away from organized religion altogether.[13]

Such was the strength of his opinion on the corruptness of the Church that he embarked on an entirely new venture, even as he clawed his way out from the depths of poverty. His first published piece of writing, *The Truth Self-Supported: Or a Refutation of Certain Doctrinal Errors Generally Adopted in the Christian Church*, appeared around 1802.[14] Here, he outlined for the first time in print a worldview that was to inflect his ultraradical politics as much as his troubled relationship with the Church. He would now follow, he declared, no law but God's law and be bound by no doctrine but his own conscience. "He then thought it his privilege and duty to admit of no doctrine, however plausible, but what he perceived in his own judgment was clearly and evidently contained in the holy scriptures . . . confident that God had . . . removed him by HIS power from a legal state of mind, into a state of Gospel Liberty, that is to say, a deliverance from the power or authority of the law, considering himself not to be under the power of the law, but under Grace." *The Truth Self-Supported* has been treated by most historians as a minor or uninteresting part of Robert's corpus, almost as a piece of juvenilia presaging his more mature "secular" output, even though he was well into his late thirties when he wrote it. This is, one suspects, at least partly because the text confronts religious rather than political authority. Yet this pamphlet was, at heart, a vindication of his staunchly antiauthoritarian worldview, expressed through the language of challenging sectarian dogma.[15]

From our (generally) more secular perspective, it is easy to underestimate how controversial some of Robert's arguments in this pamphlet were at the beginning of the nineteenth century. For example, he very explicitly rejected the doctrine of the Holy Trinity—the notion that God was constituted in the Father, the Son, and the Holy Spirit. Robert instead asserted a strongly Unitarian position, insisting that there was "ONE GOD, who is the Universal Father, and One Jesus Christ, who is the Son and Mediator, through whom, and by whom, the Father performs all his Will, yea, the whole of his Will, by his own Influence or Essence, which is called the Spirit." This may seem like splitting hairs, but by insisting on the separability and separateness of the Father, the Son, and the Holy Spirit, Robert was making a quietly incendiary claim about the very nature of human spiritual existence. The Son, he explained, was *not* one and the same with the Father, even if that was where his power came from.[16]

He was also opposed to the notion that individuals should approach those other "fathers"—ministers, priests, or preachers—to seek salvation or forgiveness for their sins. True grace, he argued, could only come from oneself. He saw the petty factionalism of the competing Christian denominations—and the apparent inability of many ministers to question their own beliefs—as preventing them from offering clear-sighted moral guidance. "Ministers in general, in our day, have their doctrines formed for them . . . for if he does not preach the doctrine that pleases the managers of his Church, he is turned out of *his* bread, and held in contempt as an apostate." Unthinking loyalty to any doctrine or school of thought epitomized what was wrong with modern religion: in his eyes, "therefore you see the necessity of calling upon God for yourselves." The essence of Robert's theological position was that personal morality should never be mediated by a person who claimed any kind of authority over another, and that shame and remorse for past sins could only be absolved by personal communion with God. This was on one level an evangelical call for believers to abandon the very notion of a traditional hierarchical church. On another, it was the moral foundation for Robert's lifelong disdain for authority of all kinds.[17]

There was also perhaps a personal undercurrent to the theology of Robert's first published piece of writing. All this talk of fathers and sons appeared to draw on his own experiences of being turned away and disinherited by his own family, most recently by Andrew in London. Consider, for example, his exegesis on Jesus

Christ as the chosen firstborn son of God, braced by biblical references: "Jesus Christ the first child of his power. *Revel.* 3. 14. . . . The first born of every creature. He is also the Exalted man. *Heb. c. i. v. 7.*" Jesus played a dual role for Robert both as the rightful inheritor of God's authority and, more obliquely, as a despised and deeply wronged man who would one day apportion justice to those who had rejected him. Perhaps most tellingly, at one point Robert depicted Jesus as a "rejected" child imbued with the power of God himself: "Jehovah, for the first time becomes a Father, and by and with the Son, created all things, and those for the Son. . . . and however he is rejected and despised, there is a day coming, when his friends and his enemies will know—the one with pleasure, the other by woeful experience, that he is possessed with power, by authority of the Father, to condemn the one, and reward the other, and appoint to each their portion."[18]

Along similar lines, for Robert the purpose of God's forgiveness was to "enflame" sinners with "a more ardent desire to be at home at their Father's house"; to be truly forgiven was to be embraced by the father, to possess "the Spirit of adoption," to become "the son and Heir of God—a joint Heir and Brother with Christ." At the heart of Robert's cosmology, then, lay a complex father-son dynamic between the all-powerful Lord and his child, who occupied a status of true legitimacy that lay beyond the power of human authorities to control. Read against his rejection by both his own father and his cosseted half-brother, it is little wonder that Robert concerned himself with the power devolved from fathers to sons and with visions of righteous retribution.[19]

Robert was a novice writer, and he was well aware that this short pamphlet was unlikely to be much of a money-maker. "Could the AUTHOR present you a Diamond in the rough, you certainly would not refuse it," read his self-effacing foreword; "do not then reject the following essential truths, on account of his unpolished ability to send them forth into the world, with their deserved splendour." There is little evidence to suggest that his pamphlet sold particularly well, and no second edition has ever surfaced. Nevertheless, this new writing venture sparked something in him. Perhaps declaring his desire to empower people to bypass their ministers, to look directly to God for moral legitimacy, was invigorating for him. He'd had enough of men in black gowns and white wigs, whom he saw as nothing more than presumptuous intermediaries, imposing their false authority over him.[20]

A violent incident on the street outside his home on October 8, 1809, led Robert into the most direct confrontation with this type of authority figure thus far. It was a Sunday afternoon, but Robert had by then stopped going to church. He had in fact been walking home from the pub carrying one of his children in his arms, with an older daughter walking alongside. As they turned the corner onto Peter Street, they happened upon a confrontation about to turn nasty. An Englishman—a man named Pierce—had been accosted by a large group of about twenty drunken people, a group of Irishmen who were, according to some witnesses, known as neighborhood troublemakers. Robert tried to defuse the situation, but suddenly the group set upon Pierce and threw him down a set of stone steps into a milk cellar. Another bystander tried to help, but he was also beaten by the group. Robert handed the baby to his daughter and tried to pull the gang away from the men, but all he got for his trouble was a couple of punches. Robert had "taken his share of three pots of ale, and one glass of gin" during his visit to the pub that afternoon, and he was not one to back down from a fight. He took off his coat, and "said he would fight one or two of them at a time," but they all jumped him at once and bludgeoned him with sticks. Had it not been for the fact that a red-coated soldier happened by and scared the assailants off, he could have died right there on the street, in front of his children.

Some of the gang were later arrested, and Robert testified against them. The defense attorney immediately seized upon him, making out that he was drunk when the assault happened and therefore an unreliable witness. While he did not deny that he had been drinking that day, Robert had a short temper with authority figures and no qualms about speaking his mind when confronted by representatives of the legal system. Anticipating a common observation about his many subsequent court appearances, a newspaper reporter noted that "the witness, having betrayed much violence of temper, during his cross-examination, was reprimanded by the Court." Indeed, the defense tried to fixate on this as a way to get the case thrown out, insisting "strongly on the violent temper of the first and principal witness" in their closing statement. It was no good; the facts of the case were clearly proven. Robert eventually had the satisfaction of seeing the defendants sentenced to six months' imprisonment for the assault, though he would always have the scars from the beating to remind him of the incident.[21]

Robert's conduct during both this altercation and the court case tells us much about the man he had become, just on the cusp of his career as a radical lecturer and writer. He no longer went to church on Sundays but instead frequented the pub, that traditional home of working-class fellowship and loose, incendiary talk about the high and mighty. It was the pub that provided him entry into the world of ultraradical and insurrectionary politics, which over the next ten years he would rise to lead. Already, he was incapable of turning his back when he saw someone in trouble, and he would rather endanger himself in an unwinnable fight than stand by and claim helplessness. He also had begun to reject, quite belligerently, the authority of his nominal social superiors, those little men in black gowns and white wigs—an instinctive social hostility that was to jibe closely with his more explicitly political views. His experiences of poverty, societal inequality, and familial rejection had toughened him up, but they had also clarified his principles. When he wrote, in *The Truth Self-Supported*, that he no longer considered himself to be under the power of the law, he was not speaking in metaphors. He was forty-seven years old, and his most radical years lay just ahead of him.

CHAPTER 5

The Press Is My Engine of Destruction

IT WAS AN OPEN secret that the tailors pissed on the soldiers' uniforms. This is how it worked: each of the rolls of cloth, stamped with a broad "R" to show they were the property of the Crown, were first weighed, and then certificates were issued with the weights written on them. When the tailors arrived at the factory in the morning, each of them got a roll of cloth with the matching certificate, to which was added the tailor's name and the date. They would take the rolls of cloth upstairs to the workshop, make the uniforms, and return them to the warehouse along with the certificate and any offcuts. The uniforms and offcuts were weighed and checked against the certificates. If the weights matched, or nearly matched, then the tailors would be paid, and they could pick up another roll of cloth, as long as more soldiers' uniforms were needed. They usually were. By 1813, Britain was simultaneously at war with the juggernaut of Napoleonic France and, again, with the upstart former colonies in North America. The conflicts, the most totalizing in British history so far, had generated a boom in several industries, including, obviously, the manufacture of military uniforms. These particular uniforms were for Britain's Spanish and Portuguese allies in the fight against Napoleon's forces on the Iberian peninsula. The certificate system was designed to stop the tailors from taking leftover scraps of cloth for their own use and sneaking them home at the end of the day. But the tailors "could make up deficient weight, and were in the practice of doing so, by making urine upon the cloth."[1]

It was not the most elegant scheme, but it worked. That is, until the manager at the military contractor's office, Mr. Stevens, caught wind of it. On October 16, 1813, he lay in wait with about twelve constables and, at his signal, they rushed the tailors as they were making their way home at the end of the day. In the confusion, several pieces of cloth fell to the ground, and nine out of the seventy subcontracted tailors were apprehended. The next morning, the officers apprehended another twenty-five suspects as they arrived for work. When he was taken into custody, Robert was heard to say that "he thought what they had done was no robbery; that some men were cleverer than others; and that should they hang a dozen a week they could not put a stop to it, for the moment a man becomes an apprentice he becomes a thief." When the tailors were arraigned before the magistrate later that day, they were asked what they knew about the thefts and if they were able to give any names. Robert's cross-examination was the longest of them all.

> Robert Wedderburn said, that he could not account for the conduct of others; he knew that in his own country, the West Indies, taylors were much given to *cabbage*, and he presumed the case was the same here. For himself, he did not pretend to more honesty than other men; but supposing he had no regard to honesty, he certainly had some to prudence, some regard to himself and his family. In the employ of [the

army contractor] Mr. Maberly, he had not held a position of trust, and nothing was so odious as the character of an informer; indeed, he would sooner go to Botany Bay than become one.[2]

Robert was not mistaken about British tailors' predilection for "cabbage," and he was likely sincere when he claimed that he thought it was "no robbery." Exactly as in the West Indies, getting to keep a small amount of excess fabric from commissions had long been one of the traditional perks of the job. Cabbage was in many ways equivalent to the customary "gleanings" from harvests traditionally allowed to rural laborers in the eighteenth century, or to the small items of stationery purloined from offices today. It was not *legal*, exactly, but it was accepted as a feature of the broader economy, and most turned a blind eye so long as the amounts involved were not significant. Indeed, in nineteenth-century slang, the term "cabbage" was synonymous with a tailor's income, and the scraps were often used to make clothes for their families. According to another newspaper report of this trial, Robert had suggested that tailors "imbibed" the practice "in the first six months of their apprenticeship, and never forgot it!" Indeed, even in the workshop in which he was employed, eight ounces of cabbage per day were permitted. As Robert quipped in the witness stand, "to say the same weight must be brought back that was given out, could only be to make him *black*." That line got a laugh from the court. "Black" was a common shorthand for dishonesty—a holdover from centuries of biblical connotations. Robert knew what people thought of him.[3]

Times were changing, and as trades like tailoring moved increasingly toward a more formalized wage-labor model, employers and subcontractors began to crack down on the practice, seeking more control over how their merchandise was used. This was just one of the many ways in which working conditions and customary benefits for laborers and artisans were degraded during the rapid industrialization of the late eighteenth and early nineteenth centuries. Tradesmen who continued to take advantage of these traditional perks were roundly criticized and increasingly liable to prosecution by their employers. Musing on Robert's words at the trial, which had been broadly circulated in the press, one commentator felt that cabbage was symptomatic of a broader malaise among workers: "What is *cabbage* with tailors, assumes other apparently harmless names in higher trades and situations. Sometimes a manufacturer is robbed in *cuttings*, and sometimes in *clippings*. Sometimes the evil appears in the shape of *chips*, and sometimes of *parings*—sometimes it goes no further than *scrapings*, and sometimes a light is thrown upon it by *candle-ends*." By the 1850s, the practice had fallen so far from favor that this meaning of the word "cabbage" was no longer widely used or even known.[4]

Of course, stealing entire rolls of fabric, as had happened in this case, went well beyond a customary perquisite. Robert was facing a significant charge, with a sentence of at least six months. Nevertheless, his comment that he preferred to be transported to the convict colony in Botany Bay rather than to inform on his colleagues was shrewd. As long as nobody "grassed," then most of them were safe. As the alderman of the court observed, "in a case of this nature, where so many were implicated, it was out of his power to discriminate betwixt the innocent and the guilty." In the end, of the thirty-eight tailors arrested in this minor scandal, only seven were convicted. Robert was not among them.[5]

Solidarity was extremely important to tailors, and not only when evading the law. There were two types of tailor in early nineteenth-century London: "flint" and "dung." Flints were members of a "club" that negotiated wages—essentially, a trade union—and were usually paid by the day in large-scale jobs like the army contractors. Lower-status dung tailors mended clothes and hawked poor-quality garments, often stitched together out of cabbage, from ramshackle wooden stalls in the "small stinking courts" off the main highways. The division originated in the 1780s, as noted in Francis Grose's *Classical Dictionary of the Vulgar Tongue*: "FLINTS, journeyman taylors, who on late occasion, refused to work for the wages settled by law. Those who submitted, were by the mutineers stiled dungs, i.e. dunghills." Robert had worked as a dung in his time, but in 1813, as implied by his refusal to inform on his colleagues, he was a member of a trade club. He would have enjoyed some social benefits, too, including the inevitable invitation to the pub after work. We have already seen how London's Black community carved out spaces for socializing and conviviality in pubs, and these spaces continued to play an essential role in working-class politics during this period. Robert was almost certainly at a pub with his trade club in 1813 when he met Thomas Spence, a man who was to profoundly change his life.[6]

At sixty-three, Spence was even older than Robert: a veteran radical with immaculate credentials. He had jumped headfirst into London politics during the great wave of activism in the early 1790s, and he spent much of his life in and out of jail for his beliefs. In contrast to most radicals targeted by British state repression during those years, Spence had held fast to his ideals and doggedly carried the torch of advocating revolutionary, egalitarian principles through the repressive 1800s and into the early 1810s. Perhaps most influentially for Robert, who still could not read and write, Spence was a bookseller and a passionate advocate for literacy and education in the fight for social equality. Since 1812, he had redoubled his efforts to reach out to poor artisans who were suffering from degradations to their working conditions and the loss of their conventional rights—in other words, men like Robert. Spence's modus operandi had always been to hold "free and easies" in pubs. At these informal and largely unstructured political meetings, poor men spoke vehemently and openly about the idiots running the country—sharing pots of beer, squinting and shouting through clouds of pipe smoke, and not just dreaming of reform but making plans to forge a better future.[7]

Robert was captivated. It was not only the way it was organized; Spence's political philosophy and vision for the future could hardly be better suited to a man of Robert's background and experience. It was all about disrupting the concentration and hoarding of excessive wealth, especially in land. At the center of Spence's ideology was the idea that all land should be held in common as a People's Farm and, crucially, that all forms of inheritance should be abolished. "The Spencean Plan," as Robert and his fellow converts—styling themselves the "Spencean Philanthropists"—called it, was a vision of agrarian communitarianism. Many of them argued that this new utopian world could only be realized through popular uprising. As part of their revolutionary outlook, Spenceans took special aim at the concept of "legitimacy" as nothing more than a mechanism to oppress the poor. As Spence himself had put it in 1803, when the revolution came, the common land "shall be deemed the equal property of Man, Woman, and Child, whether old or young, rich or poor, *legitimate or illegitimate.*"[8]

Robert was also drawn to Spence's ideas for another reason. Unlike many other reformists of the early nineteenth century, Spence did not see any reason why "Freeborn Englishmen" should have an exclusive claim to liberty. His plan for bringing land into common ownership explicitly embraced colonized people, as he outlined in a 1796 pamphlet entitled *The Reign of Felicity, Being a Plan for Civilizing the Indians of North America; Without Infringing on their National or Individual Independence.* Slavery was also an important point of reference for Spence's politics. He described the slave trade as "fraught with every mischief and Evil to the Human race." More importantly for Robert, Spence envisioned the coming revolution to be led not just by White laboring men but by a motley multitude that included "urban labourers, soldiers and seamen, beggars and prisoners, Native Americans and African slaves, women and children, Calibans and witches." Robert was inspired by this universalism and always fondly recalled "one Thomas Spence, who knew that the earth was given to the children of men, making no difference for colour or character." Here, then, was a political movement that centered Robert's experiences, reconciling his nascent working-class radicalism with the intellectual traditions of defiance that Rosanna and Amy had bequeathed to him in Jamaica and that he had claimed as his heritage from his Jacobite ancestors.[9]

Even Spence's sudden death in September 1814 could not stop the Spencean Philanthropists. Thomas Evans, another veteran London radical, took over as de facto leader of the group, organizing a large funeral procession down Tottenham Court Road, at which Spence's followers "carried the scales, as the emblem of justice, immediately after the corpse, containing an equal quantity of earth in each scale." Evans added more structure to the free-and-easy gatherings, establishing four "lodges" of Spencean debating clubs in 1815 who met on different nights of the week at different pubs around London. Robert's lodge met at the Cock on Grafton Street in Soho, but he also spoke regularly at the lodge that met at the Mulberry Tree tavern in Moorfields. By 1817 he had been elected to chair the weekly debates at the Cock, which were usually on some variation of the question posed for January 15th that year: "Would the Practical Establishment of Spences Plan, be an effectual remedy for the present distresses[?]" Upward of fifty people showed up for that particular debate.[10]

How did such an obviously extreme plan for reform—and one so closely associated with the prospect of violent insurrection—become so popular? The end of the Napoleonic Wars had worsened the already dire situation for the working poor of Britain. Robert Owen, in his report to the Association for the Relief of the Manufacturing and Labouring Poor, was fairly clear-sighted in his identification of the economic causes of the distress. Mass demobilization of soldiers and sailors meant an oversupply in the labor market, which depressed wages. At the same time, all the work associated with the war effort—work like Robert's stint making uniforms for the army contractors—suddenly dried up. Alongside this, new advances in manufacturing technology further reduced the need for labor in many traditional skilled trades. Together with this pressure on the labor market, bread prices shot up after 1815 due to a terrible harvest and the passing of the 1815 Corn Law, which deliberately raised the price of bread by preventing the import of cheap grain from abroad. In this context, the idea of a "people's farm" was understandably attractive; but in truth all flavors of radicalism experienced a resurgence in these years. In short, people were desperate, and their government appeared to be protecting only those who were already wealthy. A major symptom of the extent of public discontent manifested in December 1816, when a huge demonstration at Spa Fields in London devolved into rioting. Many Spenceans had been closely involved in planning this meeting—and indeed the riot seems to have been premeditated. The popular uprising demanded by some of them, it seemed, was close at hand.[11]

After his intervention at Owen's meeting in August 1817, Robert's star was on the rise in London's energized ultraradical underworld. Even so, a schism was forming among the Spenceans between the insurrectionists and those who sought reform via constitutional means. Robert belonged to the former camp. Government spies had been keeping tabs on him for a while, and a number of reports captured his activities in the free-and-easies during 1817, including his participation in a debate at the Mulberry

Tree on the ominous question "What constitutes Treason[?]" He also alarmed spies by "promulgating atheism" during a debate on November 13th that year, where "he boldly vociferated his opinion, that there is no Deity or a future state beyond the Grave." Robert's bravery in these debating sessions bordered on the foolhardy, especially since he was well aware that there were spies in the audience. One such informer must have been sweating a little in his seat when Robert stood up in front of about a hundred attendees and declared he knew that "the company in the room were not to be trusted, nor yet the Government, for they have a set of men whom they hire, and fill their bellies, that would hang him, or any one else if necessary." As the Spenceans discovered to their cost over the next few years, Robert was not wrong about that last part.[12]

Several of the spies who informed on Robert's tavern speeches in the months after his intervention at Owen's meeting noted that he had started selling "seditious pamphlets" at the end of each debate. The cheap political pamphlet—often just a single sheet, printed on both sides, folded and cut to make eight, twelve, or sixteen pages—was long-established as a cost-effective way to distribute radical ideas. The medium flourished in these hard, postwar years. Robert was at a disadvantage here: even three years later he had to acknowledge that "it was true he could not write, but that he had caused his ideas to be committed to writing by another person." But the ideas were what mattered, and he did not let the small matter of his illiteracy stop him from taking part in this crucial form of radical campaigning. Joining forces with Charles Jennison, a shoemaker who had been involved in trade union organizing and collected the monthly "dues" for the Spenceans, he set about producing his first periodical. The result, first appearing on October 4, 1817, was *The "Forlorn Hope," or a Call to the Supine*.[13]

Possibly recognizing the positive response he had received

at Owen's meeting in August, Robert saw journalism as a way to spread awareness of how all forms of colonial exploitation, including the enslavement of his own family, were related to the oppression of workers in Britain. His first published political article, in the first issue of *The Forlorn Hope*, demonstrated his characteristic lack of caution, even as he set out his uncompromising take on the Spencean plan. "Is not the system of a private property in land chargeable with murder?" he asked; "how can anyone account for the gigantic strides that death has taken through Ireland, a country that was able to supply your navy and army, all your colonies? and now the inhabitants are dying for want? the reasons are plain, the land is held as private property." In the same article, he intimated darkly that an uprising would soon take place in Britain, just as it had in France: "Had every man in France partook of the share of rents of their native soil, Louis XVI might have worn his head a little longer.... In vain do monarchs think to reign with peace and safety when their thrones are founded on injustice." His focus on insurrection here, and his noticeably international outlook, was just the beginning of his extraordinarily daring evocation of ultraradical politics.[14]

In his next piece, his personal investment in the links between the injustices of slavery and the hardships now faced by the laboring poor were even more apparent. Robert took special aim at the hypocrisy of both the state and the clergy: "How can the House of Commons pride themselves of possessing greatness, when they frame laws to authorise priests and princes to hold my relations as slaves?" The radical press in these years teemed with references to "slavery," but the term was almost always used as a metaphor for the sad condition of the British poor. For Robert, it was no metaphor; rather, he concentrated explicitly on the means by which "the receivers and stealers of Africans become rich" and gained political influence in Britain. He was unrestrained in his contempt for the fact that slaveholders—men like his father and brother—were put into a position to exploit the poor in Britain by the wealth they had derived from the murder of Africans in the West Indies: "The estates of such men should be called the field of blood; the money they receive from such estates, may justly be called blood-money; their savings, which they put in the [national] funds, carries with it a curse.... Will not the curse extend to their children which has commenced in their days?" Heredity and family were at the core of Robert's radical vocabulary; his rhetorical style was a mixture of the anticlericalism he had experimented with in *The Truth Self-Supported* and the haranguing, confrontational approach of the alehouse debating societies that had inspired him to take up a position as leader.[15]

Jennison could not keep up with him—in truth, he was a poor editor, and the pamphlets were littered with typesetting errors and weirdly inconsistent formatting, as well as superfluous extracts from other texts to make up for a lack of correspondence. After just three issues, *The Forlorn Hope*—aptly named, in the end—ceased publication. It was extremely common for this kind of "twopenny trash" periodical to fold shortly after launch. Robert, by no means discouraged by the failure of his first journal, had caught the publishing bug. Still dictating his ideas to an amanuensis, he moved on to a new venture within a couple of weeks. He wanted to create a print venue where he could focus on the political issues closest to his heart: the overthrow of slavery in Jamaica and the prospect of a popular uprising in Britain. In six weekly installments in the autumn and winter of 1817, he set about producing the most complete articulation of his anticolonial, antislavery, and insurrectionary political ideas of his career. They were among the most radical antislavery tracts published in English in the nineteenth century. For the title, Robert borrowed from one of his mentor Spence's favorite passages from the Bible—Matthew 3:10:

"And now also the axe is laid unto the root of the trees: therefore every tree which bringeth not forth good fruit is hewn down, and cast into the fire." It was an appropriately incendiary image.

The Axe Laid to the Root, or a Fatal Blow to the Oppressors, being an Address to the Planters and Negroes of Jamaica first appeared in late October or early November 1817. At first glance, it is an overwhelming document, comprised of editorials and correspondence from multiple authors writing in different styles, along with reprints of popular street ballads. As though deliberately to confuse a new reader, the first issue opened with a letter responding to a book review that had appeared weeks earlier in *The Forlorn Hope*. This was followed by an address to the enslaved in Jamaica advising them to resist peacefully and then an article warning planters that the enslaved "will slay man, woman, and child, and not spare the virgin, whose interest is connected with slavery." Another issue opened, without preamble, in the character of an enslaved mother speaking in Jamaican patois: "Top tife, top tife, top tife! dat England man, dat white man, de Christian buckera tiffey my pickenninney, he hungry, he go yam 'im! Oh! Der go noder, he tiffey my mamma, he be Cotolic Christian, he rosse my mamma in de fire, for yam, what me do for my mamma? Oh! Me belly ache, me die!" The periodical fizzed with different voices—some rather experimentally positioned—all competing for the reader's attention. Yet Robert had produced almost all the writing in *The Axe* himself. He just wasn't working alone.[16]

Dialogue, debate, and multiple voices were profoundly important to the Spencean way of doing politics. Spence himself had disseminated his most influential ideas in the form of a dialogue between different fictional characters, such as the straw man "Aristocrat" who scoffed at a "Mother" for asserting the political rights of women and children in *The Rights of Infants*. This commitment to polyvocality was something Robert shared intuitively. In the first issue of *The Forlorn Hope*, he and Jennison had explicitly invited "well digested argument, whether it comports exactly with the principles which may be the bias of the proprietors and conductors of the work, or in direct opposition." Robert was a debater more than a lecturer, and even as a writer he thrived in an atmosphere of diverse, and sometimes conflicting, perspectives.[17]

The working-class literary world in which Robert operated sits uneasily with our contemporary ideas about the author as an independent genius with a singular voice and a fixed perspective. Among radicals, authorship was a far more complex business. It was commonplace and expected for journalists and writers to co-produce texts, borrow from or openly plagiarize one another, or to adapt and change well-known works to give them a new meaning in a new context. In *The Axe*, for example, Robert's name or initials appear after around two thirds of the content, but he also reproduced well-known (and some not-so-well-known) street ballads, as well as excerpts from other papers. Some articles were addressed to him directly; others were addressed "to the editor"—also him—requesting "some inquiry" be made of "your *dashing* correspondent, Wedderburn" regarding, for instance, the Spencean plan. We cannot be certain, but it is entirely possible that in this instance, Robert the letter-writer was using a pseudonym to write to Robert the editor to inquire about Robert the "dashing correspondent." His very limited literacy during this period adds another layer of instability to this picture, since it means he must have been collaborating with at least one other radical to produce every word in the periodical. Yet, at least in terms of the malleability of its authorial voice, *The Axe* was not so very unusual. As the literary scholar Eric Pencek has suggested, the very instability of the authorial voice in such writings "serves to express the communal voice of a class and an ideology" rather than that of a single mind.[18]

THE PRESS IS MY ENGINE OF DESTRUCTION

What made *The Axe* unique in the world of radical publishing was its explicit focus on colonial slavery's role in the system of extractive global capitalism and the way Robert positioned the periodical as part of a wider conceptual dialogue between the enslaved in the Caribbean and the working classes in Britain. It was no less notable for the openly insurrectionary character of that dialogue. Robert had been deeply moved by the successful uprising of the enslaved in the French colony of Saint Domingue in 1791, which had resulted in a protracted war between the Black insurgents and the colonizing states of France, Britain, and Spain, leading to the establishment of the free Black republic of Haiti in 1804. The "unthinkable" nature of the Haitian Revolution led to a collective sort of trauma among Caribbean slaveholders and supporters of slavery in Britain, who frequently used associated imagery of Black-on-White violence to cow abolitionist efforts for much of this period. This is one of the reasons that British abolitionists had remained comparatively quiet on the question of general slave emancipation. Indeed, when the self-nominated "official" campaigning arm of the antislavery movement eventually reformed in 1823, it took the name the Society for the Mitigation and Gradual Abolition of Slavery, partly to distance itself from any kind of revolutionary connotations. But Robert had never been interested in being part of the official White-led antislavery movement, so he had no qualms about celebrating insurrections and uprisings of the enslaved or even about explicitly encouraging collective resistance. Indeed, when he was writing *The Axe*, an insurrection of the enslaved had taken place recently in the British colony of Barbados. Bussa's Rebellion, as it became known, had underscored the need for caution with the majority of antislavery thinkers in Britain. Robert saw it more as a source of inspiration.[19]

His most incendiary article in *The Axe*, addressed to the planters of Jamaica, is justly the most famous passage in his entire corpus. There really had been nothing like it published in English before. A short extract gives the flavor of the piece:

> Prepare for flight, ye planters, for the fate of St. Domingo awaits you. Get ready your blood-hounds, the allies which you employed against the Maroons. Recollect the fermentation will be universal. Their weapons are their bill-hooks; their store of provision is every were in abundance; you know they can live upon sugar canes, and a vast variety of herbs and fruits,—yea, even on the buds of trees. You cannot cut off their supplies. They will be victorious in their flight, slaying all before them; they want no turnpike roads: they will not stand to engage organized troops, like the silly Irish rebels. Their method of fighting is to be found in the scriptures, which they are now learning to read. . . . O ye planters, you know this has been done; the cause which produced former bloodshed still remains,—of necessity similar effects must take place.[20]

This passage, anatomizing the worst nightmares of the plantocracy, has come to define Robert's antislavery politics for many historians and literary scholars. Even today he is routinely described as a "firebrand"—someone who was content to burn down the cane fields first and ask questions later. There is certainly some merit to this description; indeed, particularly during the 1810s, he spoke and wrote like a man with little to lose, especially given the febrile and oppressive political atmosphere of those years. But this is entirely reconcilable with both the completeness of his Spencean vision for Jamaica and his hopeful utopian streak. Undoubtedly, his warning of bloody retribution for slaveholders is gratifyingly full-throated when read against the mealy-mouthed equivocations of most White British abolitionists of his generation. Nevertheless, he actually dedicated far more column inches in *The Axe* to outlining a better, post-slavery world for Jamaica than he did imagining the violent demise of the plantocracy.[21]

Robert's Spencean plan for post-emancipation Jamaica was framed as advice to the soon-to-rebel enslaved. He provided a basic outline for a profoundly democratic and egalitarian regime of governance based on freedom of conscience, common land ownership, universal suffrage (including women), annual parliaments, free education, and public juries. For Robert, the first principle of fair government was the total abolition of social rank, which he saw as the ultimate foundation of all inequality, including enslavement. "My Dear Countrymen," he wrote, "It is necessary for you to know how you may govern yourselves without a king, without lords, dukes, earls, or the like; these are classes of distinction which tend only to afflict society." He warned them above all else to avoid the mistakes that had allowed venality and corruption to creep into the British system. There, Robert claimed, governors and landlords exercised arbitrary sway over truth and falsehood through the allocation of legitimacy to some claims and the withholding of legitimacy from others.[22]

His own background of dispossession and criminalization resurfaced here, especially when he mentioned his own family's experiences: "Oh! My father, what do you deserve at my hands? Your crimes will be visited upon your legitimate offspring: for the sins of a wicked father will be visited upon his children, who continues in the practice of their father's crimes. Ought I not to encourage your slaves, O my brother, to demand their freedom even at the danger of your life, if it could not be obtained without. Do not tell me you hold them by legal right. No law can be just which deprives another of his liberty."[23]

This was as neat an encapsulation of how Robert's troubled family life had influenced his attitude to the law as any he had written. He also took aim at the inconsistent way that laws of legitimacy and inheritance were managed by the elite: "they punish in this country for stealing of children though the thief be rich, and intends the child to inherit his estates; and, at the same time, they make it right that hundreds of thousands of Africans may be stolen, and sold, like cattle, in the market." The ambiguities of British law, he said, had made it into a foolish "game" that only served to keep the craftiest sons of the "great" in employment as lawyers: "This game will always be carried on while the great manage the law, and the younger son is deprived of a share of his father's estate." Abolishing private inheritance was Robert's preferred way of preventing such a system from developing in his utopian free Black nation of Jamaica.[24]

If the men in Robert's family were a source of trauma, then his female relatives were a source of strength and rootedness. Women were central actors in Robert's plan and prominent semi-fictionalized characters in his polyvocal writing. He claimed that his information about the incipient insurrection in Jamaica came to him through his sister-in-law. (It is probably true that he had recently received an update from Jamaica from his brother's wife. Some fourteen years later, he again noted that he had met with her around 1816, adding that she had come to Britain as nurse to her aged "master," the minister at St. Peter's Anglican church in Port Royal.) The rumors about insurrection, Robert further claimed, were confirmed by another female correspondent, the mother of a plantation bookkeeper, who had told Robert that in her son's opinion, "the island of Jamaica will be in the hand of the blacks within twenty years." The fourth and sixth issues of *The Axe* were largely made up of an almost certainly fictionalized exchange of letters between Robert and his half-sister Miss Campbell, a slaveholder who (in his articles) freed the enslaved on her estates and attempted to institute the Spencean system there, falling afoul of the colonial authorities in the process. While most historians agree that both sides in this exchange were written by Robert, the extensiveness of this correspondence alone reflects the importance of female Caribbean voices in his intellectual and political framing of transatlantic revolutionary activism.[25]

The influence of Rosanna and Amy was palpable, too, in the central role Robert imagined for women in his utopian Jamaica. Strikingly, he saw women as important allies in the military defense of the island from the encroachments of slaveholding colonial powers: "let every individual learn the art of war, yea, even the females, for they are capable of displaying courage. You will have need of all your strength to defend yourself again those men, who are now scheming in Europe against the blacks of St. Domingo." Women were also identified as leaders in civil society in other key areas. For instance, they would have the crucial task of educating children in revolutionary and antislavery principles, guiding them to attain the "god-like strength" of knowledge and independence of thought. Older women were noted for their wisdom and seen as eligible to adjudicate local disputes: "every dispute may be decided in your own villages, by 12 men and 12 women; let them be above fifty." In a period marked for its paradoxes of limited and selective equality, perhaps the most radical aspect of Wedderburn's 1817 plan, then, was its faith in the judgment, wisdom, and strength of Black women as key architects of a revolutionary republic.[26]

Now in his late fifties, Robert felt he had found his calling in life: to speak for the enslaved far more radically and directly than anyone else had ever dared. "The greatness of the work that I am to perform has influenced my mind with an enthusiasm, I cannot support," he wrote. "I must give vent, I have commenced my career, the press is my engine of destruction." He took it for granted that the system of slavery in the West Indies, just like the unrepresentative and corrupt Parliament at home, could only be dismantled through destructive acts. Having honed his skills in the free-and-easies of Spencean politics, arguing with people at the pub, he brought his debating skills to bear in the form of print politics. Despite his own limited literacy, he saw that the press represented his best opportunity to enact political change that did not depend upon traditional, "legitimate" means. "Do not petition," he advised the enslaved on their preparations for resistance, "for it is degrading to human nature to petition your oppressors." He was explicit about the alternative means by which the new world would need to be brought about: "I come not to make peace; my fury shall be felt by princes, bidding defiance to pride and prejudice. Truth is my arrow stained with Africans' blood, rendered poisonous by guilt while they hold my innocent fellow as a slave, I will kindle wrath in their inmost souls." For Robert, violence was inevitable in the struggle against colonial oppression, and the press was a key means to activate it.[27]

Robert could not sustain the level of output and creative inspiration required to keep his political journal going for long. The popular abolitionist movement was in the doldrums in these years, and perhaps his focus on Jamaica was felt to be a little too remote for many working people in London, who would have preferred to focus more directly on their own problems. One Home Office spy reported that, by the end of January 1818, "Wedderburn is publishing a Pamphlet called the Axe Laid to the Root, but it has not much sale." *The Axe* folded after its sixth issue, leaving its final sentence, perhaps appropriately, unfinished. Such was the lot of the ultraradical journal. Not that this dampened Robert's optimism about politics. From the honor among thieves he had enjoyed with the tailors' union during the army contractors' affair in 1813 to the fraternity he had found in Spence's circle, he saw what solidarity might one day achieve. Robert could envision a form of solidarity that not only spoke about how enslaved people and exploited free laborers were similarly oppressed but also showed how the enslaved and the exploited might be able to share similar tools of resistance. *The Axe Laid to the Root* was Robert's first substantive political tract, and it is rightly remembered for its extraordinary evocation of violent insurrection. But it also captured something of Robert's optimism about what the future might hold for the downtrodden and illegitimate. If not quite a manifesto, it nevertheless set the pattern for his radical leadership.[28]

CHAPTER 6

Notorious Firebrand

THE ARRESTS HAD ALREADY BEGUN. In February 1817, Thomas Evans, Robert's friend and associate and the de facto leader of the Spencean Philanthropists, was arrested on suspicion of treason and held without trial for almost a year. Their ultraradical contacts Arthur Thistlewood and Dr. James Watson were picked up for the same crime in May. All were acquitted. Arthur was hot-headed enough to personally challenge the home secretary, Henry Addington (Lord Sidmouth), to a duel. No satisfaction could be gained that way; he was simply sent back to jail for a year in May 1818, on a charge of threatening to breach the peace. Suddenly, committing one's plans for revolution to paper, even revolution in the far-flung colonies, seemed like a bad idea. As Robert well understood, almost every meeting of London ultraradicals in these years was lousy with government spies. This fostered a sense of paranoia among them, especially those who favored the idea of armed insurrection to kick-start the revolution. This in turn accentuated their philosophical differences with moderates like Evans, who wanted to reform the constitution by legal means. All of it was damaging to morale and solidarity. But if Arthur, Dr. Watson, and Robert were worried about spies infiltrating the organization, they were justified. Sometimes they really are out to get you.[1]

When Evans got out of jail in late January 1818, he found that Robert had assumed a central role in keeping the Spenceans going. The two men joined forces in late spring or early summer, renting a debating room together at 6 Archer Street in Soho. Robert no doubt imagined that the discussions they co-hosted there would be like the old days at the Mulberry Tree. Indeed, the group still gathered at their old haunt, including to celebrate Spence's birthday in July, where Robert made a speech and led toasts, "accompanied by a bumper of the 'best Cordial Gin.'" But Evans was clearly shaken by his year in prison and his narrow escape from the capital charge of treason. Now he wanted the Spenceans to be a respectable group. He insisted that the Archer Street debates be calmer and more respectful and that "smoking, drinking, toasting, singing of vulgar songs and performing of burlesques no longer took place." To help ensure that the men attending behaved themselves, he announced that women were henceforth to be admitted for free. Evans's wife, Janet, herself a political radical, supported this move toward a more cordial style of debating.[2]

Robert felt that his new partner had lost his nerve. Although he was willing to behave respectfully at Evans's Archer Street debates on Monday mornings, when it was his turn to chair on Tuesday evenings, he let rip. As the spy James Hanley reported on November 2nd, "I understand this man's language is so horridly blasphemous at Archer St every Tuesday afternoon—that the Spenceans themselves are apprehensive of a prosecution—some of them wish him to withdraw his name from their Society." Robert was hardly behaving himself outside of the public meetings either: he was among ten men caught up in a mass brawl in St. Giles in September, though he escaped conviction. The cracks were beginning to show between the respectable reformer and the insurrectionary radical. The two had a rather spectacular falling out in April 1819 and decided to go their separate ways. Robert comprehensively burned his bridges with Evans by helping himself to all the furniture from their debating room. Evans heard about this and sent three heavies to accost Robert in the street while he was in the process of moving the audience chairs. Among these three men were Charles Jennison, Robert's old co-editor at *The Forlorn Hope*, and a rather hot-headed plaster-cast maker, George Edwards, whose name would shortly become infamous throughout London's ultraradical underworld. They broke down the door of Robert's home at Smith's Court and took back the chairs, despite protestations from Mary and the children. Shortly afterward, Robert published his side of the argument in two separate broadsides that he distributed about the neighborhood, attacking Evans as "an apostate" and a "double-faced politician," even insulting Janet as being a "brandy-faced Dulcina." Obviously, this marked the end of his partnership with Evans and of his time in the Spencean Philanthropists, though he maintained his Spencean ideology for the rest of his life. At least the scurrilous handbills he had printed about Evans gave him the chance to advertise his new, uncensored debating room at Hopkins Street. When he opened his new "chapel," Robert took much of the Archer Street congregation with him. Now he was in control of the agenda.[3]

Freed from the comparatively moderating influence of Evans, Robert's new chapel hosted some of the most incendiary and outright seditious debates of the time. Naturally, the audience was teeming with government spies. The Reverend Chetwode Eustace, a particularly hostile and obsequious informer, gives a sense of what kind of place it was: "I had some difficulty to discover the place for it is apparently a ruinous loft which you ascend by a step-ladder—the assemblage was perfectly suitable to their place for both Orators and Audience were with a few exceptions, persons of the very lowest description." He was right—the audiences largely consisted of men and women brought low by unemployment and poverty, disaffected and helpless people looking for a way out of their distress or at least a leader who shared their anger and frustration. Robert was more than happy to fill that role for them, to remind them that they had few legitimate and no democratic means of redress, and—most dangerously of all—to encourage them to get it by other methods. Eustace was right about the room, too; the place was a wreck. Less than a year later, when Robert was in jail, the Hopkins Street "chapel" was being used as an arena for bear baiting.[4]

Attendees paid a woman at the door a shilling, for which they received a ticket that admitted them to the lectures and debates held every Sunday, Monday, and Wednesday for one month. The topics of the debates alone demonstrate how extreme the politics were. On August 16th, for instance, the question was phrased darkly: "Is it possible for the Government to be extricated from the accumulating Perils with which it is daily surrounding itself?" By October 11th, it was more direct: "Which of the two is likely to lose the Most, the Prince who struggled to maintain his throne or the man who struggles to obtain it?" Then, two days later, a truly alarming thought experiment: "Which of the two parties are likely to be victorious, the rich or the poor, in the event of universal war?" These debates were advertised by handbills pasted to the walls around Soho and on Oxford Street with headlines such as "VENGENCE AWAITS THE GUILTY," much to the concern of some residents.

Indeed, many people, including poor people, disapproved of what went on at Hopkins Street. On one occasion, in the middle of Robert's lecture about "fat-headed parsons [who] kept harlots and houses of ill-fame," some disgruntled locals invaded the meeting to try to shut it down, leading to a physical fight between them and Robert. He was unrepentant, taking the interlopers to police court where he boldly declared to the magistrates that he "would not be governed by the laws of any country, and although a journeyman tailor, starved by taxation, he would preach that which he conceived to be right, if a rope was round his neck." This attitude could hardly have ingratiated him with his long-suffering neighbors. As one local shopkeeper complained in a letter to the Home Office, enclosing a handbill advertising one of the debates, "the michiefous tendency of this Bill and of the debates held weekly in the Temple of Sedition called the Hopkins Street Chapel need not be mentioned to your Lordship." The shopkeeper had it: there was no need to tell the home secretary that he should be concerned about Hopkins Street. He was already looking into it.[5]

For a while at least, Robert managed to protect himself from being picked up for sedition or treason in two ways. Most importantly, he framed many of his debates not only around the extremely touchy subject of domestic political reform but also around the ostensibly more legitimately debatable question of colonial slavery. On August 9, 1819, for example, Robert, advertising himself as "the offspring of an African slave" for an event publicized under the heading "Can it be Murder to KILL A TYRANT?," opened the debate on the question "Has a Slave an inherent right to slay his Master, who refuses him HIS LIBERTY?" He was clearly excited about this particular event, advertising it at a tavern meeting the night before at The Crown on East Harding Street as well as through the usual handbills pasted about the neighborhood (fig. 3).[6]

The spy Eustace was unconvinced that this was anything other than sedition disguised as antislavery: "Yesterday evening I proceeded to Hopkins St. Chapel to hear the question discussed whether it be right for the People of England to assassinate their rulers," he wrote to the Home Office the following day, "for this my Lord,

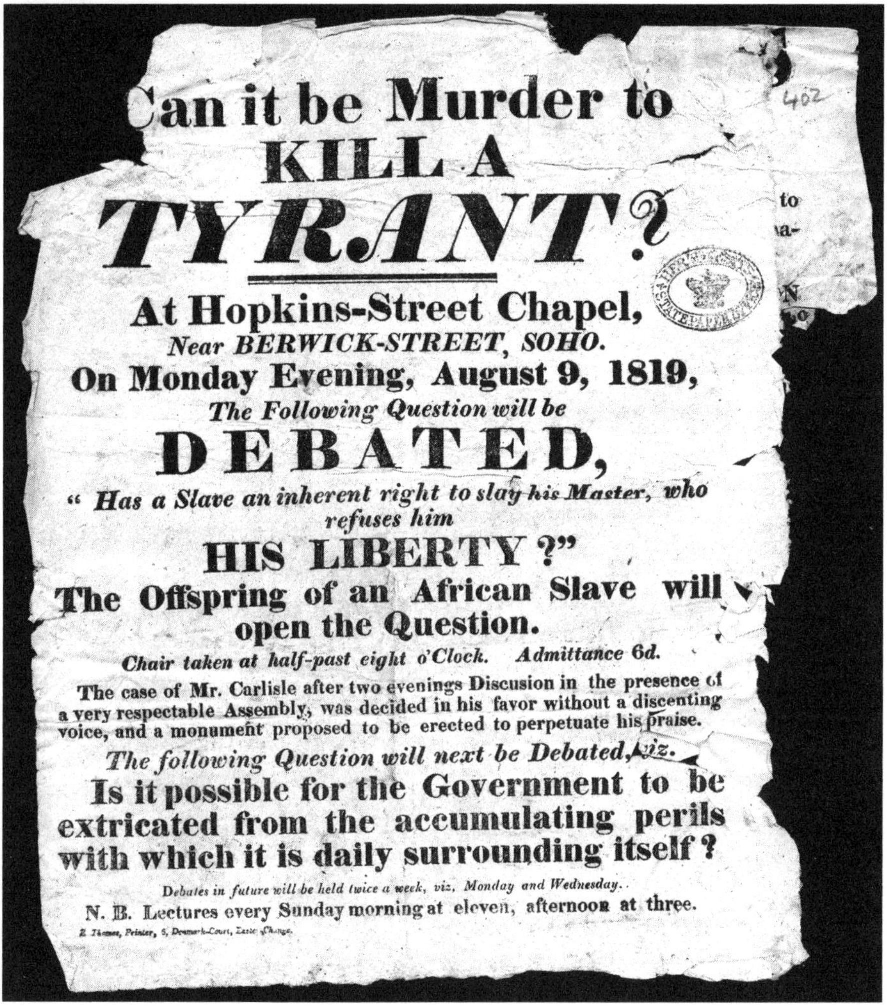

Figure 3. Handbill advertising the debate at Hopkins Street Chapel on August 9, 1819. HO42/191, 402, The National Archives (UK)

I conceive to be the real purport of the question tho' proposed in other terms." He may have been underestimating Robert's commitment to revolution in the West Indies as well as the ongoing personal connections he held with family and friends in the colony. Robert had in fact spoken very explicitly about the British state's complicity in the transatlantic slave trade, though as ever he saw it as one part of the larger problem of labor exploitation in a globalized economy: "Wedderbourne—rose—Government was necessitated to send men in arms to West Indies or Africa which produced commotion. They would employ blacks to go and steal females. . . . This was done by Parliament men—who done it for gain—the same as they employed them in their Cotton factories to make slaves of them."[7]

Another spy claimed that Robert had said "every King Bishop Priest and Potentate ought to be put to death" for failing to protect the poor and the enslaved, and even that the prince regent himself—the king in all but name—"ought to be put to death" for failing to enforce the "law of scripture" regarding colonial slavery. Equally worrying for the Home Office was that Robert stated, half-seriously, that he would be glad to incite another insurrection of the enslaved in the West Indies. When the sense of the meeting was taken, almost all the crowd voted in favor of the slave's right to slay his master, with several members of the audience proclaiming themselves ready to go to the West Indies and lend a hand. Robert leaned back in his chair and exclaimed, "I can now write home and tell the Slaves to Murder their Masters as soon as they please!"[8]

Given his extraordinary fearlessness in speech, it is little wonder that Robert ended up being arrested for sedition—multiple times. His first arrest related to the debate about the enslaved murdering their masters. On August 12, 1819, a few days after the debate, the home secretary wrote to the prince regent himself to let him know that a prosecution would be ordered against "a man of the name of Wedderburne, a notorious firebrand, for sedition." The Home Office actually had to try several different routes to secure an affidavit. In response to its first inquiry, the solicitor general and attorney general informed the Home Office that holding a meeting on the question of a slave's right to murder his master was not in itself unlawful. If officials wanted to charge him, they would need to bring in witnesses willing to testify in court to what he actually said and allow a grand jury to decide if it constituted sedition. In the meantime, Robert would remain free to return to his preaching and debating despite the arrest, thanks to a bit of help with the bail money from his neighbor and fellow radical tailor John Hill. When the case finally came to trial in September, Robert managed to convince the jury that he had been seized by "the true and infallible genius of prophetic skill" and that he should be treated as a religious prophet rather than a political lecturer. The jury bought it, and the case was thrown out on September 21st. When he appeared at the Middlesex Court of Session to reclaim the bail money on September 30th, egged on by his radical associate Richard Carlile, Robert and several others who had been acquitted of sedition charges refused to pay the court administration fee, causing a minor tumult. Anything to cause a headache for the men in power. It did not matter; he was keen to get back to his preaching.[9]

This had surely been a lucky escape, given the moment of political crisis that Britain had just entered. Large outdoor rallies for political reform had been taking place in cities all over the country for a number of years, with speeches from leading radicals and resolutions passed and printed up. In London, Spenceans were involved in organizing a number of these, including the riot at Spa Fields in December 1816, which ended up with a small contingent of radicals exchanging gunfire with soldiers at the Tower of London and demanding the release of all prisoners held there. This was unusual; the confrontation after Spa Fields was in fact deliberately engineered by more extremist elements of the Spencean society, including Robert's associate Arthur Thistlewood. The militarized nature of this uprising, as well as the increasing boldness of radical speakers and writers like Robert, set the authorities on edge all over the country. These roiling tensions came to a head at a mass meeting on August 16, 1819, at St. Peter's Field in Manchester, just one week after Robert's debate on the enslaved killing their masters. At a huge but peaceful meeting of around sixty thousand protestors, local magistrates sent in mounted soldiers to disperse the crowd. The soldiers acted with extreme prejudice, killing eighteen people, including a two-year-old child and a pregnant woman, and they injured hundreds more. The event quickly became known as the Peterloo massacre, a bitter portmanteau of St. Peter's Field and Waterloo, the battlefield where Lord Wellington scored his decisive victory over Napoleon.[10]

The massacre at Peterloo had a galvanizing effect on both the various radical movements in Britain and government repression. Where ultraradicals had before been debating the merits of sparking a popular uprising versus waiting for a more opportune moment, now they were looking to obtain the weapons. Where moderate reformers had been speaking of gradual constitutional reform, now they demanded immediate responses from the government. And where the Home Office had been keeping close tabs on both of these groups and reacting only when necessary, now officials moved proactively to arrest the ringleaders, seeking capital sentences where possible and trying to crush the reformist movements entirely. The notorious "Six Acts" were passed in December 1819, striking at the heart of all forms of radical organizing. They included a prohibition against any kind of military drilling in civilian settings, granted magistrates the right to seize private firearms, reduced the right of bail for misdemeanors (a right of which Robert had availed himself just a few months previously), prohibited political meetings of more than fifty people, introduced tougher sentences for blasphemy and seditious libel, and, crushingly, introduced a heavy four-penny stamp tax on political journalism, targeting radical periodicals like *The Forlorn Hope* and *The Axe*.[11]

In this context it is perhaps surprising that Robert was eventually brought down not for sedition or treason, but for blasphemy. During the spring or early summer of 1819, he'd had himself ordained as a Unitarian minister—meaning that he could now officially call himself "Rev. Robert Wedderburn V.D.M." This was ironic given his rather extreme and long-held hatred of the clergy, but it was also smart, since he could now believably claim that the incendiary and indeed highly blasphemous debates hosted at Hopkins Street were of a religious rather than political character. Even the hawks at the Home Office did not relish the thought of arresting preachers on matters of conscience. For this reason, Robert was able to get away with more than he usually would have, at least where nominally religious questions were concerned. He routinely denounced the clergy in eye-watering terms. For instance, during a debate on August 4th, one spy noted that he had "railed most violently against the bishops and clergy & that they deserved being burnt." By becoming a member of the clergy himself, he was able to camouflage such violent speech as the legitimate expression of Christian doctrinal differences, thus taking to absurd heights the complaint he had outlined almost twenty years earlier in *The Truth Self-Supported*.[12]

Robert's enthusiasm for an insurrectionist alliance between the enslaved in the West Indies and the working classes in Britain was of a piece with his disdain for the clergy, whom he saw as actively propping up the authority of slaveholders through organizations like the Church Missionary Society and the Methodist missions in the West Indies. His public speeches on this issue were all the more controversial because he assaulted Christian institutions—even nonconforming connections like Wesleyan Methodism—as outgrowths of a corrupt state that was complicit with slavery at home and abroad. On Monday, November 8, 1819, for example, he hosted a debate on an obviously loaded question: "Is a church establishment necessary for the preservation of religion, morality, and good order, or is it merely a political institution, and a tyrannical imposition on the people, with a view the more easily to enslave them?"[13]

Nor was this mention of "enslaving" the British poor merely a superficial reference for Robert. The following Wednesday, he proposed a follow-up debate, this time tackling the connections between Christian authority and slavery in the West Indies head-on with this question: "Which is the greater crime, for the Wesleyan missionaries to preach up passive obedience to the poor black slaves in the West Indies, or, to extort from them at the rate of £18,000 per annum, under pretence of supporting the gospel?"[14] On that night, he stood up and expressed his hope that

> they might expose the villainy of our church and state by sending out those vipers of church Missionaries to suck the blood of the poor innocent blacks in the West Indies and to make them believe that the great God was with them but instead of God it was the devil and the missionaries that was sent from London by the Secretary of State for the Home Department and for no other motives than to extort money for the great. . . . and who is this owing to why to the great heads of this Nation who are robbing the poor every day by Loading them with heavy burthens such as taxation, Extravagance and luxury.[15]

It is easy to see why such language set alarm bells ringing at the Home Office. There was only so much officials were willing to tolerate, even from an ordained preacher.

Robert must have known, so he must simply not have cared that the Home Office continued to amass evidence against him with each new debate. On October 13th, he publicly declared his intention to take up arms against the British state, "for they have declared war against the People and the Prince Regent has sanctioned it by his fine vote of thanks and has turned a deaf ear to our own grievances my motto is assassinate stab in the dark." Multiple spies heard this and reported it; it all went into the growing file of evidence. On October 28th, Robert returned to his favorite line of attack, targeting religious authority—which he tellingly still saw as a derivative of paternal authority—as a means of criticizing the government. Calling Jesus Christ a "radical reformer," he claimed that Christ instructed his followers to "acknowledge no Rabbi (no Priest) no he knew their tricks and he says stand it no longer Jesus Christ says acknowledge no Fathers why because Fathers at these days were allowed to thrash there sons at any age." As so often in Robert's commentaries on religious matters, the father figure here personified all forms of unjust authority, and of course he knew all about the physical violence that was excused under the banner of patriarchal authority.[16]

He was arrested again in November, and on December 1st he was admitted to Newgate jail to await trial for the crime of "publishing certain blasphemous works of and concerning the Holy Scriptures." Robert had slipped the net once; the Home Office would not let it happen again. There was plenty of evidence this time, and no amount of sophisticated reasoning could get him off the hook, as it had back in September. The timing of this second arrest, incidentally, was highly convenient for the Home Office: because his entry into the calendar for trials fell during the holiday period between the Michaelmas and Hilary sittings of the judiciary, Robert was allowed to be held in custody prior to trial just long enough for the new, tougher sentencing laws on blasphemous and seditious libel to come into force. It was enough to get Robert off the streets and put a permanent stop to sedition at Hopkins Street.[17]

We know now that getting arrested when he did probably saved Robert's life. He had always been at the vanguard of the insurrectionary tradition in Spencean circles, and his public speeches at Hopkins Street, like the articles he published in *The Axe*, only hinted at the true depths of his sedition. At an outdoor mass meeting in Finsbury Market on November 1st, he advised the attendants to come to the next meeting armed (for which he was sharply called to order by the other radicals present). In the more private setting of alehouse backroom meetings, he was often to be found, alongside other militant ultraradicals like Arthur Thistlewood and Dr. Watson, advocating for armed revolt. Though he was a relative newcomer to radical politics, his advanced age meant that he was treated with respect, and even some affection by the others. On August 5th, the landlord of the White Lion on Wyatt Street burst into the back room to ask the Spenceans meeting there to keep the volume of their conversation down. They had been arguing about whether they should strike now to start the revolution or wait a little longer. The landlord was friendly to their politics, but he was not stupid; he "desired them not to talk so loud, as there were people in the Gallery who said they were talking Treason, and he had noticed two Strangers there." At this, Robert sat up in his chair and addressed the room. "We care not for Strangers," he said, "if we are but friends to ourselves. I am a foreigner & a sailor, and an Old Man, but I wish I may be placed in the front Rank, as a pattern for the young ones." He said he "did not care for life, if he lost it for the benefit of his Children—they were all his Children." After so long at the fringes of legal society, Robert had finally found a social and political world that valued him. Expressing his desire to be among the "front rank" of the revolution in familial terms, he was clearly keen not only to lead but to mentor the younger members of the group.[18]

This desire was one of the circumstances that led him, ultimately, into involvement with an incident of domestic terrorism. On February 23, 1820, around twenty-five armed men gathered in a disused hayloft on Cato Street with the intention of invading Lord Harrowby's mansion on nearby Grosvenor Square, where they believed the prime minister and the entire government cabinet were gathered for a dinner. Once inside, they planned to kill all the assembled ministers, cut their heads off, and parade them through the streets of London on pikes, thus triggering the longed-for uprising of the people. They had brought with them hand grenades, swords, knives, and firearms for the purpose. The servants and other innocent guests at the dinner would not be suffered to survive the attack; they were to be considered collateral damage. The Spenceans had been planning the attack for months, anticipating the spontaneous uprising that they thought would follow with delusional confidence. But it was a trap; the ministers were not at Lord Harrowby's—the newspaper report that had stated as much had been put there by the government. There was a commotion from the front of the hayloft building, a scuffle, great confusion. The Bow Street Runners had arrived to arrest the conspirators. The Cato Street Conspiracy had been foiled. Trials and executions followed.[19]

Robert would almost certainly have been among those arrested, and quite possibly among those executed, if he was not already in jail on a blasphemy charge the night the conspiracy failed. He was seen by the conspirators as a reliable revolutionary collaborator with an eye for the practicalities of a national uprising. He had proved that much with his well-developed plans for a revolutionary Black-led Jamaican government in *The Axe*. The ringleader of the Cato Street Conspiracy—none other than Robert's Spencean "child," Arthur—had noted in one of the planning meetings at the White Lion that "he depends more on Wedderburn's division for being armed than all the rest." Moreover, Robert claimed to have connections in Ireland, and the Spenceans saw the Irish as crucial allies in the forthcoming "universal war" between the poor and the "Old Corruption" in Britain. He was also mentor to another key conspirator, a fellow Jamaican-Scottish "mulatto" named William Davidson. Robert had invited William to speak with him at Hopkins Street on a number of occasions, including the debate on Wesleyan missionaries in the West Indies.[20]

Robert and William, the two most prominent Black radicals in London, had a lot in common. Both had been born and raised exposed to the full horrors of colonial slavery in Jamaica. Both, in fact, were illegitimate, mixed-race sons of White, slaveholding Scottish-born fathers and Black Jamaican-born mothers. Both had been disappointed, though to different degrees, in their expectations of parental support and acknowledgment from their fathers, and the insufficiency of such support had contributed to both of them encountering terrible financial hardships on the streets of early nineteenth-century London. William, twenty years younger than Robert, was a cabinetmaker by trade, and like Robert was suffering from a loss of work in the post–Napoleonic War recession. He was an educated man, having studied mathematics at Glasgow University. Like Robert, he had been pressed into service in the Royal Navy at least once, and after being discharged he had entered into a state of destitution in London, pawning his cabinetry tools for money to feed his family. He applied to the gentlemanly Mendicity Society for forty shillings to redeem the tools from the pawnshop early in 1820. He used the money instead to buy a blunderbuss to kill the prime minister.[21]

Robert and William were not the only illegitimate children of slaveholding families entangled in the Cato Street Conspiracy. Arthur was White, but he was the illegitimate son of William Thistlewood, which made him nephew to the Jamaican planter Thomas Thistlewood. As we have seen, Robert's father had been the doctor on Thistlewood's estate and helped to care for Thistlewood's enslaved "wife," Phibbah, during her pregnancy. Although Arthur never met his biological uncle, he too had likely witnessed slavery up close during his service in the West Indies as a commissioned officer in the Royal Navy during the early 1790s, possibly as part of the expeditionary force sent to reclaim Saint Domingue as a slave colony for the British. According to the patchy and unreliable sources we have for Arthur's early life, he quit his commission shortly after arriving in the West Indies and escaped to the United States. After a spell in France, he, just like William and Robert, was entrapped in urban poverty and became increasingly convinced that magistrates, priests, and high-born gentlemen had no legitimacy to withhold his birthright of political freedom from him.[22]

On May 1, 1820, Arthur and William were hanged for their part in the Cato Street Conspiracy along with their co-conspirators, Thomas Ings, Richard Tidd, and John Thomas Brunt. Once dead, their heads were then removed by a surgeon's knife and held aloft to the crowd both north and south of the gibbet, one after the other: a grim, repetitive ritual. The operator in charge of removing the heads "was loudly hissed and groaned at by the mob, and some atrocious expressions were applied to him," as the reporter for the *Edinburgh Magazine* put it. "The universal groans, accompanied by some female shrieks, when he first commenced on Thistlewood, had an awful effect."[23]

Not long after, it came to light that the Cato Street Conspiracy had, in fact, been doomed to fail from the start. Much of the plan had been concocted by George Edwards, one of the men Evans had sent to Robert's house to reclaim the furniture he'd taken from the Archer Street chapel. Edwards had probably been active in London radical politics since around 1816. His plaster sculpture-making shop was next door to Richard Carlile's bookshop, and he had made a number of plaster busts of Spence for the Philanthropists. Edwards's response to worsening hardship in 1818 was to begin taking money from the Home Office in exchange for intelligence reports. He quickly infiltrated Arthur's section of the group and began to encourage them on to ever more desperate measures. He even used some of the money from the Home Office to supply them with weapons. It was Edwards who delivered the fake newspaper article announcing the dinner at Grosvenor Square to Arthur and the others, essentially sealing their fate. The deaths of these five men were deemed a fair price to pay to put a stop to the insurrectionary activities of the Spenceans.

Degraded by poverty and insulted by the very people who professed to protect them, Robert, William, and Arthur all rejected the legitimacy of the government and, to some extent, the very concept of legitimacy itself. The notion of hereditary privilege operating along the lines of "legitimate heirs," from which they had all been excluded, was a big part of this. Another of Robert's guest speakers at Hopkins Street, Allen Davenport, lampooned the absurdity of being ruled by hereditary landowners in his banned play *The Kings; or Legitimacy Unmasked* (1819), which, he claimed, the Spenceans often liked to act out when they got together. Davenport reasoned that since all monarchs ultimately derived their "kingly legitimacy" from "ruffian-force and venal sin," they would naturally try "to rule Freeman, by laws decreed for slaves."[24]

What could men like Robert, William, and Arthur, locked out

of any meaningful democratic means of redress, do about this situation? They took matters into their own hands. All three of them began merely by writing plans and giving speeches. In the pressure-cooker atmosphere of Britain in 1819, and especially after the Peterloo massacre in August, this was enough to paint a target on each of their backs. The Home Office acted swiftly and without mercy against them. There is no denying that they were all involved in plotting an appalling atrocity and that their plans showed a total disregard for the lives of the men they targeted, not to mention any innocent people who might have had the bad luck to get in their way on that night in February 1820. They had become violent terrorists. But they had a little help getting there. Arthur and William, especially, were cruelly deceived by George Edwards, and they paid for this with their lives. When these two would-be revolutionaries mounted the scaffold in May, did they even realize that their plan to wreak a classless utopia in Britain had never stood a chance? That they, in their poverty and desperation, had been deliberately led into that hayloft for the sole purpose of being caught? And when Robert appeared in court, just a week later, to receive a prison sentence for words he had spoken at Hopkins Street, did he realize just how close he had come to joining them?

PART III

Destitution

CHAPTER 7

Inside

WHEN ROBERT WAS ARRESTED in the winter of 1819, he was already in dire financial straits. Without the money for bail, which had been set at the impossibly high figure of £100, he was forced to remain incarcerated while Mary and the children struggled for food. On February 2, 1820, while awaiting sentencing, he sent out a letter, most likely to his rather unscrupulous collaborator and lawyer George Cannon, to ask for pro bono legal representation. "As I am an extremely poor man & cannot afford to move myself before a Judge for this purpose I should consider it a most particular favour if you could make it convenient to look in here the first... opportunity."[1] Undoubtedly, part of the reason for his being so "extremely poor" was down to his politics, and especially his strong words against the clergy and the Church. It had cost him business. As he put it in an advertisement for his tailoring services in 1819, "since the commencement of his labours as a public teacher, for the benefit of Society, and the advancement of useful knowledge in *Theology and Moral Philosophy*, he has experienced the neglect and dissertion of many, yea, very many of his former friends, and of masters in the trade from whom he was wont to gain employment, and thereby rendered incapable of meeting the necessary calls of common want ... left him destitute of means by the labour of his hands to support existence."[2]

Robert had long understood what it meant to be destitute, and it was not the same thing as being poor. In the pseudo-bureaucratic language of workhouses and the philanthropic societies, the word "destitute" often denoted someone who had fallen victim to vice, or was at risk of doing so. In this period, destitution was often defined as having lost God's grace. Samuel Johnson defined it first and foremost as a state of being "forsaken; abandoned," but his example was from the theologian Richard Hooker: "to fall into all such *evils* upon the face of the earth, as men, either *destitute* of grace divine, may commit, or unprotected from above, may endure."[3]

These implications carried through into the tradition of early nineteenth-century "indoor" poor relief. The stated aim of the Refuge for the Destitute in Hoxton, East London, for example, was "to provide a place of refuge for persons discharged from prisons, or the hulks, unfortunate and deserted females, and others, who, though willing to work, are unable from loss of character to procure an honest maintenance." For the evangelical middle classes, having nowhere to go and no one to turn to might reflect a character defect that was best corrected through prayer and stern instruction from one's betters. At the Refuge, potential donors were reassured that "the utmost attention is paid to the improvement of morals, and suitable admonition and religious instruction regularly afforded them by the Chaplain." Robert himself increasingly came to understand the close relationship between destitution and vice—never more so than when he himself became ensnared by both.[4]

We have already seen that the time he spent around St. Giles and Shoreditch in the late 1780s and the early 1790s was an especially difficult one for London's "Black poor" community. A generation later, the same story played out on the same streets, only in the wake of a different set of wars against France and America. In 1819, the Society for the Suppression of Mendicity lamented, "the wretched condition of many Africans and persons of colour, as well as other classes of Foreigners, who, having served this country, have lost their own without acquiring another." The street economy allowed some to support themselves. Joseph Johnson, for example, made a name for himself performing popular ballads while wearing a scale model of the HMS *Nelson* on top of his head. Charles McGee earned his crust as a street sweeper at the foot of Ludgate Hill, but he was also so well known in the area that he was the subject of a radical satire by William Hone, a striking portrait by John Dempsey, and even a light opera called *Othello, the Moor of Fleet Street*. After Robert lost his status as a "flint" following the army contractors' caper in 1813, he worked as a "dung" tailor, keeping a roof over his children's heads, in the evocative words of the historian Iain McCalman, by "patching clothes and vending pamphlets from a wooden bulk (or stall) located in one of the small stinking courts of St. Martin's Lane."[5]

For many poor men of color in London, it was more than they could do to avoid the workhouse. Again, the association between being destitute and being a potential criminal held strong in the liberal imagination. The agents for the Mendicity Society appeared to take great pleasure in 1819 when they exposed "W. B.," a "man of colour" who came to them "apparently in a strong fit of the ague" and "stated a most deplorable case of distress." They were having none of it. "One of the clerks of the Society having, however, recognised the man, his former history was produced from some original document in the Office, and he quickly recovered from his apparent ague, and at length acknowledged that he had been endeavouring to deceive the public and the Society." The officers of this charitable organization decided that "an imposter of this nature could not be permitted to go at large, and he was referred to the Police-Office, where . . . he was left to be dealt with according to the law." The combination of W. B.'s poverty and his heightened visibility as a Black man on London's streets made it that much more difficult for him, like Robert and William, to evade the grasp of these self-appointed moral guardians.[6]

So many charitable societies like this existed during the lean years after the Napoleonic Wars because they saw the extremely poor as at risk of falling under the influence of immoral and thus dangerous people. Robert's crowd was a mixture of poor artisans like himself, impoverished small business owners, and well-educated literary types. Indeed, it speaks to his natural affinity for politics and literature that he tended to gravitate more toward the latter, despite his unapologetic militancy and roughness of expression. Of the many middle-class (though poor) radical friends he made during this period, two were to shape the course of his life through the 1820s. Both of these men were considered dangerously immoral even beyond their political radicalism, though in different ways.

The first was George Cannon, Robert's lawyer. Cannon was a notoriously slippery character who published pornographic and anticlerical works under multiple pseudonyms, and sometimes under the names of his clients. The second was Richard Carlile, the bookseller. Carlile had been one of the speakers at Peterloo, and his radical activities were well known. What was most concerning about him, at least for the government, was his commitment to challenging religious authority among the poor and disaffected, which later amounted to promoting out-and-out atheism in his radical newspaper, *The Republican*. This was a profound test for the principle of the free press in a country where the political dominance of the Church of England was held in delicate tension with freedom of conscience. (Catholics, for example, were not permitted to sit as members of Parliament until 1829.) If the rallying cry of popular conservatism in early nineteenth-century Britain was "for Church and King," then Carlile, a committed atheist and archetypical *Republican,* personified for them the degeneracy at the heart of the ultraradical underworld. Unsurprisingly, he was imprisoned on blasphemy and sedition charges in October 1819, even before Robert.[7]

The influence of these two apparently shady characters collided at Robert's trial in February 1820. The charge itself related to a debate Robert had chaired at Hopkins Street on October 25, 1819, on a question concerning Carlile's trial a few weeks earlier. Robert posed the question "whether the refusal of the Chief-Justice to allow Mr. Carlile to read the bible in his defence, was to be attributed to the sincere respect he had for the sacred writings, or to a fear lest the absurdities it contained should be exposed?" At that debate, Robert had accused Chief Justice Abbott, the judge presiding over Carlile's case, of hypocrisy, because as a well-educated man he knew full well the "absurdities" that were in the Bible yet still sent radicals to jail for deriding Christianity in public. Robert's irreverent humor came through clearly enough in his speech at that debate: "Jesus Christ says, 'no man hath ever seen God,' then what a d——d liar Moses must have been, for he tells us he could run about and see God in every bush." Recalling his grandmother's punishment on suspicion of practicing obeah, Robert also railed against the story of the Witch of Endor summoning Samuel's ghost in the First Book of Samuel, which contradicted the New Testament doctrine that only God was able to raise the spirits of the dead. Also, and more to the alarm of the Home Office as we have seen, he went on to characterize Christ as a radical reformer who taught his disciples to "acknowledge no rabbi."[8]

When he was called to trial to account for this speech, Robert's defense consisted of two parts. First he extemporized a short history of the circumstances of his birth and upbringing, and he mentioned, quite respectfully, that he was a licensed Unitarian preacher and was perfectly within his rights to debate theological matters. The second part of his defense was a written paper that the lawyer Cannon had drawn up for him, filled with classical and literary allusions and further exegesis on the absurdities and inconsistencies in the Bible. The sheer range of highfalutin literary and historical references from sources in multiple languages means that Robert could not have written this defense for himself; even the judge conceded that it was "exceedingly well drawn up." Yet at the same time, to double down on the argument that the Bible was self-contradictory—and to suggest that the defendant was simply more intelligent and enlightened than the Court—can only be described as a spectacularly misjudged defense strategy for a blasphemy trial.

One of the first gambits of Cannon's speech must surely have set the jury against Robert: "Your minds are endeavoured to be prejudiced against me, by the frequent repetition of the term '*blasphemy*';—but what, after all, is the meaning of this word, so terrific in the ears of the ignorant and superstitious?" To be fair, it probably made little difference to the outcome; the judge presiding over Robert's case was none other than the man he had attacked in the speech he was on trial for: Chief Justice Abbott. In Abbott's recommendation to the jury, he baldly instructed them that as the material in Robert's defense was itself blasphemous, "you must find him guilty." The jury duly did so but recommended mercy on the strength of the first part of Robert's defense—the one he had come up with himself—on the grounds of "his not having the benefit of parental care."[9]

Robert was back in court a couple of months later, on May 9th, for sentencing. A similar scene played out again in the courtroom.

Robert first extemporized a statement referencing his grandmother's treatment under suspicion of witchcraft in mitigation of what he had said about the Witch of Endor. He was perhaps a little less cautious in his language this time, and he was called up by the sentencing judge for using language "of a nature which they could not tolerate." Then Cannon's written statement was read out, which not only refused to temper the defense's radical speech for the courtroom but astonishingly included an advertisement for Cannon's new blasphemous tract, recently published under Robert's name. The conclusion of this speech practically dared the judge to ignore the jury's recommendation for mercy and dole out a harsh sentence: "I am so extremely poor that a prison will be a home to me; and I am so far advanced in life I shall esteem it an honour to die immured in a Dungeon for advocating THE CAUSE OF TRUTH, OF RELIGIOUS LIBERTY, AND THE UNIVERSAL RIGHT OF CONSCIENCE." The judge was only too happy to oblige: Robert was sentenced to two years in Dorchester Gaol—over a hundred miles from London and well beyond the reach of impoverished visitors or collaborators—to take up a cell alongside Carlile.[10]

Cannon's legal strategy had provided himself some free advertising, but it exposed his defendant to the personal irritation of the judges. This meant that Robert's sentence was long. According to his fellow inmate Carlile, Robert's reputation as an incendiary radical and a blasphemer, and possibly his heightened visibility as a Black man and a "foreigner," meant that his time in prison was also exceptionally hard. Not incidentally, Robert's record in the Dorchester Gaol inmates' book marked him out from his fellow inmates both by explicit reference to his background and through racialized descriptions of his appearance. For example, even though he had lived in London for over forty years, his "parish" designation listed him as "A Native of Kingston Jamaica, but belongs to St. James's Parish London." Likewise, despite Robert's relatively light skin, his complexion was listed as "very dark," and his appearance was summed up by the fact that he was "a man of colour," "lusty" in stature, with "broad nostrils" and two scars on his face. We should be clear: the purely functional record of his admission to Dorchester Gaol does not imply any kind of racial animus against Robert on the part of the Dorchester authorities. Indeed, they could hardly avoid mentioning the fact he was Black when tasked with providing a short description of his appearance. But these sparse notes do emphasize the fact that Robert stood out among the inmates at Dorchester and that he was easily recognizable by the jailers, which may have made his life more difficult.[11]

Things started out well enough. Upon his first arrival at Dorchester, Robert was feted as a martyr to the cause of political reform. Cannon published a protest tract admonishing Justice Abbott, with the proceeds going to support Mary and the children. Carlile, grateful that his friend was willing to endure imprisonment to defend him, was excited to see him arrive. Indeed, Carlile's enthusiastic advocacy for Robert is what now allows us to follow him inside Dorchester Gaol. Carlile published regular updates on both of their sentences for their radical contacts on the outside. Writing by correspondence in *The Republican*, now printed and sold by his wife, Jane, Carlile noted that Robert—the "fashionable arrival at Dorchester Castle"—would be using his time inside to brush up on his writing skills before returning to public life. He even joked that the Reverend Wedderburn might take over as the prison chaplain, observing that he "is sufficiently an eccentric to amuse the prisoners."[12]

Robert's much-vaunted mastery of Christian scripture possibly led to a collaboration with either Carlile or Cannon, or both, resulting in the bitingly anticlerical pamphlet *Cast-Iron Parsons*, which was published solely under Robert's name in July or August

1820. This pamphlet cheekily suggested that, since the newfangled invention of cast iron was now being used in the structures of churches, perhaps church authorities should start making automata out of cast iron to deliver the sermons, too. The work of a clergyman had become "so completely mechanical"—and, the pamphlet commented acidly, "nothing was so much in vogue as the dispensing with human labour by the means of machinery"— that everyone would win from the arrangement: the lazy parsons would have less work to do, and the nation would no longer need to support the cost of paying so many of them.

This pamphlet certainly carried some of Robert's trademark humor, but the writing itself was quite different from both his recorded speeches and his published articles. The sentence structure was more convoluted and more grammatically conventional, and the tone was more elevated and self-consciously ironic. Take, for example, "I have even had the vanity to think that my humble lucubrations may be of importance to my country at this awful crisis of general disaffection and financial distress"; this was not the kind of sentence one would be likely to hear at Hopkins Street. In Carlile's estimation, when Robert entered Dorchester he "could not write his name, or scarce make a letter," so he could not possibly have written this text by himself. It is likely that Carlile and Cannon (who usually used the pseudonym "Erasmus Perkins") drafted it, possibly based on prior conversations with Robert. The sole attribution to Robert was probably down to the lawyer Cannon, who if nothing else was always assiduous to shield himself from legal trouble. While Robert served time in Dorchester, several more blasphemous pamphlets written by Cannon also appeared under the name of "Revd. R. Wedderburn, V.D.M.," the last of which, *High-Heel'd Shoes for Dwarfs in Holiness,* was published in May or June 1821. There is no evidence that Robert ever even saw these other publications, much less had a hand in writing them, but he seems to have been happy enough to have his name attached.¹³

Cast-Iron Parsons might have been Robert's idea initially, but his capacity to collaborate with his more formally educated contacts was severely limited by the realities of incarceration. Shortly after his arrival, it became apparent that he had been singled out by the prison authorities for special treatment. "Of the general management of the prison I do not complain," wrote Carlile from his own cell on the other side of the jail, "but the case of Wedderburn has been abominable, comparing his treatment with the common treatment of other prisoners." Instead of being allocated a cell, Robert was kept for months in the filthy entrance vestibule "where all the prisoners are thrust in before they are examined by the doctor, and cleaned." He was denied the standard prison allowance to purchase his food or fuel for the fireplace. When Carlile tried to send him some fruit via the turnkey, the parcel was returned, "with the keeper's instructions that nothing could be allowed to pass." When he was eventually moved to a proper cell, he spent the rest of his two-year sentence "confined to the Bridewell, or Ward of Solitude," with only his freezing room and a corridor of about thirty feet to pace in, for twenty-three hours of the day.¹⁴

As a man singled out for promoting dangerous ideas, Robert was not permitted to speak with any of the other prisoners for his entire sentence, though he was allowed to attend church services on a Sunday when he chose. Even the raucous *Cast-Iron Parsons* contained one dark, fleeting mention of Robert's acute boredom in "solitary confinement." Eighteen months later, conditions had still not improved; Carlile noted that the only other prisoner who "is treated any way near like the treatment of Wedderburn" was a man serving time "for bestiality, and is an altogether horrible character." Carlile organized a subscription among their radical friends on the outside for Robert's relief, and he was at least able to have his wife, Jane, send on a couple of shillings now and again to ease the burden. The overall effect of his fellow prisoner's treatment at Dorchester worried Carlile; Robert was pushing sixty, and he was beginning to look frail. "How far Mr Wedderburn may have suffered in health I cannot say, he does not appear to me to be as robust as three years ago in London, but I feel assured that if he does not take particular care of himself he will feel serious effects arising from his confinement, on entering into his former condition in life." There is no record of Mary or the children visiting Robert; Dorchester was over a hundred miles from London, and the cost of travel was prohibitive to such an impoverished family. The solitude and lack of connection with the outside world certainly took its toll on Robert's mental health. He later confided to Carlile that he had contemplated suicide during his cold and lonely internment.[15]

Robert had done extremely hard time for his crimes, but he was permitted one visitor. In the winter of 1820–21, he was visited by William Wilberforce, the former leader of the parliamentary antislavery movement. By 1820, Wilberforce's name had already become synonymous with the abolition of the slave trade, but he was arguably just as well known in radical circles as the despised figurehead of repressive government loyalism and "canting" religious hypocrisy. There was some truth to this: Wilberforce was involved with many loyalist organizations, including the infamous Society for the Suppression of Vice, which sought not only to counteract the morally deleterious effects of political radicalism on the poor but also to combat the terrible vices of drinking and swearing among the "lower orders." Wilberforce's evangelical Anglicanism, combined with his total commitment to traditional structures of authority, led him on more than one occasion to pursue religious radicals quite vindictively. He had, for instance, personally seen to it that both Carlile's wife and sister had ended up in Dorchester Gaol alongside him for the crime of continuing to print his periodical. Indeed, it was probably reading Carlile's dispatches in *The Republican* that alerted Wilberforce to Robert's desperate condition at the jail and prompted his visit.[16]

For all their political differences, Wilberforce seems to have seen some kind of potential in Robert. Typically bullish, Carlile claimed that his friend "had foiled all the arts, intrigues, and delusions of the Parson-Justices, aided by Wilberforce, to make him a Christian." Robert's account of the meeting suggested it was rather more cordial, and in 1824 he dedicated *The Horrors of Slavery* to the aging evangelical, noting that when he was "in prison, for conscience-sake, at Dorchester, you visited me, and you gave me—your advice, for which I am still your debtor, and likewise for the two books beautifully bound in calf, from which I have since derived much ghostly consolation." Scholars have speculated over what precisely was said between these two men, who seem almost diametric opposites. Surely they must have discussed scripture, and McCalman, who edited a scholarly collection of Robert's writings, has suggested that Wilberforce tried to convince him to invest his considerable talents in the antislavery cause, which is likely. We should, however, be cautious about ascribing too much influence to this conversation as an explanation for Robert's subsequent political decisions; he certainly continued to promote the abolition of slavery after his spell in Dorchester, but he also continued his increasingly disreputable ultraradical activities, even at the cost of some of his more "respectable" connections. To be sure, Robert never returned to the embrace of the Church, and, if anything, his disdain for ecclesiastical authority grew more brazen the older he got. Indeed, his children all appear to have been baptized without Robert's knowledge; Mary took their youngest,

Jacob, to be christened in January 1822, while his father was still in jail.[17]

Whatever Wilberforce said to Robert, it really did very little to alter his overall course in life. The material obligations of finding work and keeping his family alive were far more consequential determinants of the scale, if not the direction, of his political activities during the 1820s. Carlile was, in a sense, right about the toll that prison had taken on his well-being, and right when he said it would be even harder once Robert returned to his former station in life. And he was approaching the age where he would not be able to work as a tailor anymore. Robert complained frequently of poor eyesight and a bad back, and as early as 1824, eleven years before his death, he felt sure that he could not be long for this world. By the end of his sentence, he had lost both his home and his ability to work. After entering into recognizances for good behavior for three years, Robert came back to London at the end of May 1822. Struggling to find work, he immediately fell back into poverty—and some decidedly immoral company.[18]

CHAPTER 8

Outside

JUST AS CARLILE HAD PREDICTED, Robert used his time in solitary confinement to learn to write. He left Dorchester a literate man, though his handwriting continued to be blighted by his poor eyesight. Unfortunately, when he returned to London in May 1822, he found the radical scene in abeyance. With a failing radical readership and a diminishing list of willing political collaborators, he was reported to have started writing "pretty little sixpenny romances." This made good sense; his years in popular politics meant that he had contacts in the cheap print business. But this new phase of his career as an author was anything but a step toward greater respectability. A common sideline for jobbing writers and printers—especially those in legally liminal situations— was producing erotic and pornographic literature. This allowed them to appeal to wealthier clients who were willing to rough it in the less salubrious shopping districts of the city to get their hands on such titillating material. As Carlile complained in 1825, "these books and prints called obscene are got up chiefly for the use and gratification of the aristocracy." This would be Robert's new line of literary work.[1]

By March 1823, he had gone into business with Jack Mitford, a minor printer of radical periodicals and pamphlets whose sideline in pornography was rapidly overtaking his political output in both popularity and profit. The arrangement was simple; Robert would write the saucy little romances and send them to Mitford, who touched up the spelling and grammar, printed them, and put them on sale. But the two had a falling out when Mitford swindled Robert out of ten shillings in a scam involving a pawnbroker's ticket. Ten shillings was more than Robert could afford to lose, and he brought a suit against Mitford before the magistrates in February 1823. Eventually, the issue was resolved when William Benbow, a mutual acquaintance (and another publisher of obscenity), settled the debt on Mitford's behalf.[2]

The press reports of this minor legal dispute suggest how popular conceptions of both impoverished radicals and Black people living in the capital had begun to shift in the early 1820s. In the *Morning Herald,* the whole affair was played for laughs, a hilarious example of the undignified scrabbling of once-threatening radical intellectuals: "Mr. Robert Wedderburn—or Robertus Wedderburn, as he delighteth to designate himself, is a man of colour—something the colour of a toad's back; plump and puffy as a porpoise, and the magnitude of his caput makes it clear that nature had cut him out for a counsellor, had not the destinies decreed that he should cut out cloth. . . . Shelved with the rest of the radicals, he turned his thoughts to literature." The correspondent who wrote this article, John Wight, was so pleased with the way he had skewered Robert's reputation that he reproduced it the following year as part of a stand-alone collection of his "most humorous and entertaining reports" from the Bow Street police offices. In this "greatest hits" volume, Wight stated that "great care has been taken that names, which are here unimportant, should be either totally omitted, or so altered as to prevent the possibility of discovery," which, he hoped, would avoid "perpetuating the ridicule and disgrace to which individuals have, in an unlucky moment, exposed themselves." In the dozens of cases republished here for the reader's amusement, only Robert's full name and description was retained. The name of the accused, Jack Mitford, had been discreetly stricken.[3]

This was an example of a new kind of writing about the lives of the poorest on London's streets, at once fascinated and dismissive, romanticized and played for laughs. The early nineteenth century saw the popularization of picaresque "tours" through London's seamy underworld, with titles like *Vagabondiana: Or, Anecdotes of Mendicant Wanderers Through the Streets of London*. These texts introduced their readers to a diverse host of well-known London "characters," including those from the very poorest sectors of society. Members of London's Black population featured prominently in these scenes, often in crude caricature. For example, Pierce Egan's picaresque *Life in London* (1821) contained over a dozen full-color illustrations by George Cruikshank and Robert Cruikshank. In the plate entitled "LOWEST LIFE in LONDON," the text's heroes, Tom and Jerry, drink in a crowded alehouse in the East End while Black women dance with White working-class men with scarcely lighter complexions (fig. 4). The scene was described as joyous and carefree, the "group motley indeed;—Lascars, blacks, jack tars, coal-heavers, dustmen, women of colour, old and young, and a sprinkling of the remnants of once fine girls, &c, were all *jigging* together."[4]

This image of the free intercourse between Black and White in the East End boozer reminds us of the clear reality of a multi-ethnic working-class culture in early nineteenth-century London. But depicting Black bodies in a social space to emphasize the generic "lowness" (indeed, the low*est*ness) of the company also indicates the emergence of a lazy racial humor, in which dark skin was

Figure 4. Detail of "LOWEST LIFE in LONDON: Tom, Jerry and Logic among the unsophisticated Sons and Daughters of Nature at the All-Max in the East," hand-colored etching, in Pierce Egan, *Life in London: Or, the Day and Night Scenes of Jerry Hawthorn Esq. and his Elegant Friend Corinthian Tom* (London, 1821)

equated with the moral looseness supposedly endemic among the urban poor. This kind of literature expressed a fundamental anxiety about a disinhibited, diverse working-class culture spilling over into "polite" middle-class society. As it pertained to race, "mixed" families like Robert's were a core concern, which was amplified in the illustration for *Life in London* by literally using black ink to pigment both the Black women and the "mixed" child sitting on his White father's knee in the bottom-right of the frame. This was the same effect that had been applied to Robert in a caricature of his confrontation with Robert Owen in 1817, which represented him in conventionally racist terms as barefoot and with grotesquely exaggerated facial features (see fig. 1). When Robert's appearance and supposed intellectual pretentions were mercilessly skewered in the *Morning Herald*, then, Wight was drawing on a specific popular visual language, where Blackness invoked a complex package of prejudices against both the poor and people of African descent.

We might be surprised to observe that popular depictions of "race" became more pronounced and hostile toward people of African descent at the same moment that the campaign against colonial slavery once more became an issue of national attention. The newly sympathetic response to reports of insurrections in the Caribbean, from both radical and liberal London abolitionists, illustrates that at the very least a "gradualist" antislavery position was becoming widespread. In popular print media, the framing of abolition shifted subtly during the 1820s from an "if" to a "when." British radicals were, by and large, encouraged by the example of enslaved people rising up to overcome their oppressors. At a dinner marking Thomas Paine's birthday held in London in January 1824, for instance, a toast was raised to "the next insurrection of the blacks in the West Indies, and success to them." The brutal response by colonial officials to the uprising of the enslaved in Demerara in 1823, including the sentencing of the White abolitionist missionary John Smith to execution for supposedly fomenting the uprising, horrified many British readers and confirmed that gradual emancipation was the only way to ensure the safety of colonists and the security of the empire.[5]

However, White liberals and radicals alike saw no contradiction in maintaining, at the same time, that the plight of the free British laborer should take priority over the liberation of the enslaved. The tabloid-style sporting daily *Bell's Life in London*, Robert's preferred newspaper, summed up these complex views in an editorial on the Demerara uprising published on February 1, 1824:

> We should be ashamed of ourselves, if we could cease to cherish the hope of the ultimate abolition of slavery in our colonies; we rejoice in

> the example of negro capacity displayed by Haiti; ... but we contemn those pretended zealots for humanity, who can overlook the flagrant wrongs and squalid misery of millions under their own immediate care, and try to earn a spurious reputation by searching out objects of sympathy three thousand miles off. Every plan for abolition should be of the most cautious and gradual kind. The feelings and justice of mankind cannot fail to operate in some degree upon the slave-proprietors, and they will doubtless be still more influenced to a cooperation in some plan by their constant danger from their degraded labourers.[6]

This editorial sparked off a chain of articles and letters in *Bell's* on the issue of insurrections of the enslaved, including reports of a conspiracy that had been narrowly averted by colonial officials at the Frontier and St. George estates in Jamaica in December 1823. The editorials accompanying each of these articles were excoriating toward the "meek-spirited planters," who had claimed that the uprisings were a consequence of a parcel of measures introduced to mitigate the worst abuses permitted under slavery.[7]

The following week, *Bell's* reported on a meeting of "West-India proprietors" at the City of London Tavern (coincidentally, the same pub where Robert had shouted down Owen's plan seven years earlier), which had been called to discuss the recent uprisings and conspiracies. The meeting was peppered with self-regarding statements about how "respectable" and humane the present company of slaveholders were. The report was followed by another withering editorial by the paper's proprietor, Robert Bell, calling into question the "respectability" of men who bought and sold children, including their own. "We have ourselves had a wretch pointed out to us at Liverpool, many years ago, who we were informed ... had boasted of the profit he had made by a Negro-girl who had borne him three children, *all of whom he SOLD, with their heart-broken mother on his quitting Jamaica!*" Reading this account of the meeting and the editorial that followed it, Robert must have recognized so many elements of his own experience: the constant, churning reality of conspiracies and uprisings of the enslaved; the infuriating hypocrisy of slaveholders and their easy adoption of establishment "respectability"; and above all, the casual discarding of enslaved women and the illegitimate children they bore to planters.[8]

Although he had been careful to avoid controversy since his release from Dorchester, Robert could not forbear responding publicly to this article. On February 20th, he walked to the offices of *Bell's* and dropped off a letter detailing some of the outrages that he himself had witnessed as a child. On February 29th, Bell published Robert's letter as evidence against some "abuse" he had received in response to his paper's strongly antislavery stance. As had been his practice since the summer of 1817, Robert openly named his father, along with Boswell, as Rosanna's abusers, and he detailed some of the sexual and physical violence his mother had endured at their hands. He was also characteristically unrestrained in his description of the moral depravity of slavery in Jamaica: "I HAVE SEEN MY POOR MOTHER STRETCHED ON THE GROUND, TIED HANDS AND FEET, AND FLOGGED IN THE MOST INDECENT MANNER, THOUGH PREGNANT AT THE SAME TIME!!!" The public force of Robert's all-caps accusation, along with the fact that the plantation businesses of "Wedderburne, Colvill and Co." had been mentioned by name in the paper the preceding week, brought this letter to the attention of Andrew Colvile, heir to James Wedderburn's fortune and estates in Jamaica and Robert's half-brother.[9]

Bell's was not the kind of newspaper that a man in Andrew's station of life read regularly, and he noted rather dismissively that the issue containing Robert's letter had been "put into" his hands about a week after it was first published. When he did write in response in mid-March, he hinted at a defamation lawsuit against

Bell and demanded that his own letter be published along with a retraction and apology. The letter rehearsed the story that James—who had died in 1807—told him when Robert had approached Andrew in London for help back in 1801: Rosanna was nothing more than a troublesome "negro woman-*slave*"; he had never had sex with her; Robert was therefore not his son; and the whole story was obviously made up so he could get money. To this, Andrew added an aside of his own: "upon the slightest enquiry you would have discovered that [Robert's letter] referred to a period of between sixty and seventy years ago, and *therefore* is not applicable to any argument upon the present condition of the West Indies." This was probably the strongest part of his argument, though it did rather undermine his main point that Robert's letter was merely self-interested "slander." Bell—like many newspaper editors, often quite hard up for content—was very happy to publish Andrew's letter. But he did not take kindly to the attempt to silence him by the threat of legal action. Instead of the demanded apology and retraction, Bell doubled down on his support for Robert's version of events. Bell's reply amounted to a reiteration of the original charge Andrew had sought to refute: "A father's marriage makes him *not the less the father of his own children*, in the eye of Heaven, though borne to him by his Slaves." That was just what Robert had been saying all along.[10]

With a friendly editor in a major London newspaper on his side, Robert pushed his advantage to get the last word in the exchange. He was open about his motivations: "I deem it now an imperative duty to reply to the infamous letter of A. Colvile, *alias* Wedderburn, and to defend the memory of my unfortunate mother, a woman virtuous in principle, but a Slave, and a sacrifice to the unprincipled lust of my father." Unlike Colvile, Robert was able to cite sources and evidence for his version of the events that transpired in Jamaica, including the location of his own manumission record signed by James, "in the Government Secretary's Office; where it might be seen to this day." He was also able to settle a couple of old scores by exposing both James's and Andrew's astonishingly callous treatment of him when he came to them in distress, seeking help to feed his starving family. His sign-off was characteristically defiant: "if *my dear brother* means to *show fight* before the Nobs at Westminster, I shall soon give him an opportunity, as I mean to publish my whole history in a cheap pamphlet, and to give a public specimen of the inhumanity, cruelty, avarice, and diabolical lust of the West-India Slave-Holders." This "cheap pamphlet" was, of course, *The Horrors of Slavery*.[11]

Robert had not published anything for a while, but nowadays he had contacts in the pornography business whose printing apparatus he could use. In May he registered himself as a printer at 23 Russell Court, where William Dugdale had long produced a range of radical pamphlets filled with obscene libels against government ministers, alongside more specialized smut fixated on naughty priests and flagellated arses. As one might imagine, Dugdale was set up to reproduce images as well as text, meaning that Robert could also include an image of himself—the only realistic portrait of him to have survived (fig. 5). As we have already seen, when it came to writing the text itself, Robert was far more committed to telling Rosanna's and Amy's stories than relating his own "history" as he had promised during the exchange with Andrew. When he had gone through all the details, he also included the original letters that had been published in *Bell's*, again defying Andrew to take him to court so he could prove James's behavior as a matter of public record: "I have now fairly given him the challenge; let him meet it if he dare." Closing the account, he hinted at a continuation of the story: "In a future part of my history I shall give some particulars of the treatment of the blacks in the West Indies, and the prospect of a general rebellion and massacre there,

Figure 5. "Robert Wedderburn, Son of the Late James Wedderburn Esq of Inveresk," monochrome engraving, in Robert Wedderburn, *The Horrors of Slavery* (London, 1824)

from my own experience." Although this second installment appears never to have materialized, the mention of rebellion was a fitting end for his testament to his mother's and grandmother's memory. The exchange in *Bell's* had begun with a notice of an insurrection in the West Indies. Though his circumstances had changed somewhat, he continued to draw inspiration from the rebellious enslaved, both men and women. With that in mind, Robert's decision to dedicate his account to William Wilberforce, the conservative icon of both the antislavery and antiradical movements, was appropriately—if unintentionally—confrontational.[12]

Perhaps this confrontational approach was becoming an issue for Robert. He remained an active member of the radical scene throughout this period, but he appeared increasingly out of place. The latter half of the 1820s saw him lose more and more influence, and more and more of his friends and contacts in the radical movement. By comparison to the rough-and-ready plebian culture of the 1810s, the new breed of radical intellectuals now emphasized a reliance on self-improvement and an alternative working-class sense of respectability, based on the decidedly masculinist ideal of total independence of thought and action. Robert's desperate poverty, rumbustious temper, and unrepentant anticlericalism, as much as his close association with seedy characters and smut-peddlers, all left him out of step in this "march of intellect."[13]

Robert was trapped in a vicious cycle: the less respectable he appeared, the less able he was to gain respectability. The progressive loss of his influential contacts in the political underground during this period led him into ever-seedier circumstances. Carlile stood by him the longest, helping him to open up a new debating house at 12 White's Alley, off Drury Lane, in April 1828, an attempt to rekindle the glory days of the Hopkins Street chapel. The Home Office was still keeping tabs on him, and just before

White's Alley opened, one spy reported that "Wedderburn has been trying all he can to get a place to preach in. . . . when he shall get a place his society is to be called Diabolists or Worshippers of the Devil"—a commentary on the absurdity of praying to influence a God who was omnipotent and omniscient. The chapel's first debate opened with Robert delivering a "liturgy" that he and Carlile most likely wrote together, in which he argued that it made far more sense to pray to the devil, whose power was limited and who might therefore be more willing to listen to one's entreaties. In the event, the White's Alley chapel was a damp letdown. The room itself was redolent of Hopkins Street, in that it was a dilapidated old carpenter's workshop, over the door of which Robert had hung a handwritten sign reading "The New Assembly Room." Twenty-eight people attended the grand opening debate, though there was room for over two hundred. Most of these were friends and family, including two of Carlile's very young children and Dugdale the pornographer.[14]

Robert no doubt had visions of a packed house, filled with outraged and scandalized patrons trying to shout him down. What he got was indifference. A couple of weeks later, only six people were present at White's Alley—including Robert himself and a government informant. All the extemporized, passionate speechifying, righteous anger, and willful controversy that had made his name as a "notorious firebrand" a decade earlier now looked undignified and counterproductive. Many British radicals wanted concrete, achievable plans for political reform, and a consensus was forming around the extension of male suffrage and limiting working hours for children in the cotton factories as strategic priorities. The only people willing to help Robert and Carlile in their "Christian Diabolist" experiment were, in the estimation of one spy at least, "all very low who have long known him." These included such undesirable company as John Edgar, an elderly clogmaker who was a figure of fun in the neighborhood because his wife, a nineteen-year-old prostitute named Matilda, was very publicly cuckolding him with "a young strapping journeyman baker."[15]

Even these friends didn't stick around much longer. When Carlile sent an account of Robert's liturgy to the deist and new-generation radical Robert Taylor, then in prison on blasphemy charges, his response was a master class in the backhanded compliment. "I have laughed most heartily at the exquisite sarcasm of the Diabolical Liturgy," he wrote. "If Wedderburn's measure of talent were but served up in a better looking vessel, or some that have ten-fold his talent would but bring it forth with half his courage and honesty, we would not want rich intellectual feasts."[16]

Once again, coded references to Robert's appearance stood between him and the measure of respectability that was suddenly so highly prized by British reformers. He just could not attract the right kind of people. The last straw for his White's Alley meeting room came just a couple of months after its opening, when a heavily intoxicated passerby interrupted the barely attended Sunday afternoon meeting by incessantly hammering on the door. It was embarrassing. This was not worth the five shillings per week rent that Robert was paying on the place; the following Wednesday he informed Carlile that he was giving up the White's Alley room. At the final meeting the following Sunday, according to the informer, "only five persons attended and a sort of abusive conversation took place for about an hour. No proposition for other meetings or for any other purpose took place, nor do I find there is anywhere else."[17]

It may already have been too late for Robert to make any kind of a comeback. Family had always been his primary source of strength and comfort, but even they seem to have deserted him. Even in the prime of his influence in the late 1810s, he had depended on Mary and the two girls, Hope and Lydia, to supplement the family income by selling their paper flowers. But the girls had grown up now and moved on. The fact that Mary had taken their son, Jacob, to be baptized while Robert was still in jail—almost certainly against his wishes—signals a rift between them, if not an estrangement. We have no record of Robert mentioning his wife or children after *The Horrors of Slavery* was published in 1824. Even if he and Mary were still together, there was no way the marriage could survive Robert's movements after White's Alley. By the winter of 1828 he was letting out bedrooms in a broken-down tenement on Featherbed Lane to make ends meet. As one police officer tactfully put it, "I believe it is a house let out to girls of the town." These were desperately poor women whose clientele were barely better off. One of Robert's tenants, Mary Ann Barrand, was arrested for grand larceny in November 1828 when one of her clients hid a stash of stolen property under her bed. Robert himself acknowledged that his new lodgers "were addicted to drunkenness and noise." But drunkenness and noise were not what got him into trouble. He was arrested for brothel-keeping on June 1, 1830, and went to trial in early November.[18]

Robert had not lost his habit of making matters worse for himself in court. His defense speech at the trial—"the most extraordinary speech that perhaps ever was made under similar circumstances," according to one witness—not only ended up plastered all over the London papers but was also noted in the regional press around Britain.[19] Disregarding his legal advice to plead ignorance, Robert instead went on the offensive. He accused the presiding judge of being a frequent visitor to the house, whose "own favourite Carrotty Eliza, who 'padded the hoof' in Fleet-street, met him there times out of mind." From there the trial devolved into a farce, with various officers of the court attempting to stop

Robert from speaking while he deliberately provoked them, much to the amusement of the gallery.

> THE RECORDER.—Defendant, have some regard for decency. Do not take the opportunity which your defence affords you, to libel respectable men. . . .
>
> WEDDERBURN.—Pooh, man! I know what I am about. I am addressing the Jury, and must not be interrupted. I shall now give you facts enough.

At this stage Robert's language evidently became too strong for the *Morning Advertiser* to print. The journalist covering the case instead paraphrased Robert's testimony that "he had about six months ago taken the house in question for the purpose of letting it out to women of a certain class" and that in his preaching days "he had seen quite enough of what was called modesty, to induce him to try the other sort." Just as he began "to touch upon Christianity in a very revolting manner," the Recorder of the Court was forced to intervene. Now the *Morning Advertiser* journalist could not resist quoting their back-and-forth directly:

> THE RECORDER said, do not add to the offence you are committing against the laws of decency, the crime of blasphemy.
>
> WEDDERBURN.—Pooh, pooh! I know what blasphemy is well enough, I suffered for it two years. Well, I was talking of the modest ladies, so as I was disappointed in them, why, as I told you, I went amongst those who were everywhere hunted down. I compassionated them, and I resolved to protect them as far as I was able; so as I was not able to live by the one house, why I took another.—(Roars of laughter.)
>
> THE RECORDER.—I caution you that you—

WEDDERBURN.—I wish that you would let me alone; you can punish me afterwards just as you please; sure I know you well enough.

At this point, the *Morning Advertiser* paraphrased him addressing the jury directly, including his demand that they "must see, that, although he let rooms to ladies of easy virtue, he did not come under the denomination mentioned in the indictment." Robert seemed to be having a great time. He was just declaring that the court aldermen had been too drunk to hear the case on the originally appointed date when his beleaguered court-appointed counsel, Mr. Smith, stood up and began to make an appeal to the judge. Robert shouted down his own defense lawyer, too. "Don't interrupt me," he snapped; "I love this country, because I am opposed to tyranny and oppression of all sorts, and I shall always stand up in defence of the British Constitution.—(Loud laughter.) I am not a brothel-keeper, nor the keeper of a disorderly house, but I keep, and I shall keep as long as I can, a house of refuge for destitute prostitutes." Unsurprisingly, the jury instantly found him guilty, and he was sentenced to twelve months' hard labor in Giltspur Street compter, a small prison near Newgate. At the end of the trial, Robert put his hat on in front of the judge—a traditional gesture of defiance—and walked out of the courtroom.[20]

Robert's knowing accommodation of prostitution was not unusual for a down-on-his-luck artisan radical with few friends left. Given how poor he was, one wonders if he had gotten himself thrown in jail deliberately, just to have free bed and board for a year. Yet his claim in court to be a supporter of destitute women may not have been as cynical as it might first appear. His characterization of sex workers as victims of circumstance who were "everywhere hunted down" was in keeping with his lifelong respect for women who fell afoul of legitimate authorities. Destitution and friendlessness may have been what drove his lodgers into prostitution in the first place, but many preferred to live in houses like the one on Featherbed Lane over the alternative, which was almost certainly the workhouse or hospital. The court and the newspapers might paint Robert as nothing more than a common pimp, but he was adamant that he simply gave women a place to live, with no questions asked about any potentially "immoral" behavior they might resort to. He could not plausibly claim that he didn't know what went on at his lodging house. But he at least gave the women living there the option of a life outside the direct supervision—and condemnation—of the authorities. Robert rejected the kind of moral judgment and harsh discipline that he and his family had experienced during their own periods of destitution. His cheap and discreet lodgings offered women a place to simply exist in peace: to get on with their lives as best they could without being constantly admonished for how forsaken—how destitute of God's grace—they were. Robert's gleefully disrespectful performance in court suggests that he stood by his own moral judgment, even at the cost of his freedom.[21]

CHAPTER 9

Outsider

BEHIND BARS AGAIN, THEN. The first stint from 1820 to 1822 had been physically and emotionally devastating for Robert, and now he was a decade older and had fewer friends than ever to help look after him. Mary and the children were gone. Among young, respectable London radicals, now looking toward a reformed Parliament where they might sit as MPs, a conviction for running a brothel was profoundly embarrassing. What kind of serious politician would want to be associated with someone like that? Robert's days of chairing tavern meetings were over, even if he didn't know it yet. Indeed, it speaks to how obscure he had become—and perhaps to the way that assumptions about race were solidifying in British popular culture—that he was confused for his onetime protégé William Davidson in newspaper reportage of his 1830 trial. In 1820, Robert had been sent from London to an infamous jail in a far-off county—"the *English Bastille*," Carlile had called it—and he had been seen as either a dangerous enemy of the state or a heroic prisoner of conscience, depending on who you asked. Now, he was a petty criminal immured in the local compter. Nevertheless, falling beneath the notice of the Home Office had its consolations. Giltspur Street was not Dorchester; here, Robert was just one of the common prisoners, and while no one on the outside was arranging financial support for him, at least no one on the inside was actively trying to break his spirit.[1]

He was convicted to hard labor, which, given his advanced age, probably meant using his existing skills to help make or mend prison uniforms, working from his cell. This left him with the evenings to himself, which he soon began to use to write. He knew just what he wanted to say and to whom he wanted to say it. The topic dearest to his heart, the abolition of slavery, had been all over the news in the six months leading up to his conviction. Back in May, a huge, oversubscribed meeting of the reformed Anti-Slavery Society had moved, amid a deafening chorus of cheers, to petition Parliament to take immediate action to begin emancipating the enslaved. The former Society for the Mitigation and Gradual Abolition of Slavery had now dropped the words "Gradual" and "Mitigation" from its name, signaling the organization's new strategy. The strength of public feeling on this issue had surprised the society's directors, who included cautious gradualists like the aged Wilberforce and an ambitious career politician named Henry Brougham.[2]

Although Robert had met Wilberforce personally, it was Brougham's speeches at the May meeting of the Anti-Slavery Society that seem to have most caught his attention. For one thing, Brougham had used one of Robert's favorite Bible verses when he reiterated his earlier demand that planters "lay the axe to the root" of slavery. More substantively, he had been very explicit in linking the abolition movement with the ongoing campaign for parliamentary reform and relief for the distressed poor in Britain. At the meeting, he pointed out that it would be "grossly inconsistent" for abolitionists to "neglect the misery that was near their own door, while they were holding out . . . a helping hand to the wretchedness that was beyond the Atlantic." This was compatible with the vision for transatlantic solidarity that Robert had always cherished. Finally, Brougham shared his recognition that optimism in reform should be tempered with realism, stressing the need for a careful, detailed plan if the society wanted to convince Parliament to enact emancipation. He was "all for going on prudently and cautiously indeed, with a due regard to all interests, and disregarding none," Brougham had said, "*but go on we must and go on we shall.*"

There was much cheering and patting of backs at the end of this meeting of the Anti-Slavery Society—they had resolved to campaign for the immediate end of slavery, after all. But no one quite knew *how* it should be done. The final result from all the speeches and cheers was a petition to the House of Commons that had plenty of urgency but not much in the way of practical detail. They demanded that Parliament "proceed forthwith to devise, and adopt, and enforce the best and wisest means of ensuring [slavery's] universal extinction throughout the British Empire." The only concrete measure suggested in the petition, passed thanks in part to the advocacy of Daniel O'Connell, who had championed the successful campaign for Catholic emancipation in 1829, was that Parliament should appoint a specific date after which all children born in any of the British dominions would be free.[3]

The destination was set, and it was agreed that the journey to emancipation should be undertaken in all due haste, but the course had yet to be charted. Hundreds of thousands of people were still the legal property of slaveholders; how could these powerful and influential men be legally and safely dispossessed of their "human property"? Moreover, recalling the region's recent history of insurrection and revolution, even many "immediatist" abolitionists in Britain still thought that an overnight transition to freedom would endanger the White inhabitants in the West Indies and that the enslaved first needed to be *taught* how to live as free men. The safety and wisdom of abolishing slavery became a political wedge issue at the general election held in August 1830, almost to the same extent as parliamentary reform. During his campaign for Wilberforce's old parliamentary seat of Yorkshire, Brougham emerged as a particularly convincing advocate for a carefully managed transition to both an extended franchise for men and freedom for the enslaved. When he was elevated to lord chancellor under Earl Grey's premiership in November 1830, his reputation as a champion for both antislavery and reform causes was well established. Never one to be overawed by titles, Robert addressed his final published piece of writing to the new lord chancellor, now properly styled Lord Henry, first Baron Brougham and Vaux, with his own suggestion for how slavery could finally be laid to rest.[4]

In some ways, *An Address to the Right Honourable Lord Brougham and Vaux . . . Suggesting an Equitable Plan for the Emancipation of the Slaves* continued on the same themes Robert had established in his earlier writings and speeches about slavery. He testified once again to some of the horrors his mother and grandmother had endured, again naming James as his father and one of the perpetrators. As ever, he emphasized the significance of owning and managing the land as a prerequisite for true freedom—indeed, as he boasted in a letter to an associate two months later, he could still recite the "fundamental principles of Mr. Spence's plan" from memory. He redoubled his criticism of the Methodist missionaries he had seen extorting money from the enslaved in Jamaica. He paid close attention to the conditions of the laboring poor in Britain and even referenced the terrible hardships witnessed in Ireland as a result of mismanaged colonial policy. All of these were topics he had handled before. Yet, for all these thematic consistencies, the tract itself represents an abrupt tonal shift in

Robert's antislavery writing, perhaps even a betrayal of his ultraradical sensibilities in favor of the kind of pragmatic compromise that Brougham was seeking. Ever since his harrowing spell in Dorchester, Robert had done his best to keep his opinions on British politics separate from his antislavery work. But even taking this into account, the *Address to Lord Brougham and Vaux*, the last tract he ever published, seemed to be a desperate lurch for the kind of respectability that he had always disparaged.[5]

In 1817, when he blazed his way into London's radical underground and its widely read newspapers, he had called for a Haiti-style revolution and the establishment of an egalitarian, militaristic free Black republic in Jamaica. Now, a little over a decade later, he promoted a gradualist approach founded on the equitable compensation of slaveholders. "It is quite just to set the slave free," he now argued, "and it is equally unjust to rob the master of his value." He attacked "those ignorant fanatics, who were so frequently troubling parliament with petitions against slavery," without "any consideration of the West-India proprietors' right by law." Would "these lovers of emancipation subscribe to pay anything to the owners?" he asked. "I answer no." Robert's "equitable plan" itself was also a far cry from the revolutionary utopian vision he had put forward in *The Axe Laid to the Root* in 1817. Although he still maintained that the work of emancipation should fall to the enslaved themselves, now his position offered very different implications for the institution of slavery and the social order of Jamaica. "I hold it right that a slave ought to have a law made in his favour, to demand his release from his master when he can purchase his freedom, or that he can choose another owner." Once freed, the formerly enslaved would be entitled to buy their own children. This, then, was to be gradual emancipation by self-purchase: a system that would leave the essential structure of slavery in place but hollow it out, ever so carefully, from within.[6]

Overall, the *Address to Lord Brougham and Vaux* may seem like a sad climbdown from the incendiary ideas that Robert had expressed fourteen years previously. He struck a strangely conciliatory tone with a group of people whom he had declared multiple times in the past deserved to be murdered along with their children. "I doubt not that the planters will assist the slaves in procuring their emancipation by all possible means," he wrote; "for I never knew any of them but who were gentlemanly and kind in all their ways;—it is the overseers who are so frequently severe, which occasions the slave to rebel and to destroy them. The late Right Honourable William Pitt has said, 'that individuals farming an estate and slaves, had extorted labour from them more than nature could bear, and which mainly contributed to insurrection'; if such practices now exist, they should be immediately abolished." It is difficult to imagine the Robert Wedderburn of 1817 or 1819 citing the wisdom of William Pitt, much less alluding to slaveholders as "gentlemanly and kind."[7]

However, it is important to acknowledge that the threat of insurrection remained a central part of the equation for Robert. Under his new plan for gradual emancipation, the threat of violent insurrection could act as a kind of constitutional balance, safeguarding against excessive punishment by an overseer on the new plantations, "for his life would be in danger if he exceeded what the slave deems necessary; the fact is, they have set fire to the fields of cane, and thereby have brought the white man to the extinguishing of it, and then destroyed and committed these task-masters to the flames. When disposed to exercise their vengeance, they do not send previous notice, as the poor incendiaries have done in this country of late." We might recognize a hint of the old Robert in this last aside, comparing the suppression of the insurgent poor in Britain to the organized insurrections of the enslaved. Yet he now adopted the much more conventional complaint made by many

British radicals: that (in his words) "the condition of the slaves were far superior to European labourers." This crude and misleading calculus, which he had so inspiringly rejected in his Hopkins Street days, was now at the core of his argument against abolishing the institution of slavery.[8]

"Charity," he claimed not once but twice in this short pamphlet, "ought to begin at home." His advice to the British nobility and gentry who lent their support to immediate abolition was to "consider the free poor of their own country, before they reduced the slaves to the same state of starvation, by making them free." He even acknowledged that he had tried in the past to convince four different enslaved people to leave their masters when they came to Britain, just as Joseph Knight had left his uncle John. But only one, an eighteen-year-old with "a severe and cruel master," consented to stay in Britain, with all the others including his own sister-in-law "preferring slavery in Jamaica, to freedom in this country." Perhaps this claim was true; if so, it raises desolating questions about how some enslaved people negotiated their decisions when presented with the prospect of freedom without family, security, or safety. It was just as likely, though, that the pain of his own dispossession and constant criminalization had finally gotten the best of Robert. His deployment of the supposed protections allowed for the enslaved in Jamaica reads like a litany of all the hardships he had endured since coming to Britain: "In a state of slavery, there is no seizing for rent or taxes, no casting into prison for debt, no starving families obligated to destroy themselves, or their offspring, for want of provision . . . no mourning widows, or parent bereft of their sons; no remorse for crimes, that being unknown to them." From his cell in Giltspur Street, he seemed to be pondering what British freedom had done for him recently.[9]

In emphasizing this last point at least, Robert was most likely trying to maneuver himself back into the fold of a British radical movement that had moved on without him. Many respectable radicals viewed the parliamentary abolitionists as a bunch of out-of-touch liberal elites who knew but certainly did not care about the White working class "at home." The West India lobby had been trying to deflect metropolitan attention away from the horrors of colonial slavery by saying that enslaved Africans had it easier than British laborers since at least the 1780s. As we have seen with *Bell's Life in London*, these ideas had been seeping into both liberal and radical commentaries on colonial slavery since the early 1820s, even when their arguments were supportive of enslaved people's struggle for freedom. The purchase of proslavery ideas among the working-class radical movements of the period was further promoted by the personal unpopularity of Wilberforce and other prominent evangelical parliamentary abolitionists and a growing sense that their priorities were backward. Populist strategies highlighted the appalling plight of children working in cotton factories, appropriating the language of "slavery" to diminish colonial brutalities by comparison.[10]

The radical shift against evangelical abolitionists certainly touched Robert's former circle. For instance, even while he was supporting Robert's efforts to set up the White's Alley debating room in 1828, Carlile was decrying the antislavery movement as an unwelcome distraction from the more important issue of the exploitation of child labor in British factories. Introducing a widely reprinted narrative of a "child factory-slave," Carlile claimed that the "*black humanity* of Mr. Wilberforce seem to have been entirely of a foreign nature. . . . And yet, who shall read the Memoir of Robert Blincoe, and say, that the charity towards slaves should not have begun or ended at home?" This was just the tip of the spear. Like his famous radical journalist colleague William Cobbett, Carlile disdained the hypocrisy of middle-class abolitionists, and this contempt eventually metastasized into resentment for the enslaved themselves, for the crime of distracting attention from the supposedly more serious issue of British labor conditions. Carlile's criticisms of Wilberforce eventually deteriorated into promoting racist ideologies. By 1833, no longer in touch with Robert at all, he was working directly with slaveholders to publish their proslavery tracts cheaply for a broader readership.[11]

The strange recantation of his formerly uncompromising position on slavery reflected Robert's attempts to regain relevance in this context, without abandoning his commitment to freedom for the enslaved in the West Indies. But this was, perhaps, too little, too late for the elderly and now irredeemably unrespectable Black radical. The incipient racism in some quarters of the reform movement was possibly a factor in his alienation, though it is important to note that this was by no means universal among all reformers. The bigger problem for Robert was his long and still growing criminal record. It is telling but not surprising that the *Address to Lord Brougham and Vaux* was published by John Ascham, who was known at this stage of his career primarily as a pornographer. After a decade of associating chiefly with these types, Robert could only be a liability to a radical circle that had parted ways with both the rough-and-ready debating style of earlier years and what many of them saw as a morally long-sighted antislavery movement. From here on, he was to be tolerated rather than embraced. Stepping from the Giltspur Street compter into the wintry London air at the end of his sentence in November 1831, Robert was greeted by no one. Now approaching seventy, and largely alienated from his family and radical contacts, he had little choice but to pick up where he'd left off.[12]

At about nine o'clock in the morning on February 11, 1832, Mr. Davis, the landlord of the Distiller's Arms pub on Saffron Hill, heard cries of murder coming from nearby Field Lane. He ran down the alleyway, where he found a crowd of people gathered outside number 8. They could make out a woman's voice coming from inside, faintly crying out for help. Joined by two police constables, Waddington and Curty, Davis proceeded down the side-passage and burst into the house. Inside, they found that a pornography shop had been set up in the front room, peddling notorious obscene books, including *The Amatory Adventures of John Wilmot, Earl of Rochester,* and John Cleland's *Fanny Hill.* The windows were lined with obscene pictures. Robert was sitting in the shop with two young lads aged between fifteen and seventeen. In the back, they found a windowless cellar, the floor and walls "covered with wet filth," with a pig trough of stagnant water to one side and the necessary buckets to the other. Near the door, a young woman around thirty years of age lay bound hand and foot, with the cord twisted tightly round her neck. She appeared to be in a stupor, on the verge of dying of asphyxiation. She was covered in bruises and her clothes were torn. Davis unbound the cord around the woman's neck and carried her out to the lane. She fainted, and she was taken to the Saffron Hill workhouse to recover. More police constables arrived. Robert stood up from his chair and declared that he was the one who had tied up the woman. He was taken into custody, along with the two boys in the shop, a third lad sleeping in bed upstairs, and the housekeeper.[13]

At the Hatton Garden police office, the prisoners were processed swiftly. The official Police Court report of charges is perfunctory: "Robert Wedderburn, Ann Atkinson, John [G]unningham, William Ros[e], and George Mason, with assaulting Mary Ann Middleton, so that her life is considered in danger.—For examination on Thursday next." Newspaper reporters, hanging around the court looking for stories, were eager to record the juicy details. The victim, Middleton, was obviously not well enough to testify, so the magistrate examined the witnesses and defendants instead.

Davis described the dramatic rescue and the state of the house, adding that he had heard about Robert's previous indictment for keeping a "disorderly house." Waddington, the constable, corroborated Davis's account and produced some of the pornographic books and pictures he had confiscated from the shop. The magistrates moved on to examine the defendants. The housekeeper, Atkinson, said that she had only worked at the house for three weeks, but she knew that the women who lodged there "get their living in the streets." She said that Middleton had come into the house raving drunk on Friday night and thrown knives at Robert. The boys, Mason and Rose, were then called. They confirmed that they were lodgers in the house, too; that they had gotten out of bed earlier that morning to find Middleton bound in the cellar; and that Robert had said he had done it. Finally, Robert was called to make his statement. He said that Middleton had been a lodger in his old house in Featherbed Lane. She had shown up at the Field Lane house in the early hours of Saturday morning, "and told me that she had been released from the Borough Clink. She had a cut on her head, and she was quite mad." He said that she had been throwing objects around, pouring kettles of water over the other lodgers, and pulling the blankets from the beds. He had been obliged to tie her up to stop her from hurting herself and others. The magistrate remanded Robert and the other defendants in custody until Middleton could give her side of the story.[14]

On February 20th, Middleton had recovered enough to testify, though her voice was still hoarse. The widespread news coverage of the case had had predictable effects. When Robert and the others were brought from the cells up to the Police Court, a crowd had assembled outside, hissing and groaning at them, baying for blood. In the courtroom, Middleton provided a harrowing and lengthy statement. She testified that she had shown up at the house at Field Lane around seven o'clock in the morning on the day in question and asked for a room to be made up. She said that the housekeeper, Atkinson, after helping her unlace her stays, "thrust her hand down my bosom to try if I had any money concealed there." At this point, Robert had dragged her into the cellar, where she was subjected to a sustained and violent sexual assault by two of the boys, Gunningham and Rose. Each of the multiple newspaper reports of the trial deemed parts of her statement "unfit for publication," heavily implying that she had testified to being raped or assaulted by penetration with an object. Middleton also stated that Robert had helped to restrain and silence her during this attack and that he had exclaimed that "my crying would not avail me, as that was Field-lane." Finally, when they left her alone, she managed to crawl to the door and raise the alarm, until Davis and the constables came in.

In his defense, Robert provided what the newspapers described as "a confused statement, in which he stated that he had no ill will or malice towards the prosecutrix, or any cause to ill use her." He reiterated his earlier statement that Middleton had come in drunk and violent, that she had taken up a knife, and "threatened the boys, and then to cut her own throat, and said she would burn herself to death." Then, he said, she held her head close to the fire until her hair began to smoke, at which point he stepped in and restrained her for her own safety. "However illegal my conduct may have been," he declared, "my motive was good."[15]

Character and reputation were important parts of criminal justice in the early nineteenth century, and they had a major impact not only on the outcomes of trials but on sentencing. At this trial, Robert's own reputation had been a major issue, with several witnesses mentioning his previous conviction for running a brothel. It is not immaterial, either, that the newspaper reports of the first hearing introduced him by reference to his dangerous past as a political radical and suspected atheist. At the second trial, Davis mentioned pointedly that the boys, Gunningham and Rose, "were well known about the neighbourhood" as petty thieves and that he had ejected them from his pub once, when one of them had cheekily called for a pipe of tobacco. Middleton noted that Robert and these two boys had become acquainted while they were all inmates in Giltspur Street compter. (As former convicts, they could not expect the benefit of the doubt.) Foolishly, the boys immediately declared they had never been in prison—an outright lie that was instantly disproved by one of the constables, who knew that Gunningham had only been released from Giltspur Street three weeks previously. With all these factors taken into account, Robert, Rose, and Gunningham were all found guilty, while the other two defendants, Mason and Atkinson, having demonstrated a reasonably clean character, were discharged.

The moral censoriousness of the court applied also to victims. During the course of the trial, it had become clear beyond doubt that Middleton was a prostitute. Even her own account—that she "got her living" by being "assisted by a gentleman, who is my friend"—was a clear euphemism intended to convey this meaning without technically incriminating herself. This was an important development because the moral stigma attached to such women affected the extent to which she was able to pursue a criminal prosecution for rape. Since she had been taken into the workhouse for medical treatment, it was up to the Overseers of the Poor to decide whether to refer the case to a higher court or to simply allow the magistrate at Hatton Garden to exercise his very limited discretion and summarily mete out the much lesser punishment for common assault. The magistrate himself pleaded with them to take the case forward for a higher prosecution, but they were simply not interested. He was disappointed, stating "I can only say that this is a fit case for prosecution. The prosecutrix, by her own account, is an unfortunate woman, and it is only her situation in life that induces the magistrates to inflict summary punishment" for the assault only. Even though they had been convicted of a violent and sustained assault, Robert, Rose, and Gunningham were each fined only five pounds, defaulting to a two-month prison sentence if they could not afford to pay.[16]

The "official" police records at Hatton Garden state nothing more than the fact that Robert, Rose, and Gunningham were convicted of "violently assaulting and beating" Middleton, while Atkinson and Mason were acquitted. The proceedings of the trial and the way it was reported in the newspapers present the historian with an appalling ethical dilemma. Middleton's disclosure—the version we have access to—is damning toward Robert for his role in the assault. We must take it seriously and believe her. At the same time, for us to do this, we must also accept, and to an extent endorse, journalistic sources that we know had long been compromised by personal, sometimes racialized animus toward Robert. Indeed, this period has been recognized as one in which newspaper editors and readers alike increasingly visualized a frightening "criminal class," driving an increase in sensationalist reporting of crimes committed by the very poorest—and a degree of creative license on the part of court journalists when representing "undesirable" elements like Robert. As a result, trial reportage, particularly for cases that were deemed salacious like this one, is not generally prized by historians for its forensic accuracy. The reports of the two Middleton trials all broadly align in the key facts, but none of them matches the others in terms of the precise wording used or indeed *whose* testimony was reported "in full," whose was paraphrased, and whose was omitted completely. Middleton was introduced in one report as "Mary Ann Jevitt, *alias* Ann Myddleton" and in another as "Mary Anne Middleton *alias* Tibbutt." In most of the reports, the names of the accused were misspelled or wrongly transcribed—Gunningham was rendered as "Dunningham," Rose became "Ross," and Robert became "Richard Wedderburn." Should this evident lack of care with the details—in addition to the fact that Robert's bad reputation (and possibly the color of his skin) had already made him a target for journalists—factor in how we appraise this complex sort of historical evidence?[17]

We know that newspapers tended to plagiarize one another during this period, so the same mistakes could be copied over multiple independent articles, essentially corroborating false information. We also know that journalists employed tricks to imply details that may not have necessarily been stated in court. The key piece of testimony, in which Middleton stated precisely what happened after she was restrained in the cellar, was cut from *all* of the newspaper reports on the grounds that it was "of the most disgusting nature, and unfit for publication." This leaves readers to draw for themselves the obvious conclusion of a sexual assault. But it was also a well-established journalistic tactic to stoke readers' outrage on the back of less-than-conclusive evidence.[18]

Back in November 1830, for instance, the *Morning Advertiser* had carried a letter of complaint regarding a misleading report about another assault case. The original article had stated that the defendant had first verbally insulted a young sailor following a mutiny and had then proceeded to commit "an assault of a nature which we (the Editor) cannot describe." The defendant in this case was understandably outraged that he had been all but accused of sexually assaulting a young man in the press, when he had in fact "only" struck him with his fists. The paper stopped short of a retraction, but it did print his solicitor's statement that their insinuation was "calculated to cast a foul stigma on his character" and that in fact "no such evidence was given . . . as is reported in your paper, nor was any statement made throughout the whole of the trial to any such effect." This instance demonstrates that we must remain extremely cautious about taking newspaper trial reports at face value as representing what was said in the courtroom. Much less can we treat them as windows into the reality behind contested versions of events.[19]

With that said, several reports of Middleton's testimony explicitly stated her clothes were pulled up over her head during the attack, a detail which leaves very little to the imagination and was unlikely to be completely fabricated. Even if we were to adhere to the most generous possible interpretation of the newspaper reportage—and I am not convinced that we should—then it is still a matter of public record that Robert very nearly killed Middleton by restraining her with a cord and throwing her into a cellar. For all their limitations as historical evidence, all the newspaper reports broadly agree on these essential facts, and none of them tend toward acquitting Robert of a central role in what was undoubtedly an appalling act of violence. Only his own statements run counter to Middleton's reported claims that he was an accessory to the sexual assault itself.[20]

Whatever really happened in that cellar, as far as the public were concerned, Robert was a monster. When he and the two boys were escorted from the court back to the prison at Clerkenwell, the crowd outside made its feelings known, hissing "indignant execrations" and pelting the defendants with "mud, stones, turnips, cabbage-stalks and every kind of missile." All the reports agreed on one final fact about this trial: Robert bore the baying of the crowd with calm firmness "and merely made a feint with the head, and shrugged up his shoulders, when anything struck against him." It is a wretched parting image of a man who, in younger and more optimistic years, had disregarded threats of legal sanction at every turn to defend the reputation of an "unfortunate woman" whom he honored and admired; who had dared to challenge his enslaved family to rise up and take their own freedom by force;

who had sought to find a way for all his oppressed countrymen, in Britain and the West Indies alike, to believe themselves free and equal to anyone, without a thought for status or title.[21]

Government spies still occasionally deigned to report Robert's movements back to an uninterested Home Office, though now he merited only a fleeting mention and only when he came into contact with more dangerous figures. The last time he was spotted in radical circles was in the audience at a lecture given in March 1834 by Robert Taylor—the man who had wished that Robert's "Diabolical Liturgy" could have come from a "better looking vessel." "Wedderburne the coulerd man & others of that school" were among the 250 or so people present—an audience about the same size as the ones Robert used to draw at Hopkins Street. Back in 1819, he had commanded the room with his rough charisma, raising belly laughs or scandalized grumbles at whim, reading the room and speaking always on the spur of the moment. Now, in 1834, he was out of touch. Robert was barely noticed and certainly not invited to speak: a lonely figure on the fringe of a movement he had once led. He died in poverty and nearly total obscurity in late December 1834 or very early January 1835—though not without the satisfaction of seeing the bill for the emancipation of his "oppressed countrymen" passed in Parliament and enacted on August 1, 1834. He was buried at Bethnal Green in London on January 4, 1835.[22]

Robert understood that destitution denoted both material hardship and a fall from grace. Like so many people of his generation, much of his life had been defined by want: the want of money, the want of friends, the want of luck. Yet even in his humble station, he faced and overcame terrible material hardship to rise to a position of extraordinary prominence, an achievement that few other people could claim. Likewise, very few, even within the plebeian radical circles in which he moved, could claim such a spectacular fall from grace. Robert's spiral into destitution was precipitated by the vindictive and even spiteful way he was treated during his spell at Dorchester Gaol between March 1820 and March 1822. It was worsened by some of the questionable decisions he made—particularly his increasing entanglement in London's sex industry through his shady contacts in the world of pornographic publishing. He had to bear the responsibility, and the consequences, for that.

But his progressive alienation from respectable radical circles may also have to do with broader cultural shifts in how working-class radicals saw themselves, and how they defined who belonged and who did not. The spreading normalization of anti-Black caricature in popular culture during the 1820s and 1830s is one part of this. The story is further complicated by the increasingly nationalist and xenophobic approach to political rights that some of Robert's contacts favored, and by their deliberate rejection of abolitionism on the grounds of class interest in the late 1820s. Robert's attempts to stay relevant in this context, including his disappointing lurch toward gradualism and slaveholder compensation in *An Address to Lord Brougham and Vaux*, might perhaps indicate how isolated he had become toward the end of his life. His involvement with the brothels at Featherbed Lane and Field Lane, along with his terrible actions on the morning of February 11, 1832, might suggest that his need for money to survive made him unscrupulous and willing to exploit vulnerable women for profit. But his dark final years are also symptoms of the fact that he had no one left to turn to in the radical movement.

While the destitute and seedy circumstances of his final years provide a sad coda to an otherwise inspirational story, it is precisely this complexity that makes Robert such a compelling figure. The realities of destitution in early nineteenth-century London were not pretty, and Robert was not the only one who needed to make difficult compromises to survive. But it was also his destitution and the rebellious and violent temper that he had inherited from Rosanna and Talkee Amy that rendered him visible within the bureaucratic edifice of the carceral state and the records of popular culture. His ever-challenging, unpredictable, and frequently unlawful behavior left behind enough traces for us to reconstruct his progress from the center to the margins of a movement that, for a few brief spells in time, could envisage true solidarity between exploited laborers at opposite ends of the Earth. In that respect, Robert's various encounters with and deep personal experience of destitution lend him a strange kind of strength. In 1823, a newspaper report described him as a "breeches-maker, Field-preacher, Radical Reformer, Romance writer, Circulatory Librarian, and Ambulatory dealer in drugs, deism and demoralisation in general." It was intended as an insult, but he would probably have been rather proud to read this description. It might well serve as his epitaph.[23]

EPILOGUE

Legacy

WE REALLY SHOULD NOT KNOW this much about Robert Wedderburn. He sits uneasily in the constellation of famous Black writers of the eighteenth and nineteenth centuries. He lacked the entrepreneurial and political savvy of a self-made man like Olaudah Equiano. His literary talents were notable, but only an overgenerous appraisal of his writing skills could elevate him to the caliber of a Phillis Wheatley. He was witty, but not as urbane or charming as Ignatius Sancho. He was an impressive scholar of the Bible, especially taking into account his limited literacy, but he was not as much a master of scripture as John Jea or Boston King. Unlike all of these writers, he seems to have been completely uninterested in proving his respectability or any rarefied learning: he does not want to impress us. That, perhaps, is what makes him such a beguiling intellectual.

In this respect, the contemporaneous Black author he had most in common with was Mary Prince, the first enslaved woman to publish an autobiography in Britain—the abolitionist tract *The Life of Mary Prince* (1831). Like Robert, Mary was uninterested in downplaying or sugarcoating the less respectable elements of her life, as evidenced when she openly and unashamedly discussed her premarital sexual encounters in a public court case in 1833. Yet she was even more exposed to misrepresentation from without than Robert. She was relentlessly patronized by her White abolitionist editor, Thomas Pringle, who made heavy-handed interventions in her autobiography, representing her as a passive victim without agency or self-interest. As she and Robert were both at pains to attest, women who had been enslaved were seldom the poster-children for passive victimhood that White abolitionists often made them out to be.[1]

It was his impulse to testify to the messy, defiant, and indeed sometimes problematic realities of enslaved women's actions that first separated Robert from the common rank of London ultra-radicals in the summer of 1817. Much of the rest of his life as an author was spent investigating this theme, even if his extremely controversial political views were to have a greater impact on how he was perceived at the time. He was just one among many would-be reformers broken on the wheel of British state repression in the aftermath of Peterloo and the Cato Street Conspiracy. He was disgraced by his convictions in 1830 and 1832, and his death went unnoticed in both the mainstream and radical presses. In the century and a half that followed, Robert languished in the oblivion of a hostile archive—the wages of a destitute man's challenge to the legitimate authority of slaveholders, judges, ministers, and politicians. Indeed, it was only when historians turned to scrutinize the records of antiradical state repression that the true significance of his work began to emerge. Ever so slowly over the past fifty years, scholarly and popular interest in Black British history, always closely allied to working-class history, has brought him center stage.

Robert was all but excluded from the classic social histories of the British urban poor. He warranted just a passing mention in E. P. Thompson's magisterial *The Making of the English Working*

EPILOGUE

Class (1963), as "a coloured tailor" who "promoted a little ill-printed journal" called *The Forlorn Hope*. Beyond that, he was relegated to the background—not even really a supporting character in the grand drama of the emergence of working-class consciousness. Though they were by no means hostile, Thompson and his contemporaries in the 1960s were simply not that interested in Black lives, partly because of the prevailing view that one could not be both Black and fully British. Yet even so, the dominance of "class" in British history departments from the late 1960s to the late 1980s—in no small part attributable to the early impact of Thompson's work—laid the foundations for histories of "race" to also be treated as a crucial social and cultural factor in Britain's "history from below."[2]

This in itself was an accident of history. "Black British" as a political identity was at this time undergoing its most important period of transformation to date, driven by the migration of thousands from the Caribbean in the decades after the Second World War. By the early 1970s, various forms of left-leaning Black radicalism, including Black Pantherism, were established in the United Kingdom. This distinctive British Black radicalism flourished in response both to the increasing hostility of the British state toward Caribbean migrants and their families and to worsening social discrimination, stoked by populist White nationalism. The promotion of Black history in Britain during this period was a direct and conscious response to the likes of Enoch Powell and the neofascist National Front, borrowing from an American radical tradition to tell histories of both White prejudice and Black resilience. Indeed, some of the first major works of what we now call Black British history—notably Folarin Shyllon's self-defined "propaganda of the truth," *Black Slaves in Britain* (1973) and *Black People in Britain* (1977)—were funded and published under the auspices of the antiracist think-tank the Institute for Race Relations. But if the seeds of Black radical history writing had been transplanted from the United States, the soil in which they took root in Britain was a Marxist social history tradition—one that centered class consciousness and adopted a resolutely *national* frame of reference. Black British history as a subfield arose in response to a relatively parochial understanding of class struggle, but it was framed in the context of an increasingly global understanding of antiracist solidarity.[3]

Conditions were therefore perfect for historians to "discover" Robert when the early, classic works of Black British history were being published in the 1970s. However one interprets it, his life and work make a striking case for the ways in which *British* working-class "origin stories" could be reconciled with anticolonial history and antiracist activism. One would be hard-pressed to identify a more organic Black British "working-class hero" to make the case that contemporary racism and class injustice were rooted in the era of transatlantic slavery. Robert is a gift to flag-waving Marxist historians of race and resistance in Britain, proof of everything they so much want to see in Britain's past. Yet among the pioneering scholarship of Shyllon, Edward Scobie, and James Walvin that appeared in this crucial decade, Robert does not feature at all.[4]

The problem was perhaps one of historical methodology. Robert's legacy had been so thoroughly buried by the punitive state that his work became visible to scholars only in the early 1980s, once they turned their attention to histories of surveillance and repression. This development in history writing, at least as far as it pertained to race, came in response to a growing sense that Britain's contemporary Black population had come under siege. The far-right National Front had been in the news for its violent harassment of Black men in cities across Britain, while the racism of the Metropolitan police had grown notorious. In the wake of the

EPILOGUE

botched police investigation of the New Cross massacre in 1981 and the passing of the British Nationality Act the same year, many Black British communities were rightly cynical about the hostility of the British government toward them. In this context, most modern readers came to know Robert first and foremost as an example of how Black men who stepped out of line had always been targeted by the British state. Thus Peter Fryer, in his seminal *Staying Power* (1984), introduced Robert as one of history's Black "radicals who suffered for their beliefs and activities" and one of the heroic working-class figures "imprisoned for freedom of speech." Likewise, in 1987 Ron Ramdin's *Making of the Black Working Class in Britain* (whose title acknowledges a debt to Thompson while highlighting a clear deficiency in the original) introduced Robert through his willingness to face prison for his political beliefs.[5]

In these years, historians of radicalism made increasing use of spy reports and prosecution records to gain access to the more militant aspects of Britain's early nineteenth-century political underworld. Here, rather than in the tradition of Black British history per se, is where Robert really staged his twentieth-century resurrection. He and his Hopkins Street chapel feature centrally in David Worrall's excellent book *Radical Culture: Discourse, Resistance, and Surveillance* (1992). But without a doubt the historian we have most to thank for bringing Robert's work to a modern readership is Iain McCalman. First in his PhD thesis submitted in 1984 and then in his masterful *Radical Underworld* (1988), McCalman trawled thousands of pages of handwritten reports by government informers to disinter the inner workings of the Spencean underworld, buried for so long by the Home Office. He clearly knew that, even in a scene populated by many larger-than-life characters, Robert was a figure of extraordinary historical and literary interest. Two years before his monograph came out,

McCalman published an article in the journal *Slavery & Abolition* that thirty-five years later remains an essential reference for any serious work on Robert's world. McCalman's archival scholarship is both dizzyingly expansive and exactingly rigorous; both the article and *Radical Underworld* are packed with hundreds upon hundreds of citations to Home Office records that document Robert's actions in London from 1817 to 1820 in minute detail. Every scholar who has published anything on Robert Wedderburn since 1986 is deeply indebted to McCalman's dedication and historical skill in bringing his political activities to wider notice.[6]

Radical Underworld was deservedly praised by pretty much everyone upon its original release, but McCalman also possessed the humility to acknowledge where its limitations lay. In the 1993 reissue, he recognized that he stood to gain much from the insights of literary criticism, and in particular from a rigorous scrutiny of how language shapes historical meaning in the construction of non-canonical writings such as Robert's. He might also have noted that scholars up to that point had primarily understood Robert's work and experiences through a restrictively national framing—as a radical whose life could be understood almost entirely with reference to British social history. Indeed, McCalman partially addressed both of these limitations in his extended introduction to *The Horrors of Slavery and Other Writings* (1991), in which a selection of Robert's works was reproduced in an accessible format for the first time. This introductory essay, itself a major work of original research on Robert's life, framed him as the crucial connection point between a tradition of "respectable" Black anglophone writing typified by Equiano, on the one hand, and the rowdy, unruly face of the revolutionary Atlantic world on the other. McCalman's pivotal interventions thus anticipated a shift in how Robert came to be understood by scholars: once considered a particularly "pungent" radical orator who exemplified the

EPILOGUE

essentially *British* story of class struggle and antislavery, he is now deemed the most uncompromising and distinctive abolitionist of the "Atlantic proletariat"—an archetype of the "organic," self-taught, and homegrown radical intellectual.[7]

The 1990s saw Robert emerge at the center of a new way of thinking about the African diaspora, now in the context of the revolutionary Atlantic. Thanks to the efforts of the radical historians and literary critics in the 1990s, it is now the default position to define him, in the words of the historian Peter Linebaugh, "as a revolutionary who is able to bring to England experiences from the other side of the Atlantic." Robert's status as a bona fide "revolutionary," rather than a mere rabble-rouser, has been taken for granted in everything published about him ever since; so much so, in fact, that nowadays it is easy to forget that our posthumous recognition of his historical significance—one hesitates to call it *historical legitimacy*—was only made possible by resetting our focus on the connections between Caribbean and British radicalism. In light of this new framing, Robert's life and work no longer just linked the colonial metropole to the "peripheral" slaveholding societies of the Americas, but now indicated how Black cultural identity emerged from an Atlantic, and not solely British, framework. It is no coincidence that during the same year, in the first chapter of his foundational text *The Black Atlantic*, the sociologist and cultural theorist Paul Gilroy also located Robert—alongside William Davidson and the Chartist William Cuffay—as a core influence in the emergence of Black international radicalism.[8]

Gilroy's work, a study of and argument for a distinct Black Atlantic consciousness that existed outside of the national histories in Europe and the Americas, was transformative for many different fields in the humanities and social sciences. It clearly influenced *The Many-Headed Hydra*, an ambitious and rollicking history of the revolutionary Atlantic world, where Linebaugh and Marcus Rediker remade the case for Robert as "a strategically central actor in the formation and dissemination of revolutionary traditions, an intellectual organic to the Atlantic proletariat." In these crucial studies, Robert emerges from the gargantuan machinations of transatlantic slavery, anticolonial resistance, and revolutionary insurrection as an especially vivid human emblem, both of the radicalism engendered by the paradoxes of the Enlightenment and of the irresistible democratic impulses unleashed by the Age of Revolutions. Robert's work was a primary transmitter of Caribbean insurrectionary thought into London radical circles. His close attention to the Haitian Revolution and his insight in situating this and the uprisings in Barbados and Demerara in an Atlantic, rather than Caribbean, context make him a standout figure in the history of early nineteenth-century radicalism.[9]

For some, Robert represented a radical, uncompromising counterpoint to an increasingly focus-grouped and oddly nationalist vision of British cultural pluralism encouraged by the New Labour government: "saris, samosas, and steel bands," as it was often dismissively described. Surprisingly, the intellectual and political project of multiculturalism remained quite resilient in Britain in the 2000s, perhaps as a censure to the Islamophobic populism of the new, post-9/11 northern Atlantic world. While sociologists grew more cynical about the limitations of New Labour's superficial "multicultural Britain" agenda, historians and literary scholars in the United Kingdom and the United States sustained and expanded a healthy scholarship on how metropolitan cultures and politics were influenced by migrant communities, and especially intellectuals of the African diaspora. Once again, these waves of Black history and Black literature scholarship recursively influenced and were influenced by broader social trends.[10]

These were the years in which Olaudah Equiano approached

EPILOGUE

"exit velocity," almost (though perhaps not quite) joining that small pantheon of pre–Civil Rights era Black personalities who become household names on both sides of the Atlantic. Bolstered by the nationwide bicentenary commemorations in 2007 of the Abolition of the Slave Trade Act, Equiano became an important representative figure during these years, not only of the inhumanity of the slave trade but of the leadership of Black intellectuals—and the influence of African and Black Caribbean intellectual traditions—in the campaigns to abolish it. Up until about the mid-1990s, Equiano was usually mentioned alongside Robert as part of the unbroken thread of antiestablishment Black radicalism running throughout modern British history. But then, with his dignified portraits and his eloquent prose, he was suddenly appropriated as the "respectable" face of African-led metropolitan antislavery. During the bicentenary year of 2007, this brought with it the accoutrements of state approval: along with Ignatius Sancho, Equiano became one of the first two named people of African descent to feature on a British postage stamp. Likewise, he entered the national curriculum for history in 2008 (only to be taken back out as part of the Conservative education secretary Michael Gove's widely criticized reforms in 2013).

This abrupt embrace by the establishment is possibly due to Equiano's avowed admiration for British tolerance and his readiness to work within existing structures of power to achieve his aims—both key tenets of the (neo)liberal multiculturalism espoused by New Labour. Moreover, his personal journey from enslavement to self-made bourgeois respectability, and of course his leadership in the popular antislavery movement, was spun as a good news story, attesting to the redemptive potential of a culturally pluralist iteration of Western liberal capitalism. In retrospect, it is difficult to imagine the impoverished and often rebarbative Robert ("my motto is assassinate stab in the dark") being thus honored by the state at that particular moment of national self-reflection.[11]

Robert retained more of a "cult" following in the first decade of the 2000s. Those who knew about Robert Wedderburn, knew. Partly because he embodied a classed, raced, but defiantly insurgent identity that was neither wholly British nor wholly Jamaican—what postcolonial theorist Homi Bhabha called "cultural hybridity"—many saw in him the fulfillment of an ideal type of Black resistance from the margins. It was precisely his stubborn refusal to fall into easy, predetermined categories, both in his writing and in his identity, that explained his attraction for scholars and certain sectors of the public during the multicultural 2000s. If Equiano had been repackaged as a liberal hero who represented Britain's innate national capacity for tolerance, decency, and cultural plurality, then Robert was seen as his anti-capitalist Jungian shadow-self, standing for the insubordinate and irreducibly "hybrid" world of the Black Atlantic. For the bicentenary year, the contemporary artist Paul Howard produced a new portrait of Robert—a full-length photographic re-creation featuring the actor Lloyd Gordon. Howard's piece reveled in his subject's reputation as an avenging hero; he was depicted as "shabby but magnificent, a machete at his waist, an axe at his feet ... and a copy of the 1831 weekly journal The Poor Man's Guardian" close at hand. The portrait was hung at the Docklands Museum in London, directly facing—or rather, confronting—a nineteenth-century portrait of the slaveholder George Hibbert; it was the very avatar of a defiant, hybrid cultural identity.[12]

What made Robert basically unacceptable as a state-endorsed national hero at the time of the bicentenary has proven his most valuable quality for scholars interested in how slavery "made" the modern world. Approaches to his work have proliferated in the 2010s and 2020s, from the reassessment of contemporary legacies of colonialism to the recentering of social class in historical analysis. My own work has sought to clarify Robert's full contribution to grassroots British radicalism, as part of the broader argument that British popular politics were to an extent defined by Black intellectual leadership. But this is just one way he continues to reshape how we understand Britain and the Caribbean's entangled pasts. Alongside ongoing interest in his status as a radical Black Londoner, Robert has become important to new accounts of Scotland's role in British colonial history, acting both as an inspirational symbol of resistance and as a reminder of how much these legacies still shape the nation today. Literary scholars increasingly recognize his important contributions to the genre of "Haitian gothic" writing. At the same time, his accounts of Rosanna's and Amy's experiences are helping Caribbean historians to understand patterns of resistance in colonial Jamaica. Scholars and activists alike now turn to Robert's work—or at least his work before *An Address to Lord Brougham and Vaux*—as an example of how the lessons of anticolonialist opposition in the past can inspire us to solidarity in the present. To borrow the words of the literary critic Shelby Johnson, Robert's "prophetic vision" of a radically leveled world economy depended not upon individual heroes but the actions of "diverse speakers and unexpected collaborators."[13]

In our atomized and terminally online times, Robert's insistence on the need for radical solidarity over liberal individualism sounds out like a clarion call through the fog of an obscured past, a nearly forgotten, brief moment when another world seemed possible. It is fitting that he is more and more often seen by scholars as an important figure for our understanding of the relationship between slavery and capitalism. His apparently intuitive understanding that racialized capitalism was the common denominator in the exploitation of workers around the world—from enslaved people in Jamaica to factory workers and dung tailors in London—has inspired scholars to explore how early socialist ideas were articulated in relation to empire. It seems difficult not to see ourselves reflected when we look at the world that made and then so spectacularly unmade Robert's reputation. Within the ongoing omni-crisis of late-stage capitalism, food banks, unaffordable housing, resurgent state-condoned racism, and paid-for political gaslighting operating at an industrial scale, Robert's outright rejection of any authority derived from the violent expropriation and hoarding of land and resources is now very much back in vogue.[14]

The language that scholars have used when describing Robert's radicalism—"organic," "natural," "earthy," even "pungent"—speaks to an enduring sense that he embodies a pure form of radicalism: radicalism as it should be. His prophetic vision of a world without slavery or poverty was predicated on the idea that solidarity between colonized and exploited peoples was not only possible and desirable but inevitable. While he learned, to his cost, toward the end of his life that such solidarity could not be taken for granted, Robert remained optimistic about the capacity for poor and enslaved people to find common cause in the pursuit of freedom and equality. Until his death, he believed that they might one day even be successful. For this belief, he was once derided as naïve, even deluded. But he was more of a realist than people gave him credit for. He understood from the example of Haiti the need to plan carefully to defend anything that might be gained from an insurrectionary movement for freedom. He learned from Barbados and Demerara, and from William Davidson and Arthur Thistlewood too, that insurrections most often ended up with bloody reprisals, with severed heads held up to the crowd or fixed on a spike over Temple Bar. He learned from his father and his half-brother Andrew that the law is no guide to conscience and that power has a habit of legitimizing itself as it reproduces. Most im-

EPILOGUE

portantly, he learned from Rosanna and Amy that sometimes it was worth the punishment to thumb one's nose at authority, to unsettle for a moment the complacent, self-regarding assumptions about justice and honor held among a pack of slaveholders. Seemingly doomed acts of defiance in the face of overwhelming odds can yield major effects further down the line. In Jamaica they have a saying: "If you are the big tree, then we are the small axe." There is nothing naïve about that.

NOTES

Prologue

1. Robert Owen, *Report to the Committee of the Association for the Relief of the Manufacturing and Labouring Poor* (London, [1817]), 6; Robert Owen, *The Life of Robert Owen*, 2 vols. (London, 1857), 1:113–115; Michael Morris, "The Problem of Slavery in the Age of Improvement: David Dale, Robert Owen, and New Lanark Cotton," in A. Benchimol and G. McKeever, eds., *Cultures of Improvement in Scottish Romanticism, 1707–1840* (Abingdon, 2018), 111–131; Owen, *Report*, 18.

2. *The Star*, August 22, 1817.

3. *Suffolk Chronicle*, August 23, 1817; *The Star*, October 30, 1809.

4. *Suffolk Chronicle*, August 23, 1817; "Dorchester Prison Admission and Discharge Records, 1782–1901," NG/PR1/D2/1, 111, Dorset History Centre.

5. Robert Wedderburn, *The Horrors of Slavery* (London, 1824), 9; Robert Wedderburn, *Truth Self-Supported: Or, a Refutation of Certain Errors Generally Adopted in the Christian Church* (London: W. Glindon and G. Riebau, [1802]), 4; "Register of marriages, 1754–1785," P69/KAT2/A/01/Ms7891/1, Saint Katherine Cree: City of London, London Metropolitan Archives (hereafter, LMA); "Robert Wedderburn," October 3, 1795, MJ/SP/1795/10/034, Middlesex Sessions of the Peace: Court in Session, LMA; "Register of Baptisms," July 15, 1816, DL/T/036/024, Holborn St Giles in the Fields, LMA; *Truth Self-Supported*, 1.

6. Iain McCalman, *Radical Underworld: Prophets, Revolutionaries, and Pornographers in London, 1795–1840* (Cambridge, 1988), 50–73, 128–152; "15 January 1817," HO42/158, 229, Home Office: Domestic Correspondence, The National Archives, London (hereafter, TNA).

7. *Morning Post*, August 22, 1817.

8. For a typical hagiographical piece of mid-twentieth-century historiogra-

phy, see Ernest Marshall Howse, *Saints in Politics: The "Clapham Sect" and the Growth of Freedom* (Toronto, 1953). A famous exception to this general trend is Eric Williams, *Capitalism and Slavery* (New York, 1944), although this was not published in Britain until 1964. For a more penetrating analysis of the idea of a "national sin," see John Coffey, "'Tremble, Britannia!': Fear, Providence and the Abolition of the Slave Trade, 1756–1807," *English Historical Review* 127 (2012): 844–881. For a recent populist use of abolition to obfuscate the history of British slavery, see the speech given by Suella Braverman (then the Conservative home secretary) at the "National Conservatism" conference in May 2023, during which she baldly stated that "the defining characteristic of our relationship with slavery is not that we practiced it, but that we led the way in abolishing it." National Conservatism, "Suella Braverman: The Value of Conservatism," YouTube video, 35:34, May 17, 2023, https://youtu.be/NS5nh1aD-qM (accessed November 15, 2023).

9. See Ryan Hanley, *Beyond Slavery and Abolition: Black British Writing, c. 1770–1830* (Cambridge, 2018). For Equiano and respectability, see Vincent Carretta, *Equiano the African: Biography of a Self-Made Man* (Athens, GA, 2005); Cassander L. Smith, *Race and Respectability in an Early Black Atlantic* (Baton Rouge, 2023), 85–117.

10. For a small sample of this extensive scholarly debate, see Tom Scriven, "Slavery and Abolition in Chartist Thought and Culture, 1838–1850," *Historical Journal* 65:5 (2022): 1262–1284; Ryan Hanley, "Slavery and the Birth of Working-Class Racism in England, 1814–1833," *Transactions of the Royal Historical Society* 26 (2016): 103–123; Zach Sell, "'Worst Conceivable Form': Race, Global Capital, and the Making of the English Working Class," *Historical Reflections* 41:1 (2015): 54–69; James Epstein "Taking Class Notes on Empire," in Catherine Hall and Sonya Rose, eds., *At Home with the Empire: Metropolitan Culture and the Imperial World* (Cambridge, 2006), 251–274; Marcus Wood, *Slavery, Empathy and Pornography* (Oxford: Oxford University Press, 2002), 141–180; Don Herzog, *Poisoning the Minds of the Lower Orders* (New Haven, 1998), 397–402; David Turley, *The Culture of English Antislavery, 1780–1860* (London, 1991), 104–189; Seymour Drescher, *Capitalism and Antislavery: British Mobilization in Comparative Perspective* (London, 1986), 89–110; Betty Fladeland, *Abolitionists and Working-Class Problems in the Age of Industrialization* (Baton Rouge, 1984); Seymour Dresher, "Cart Whip and Billy Roller: Antislavery and Reform Symbolism in Industrialising Britain," *Journal of Social History* 15:1 (1981): 3–24; David Brion Davis, *The Problem of Slavery in the Age of Revolution* (New York, 1975), 343–468.

11. "Examination of William Plush," TS11/45/167, TNA.

12. For the broader social history of British abolitionism, see, inter alia, David Richardson, *Principles and Agents: The British Slave Trade and Its Abolition*

(New Haven, 2023), 118–248; Michael Taylor, *The Interest: How the British Establishment Resisted the Abolition of Slavery* (London, 2020); Srividhya Swaminathan, *Debating the Slave Trade: Rhetoric of British National Identity, 1759–1815* (Farnham, 2009), 171–218; David Brion Davis, *Inhuman Bondage: The Rise and Fall of Slavery in the New World* (Oxford, 2006), 231–249; Peter Linebaugh and Marcus Rediker, *The Many-Headed Hydra: The Hidden History of the Revolutionary Atlantic* (London, 2000), 248–287; John R. Oldfield, *Popular Politics and British Anti-slavery: The Mobilisation of Public Opinion Against the Slave Trade, 1787–1807* (Manchester, 1995); David Turley, *Culture of English Antislavery*, 108–195; Robin Blackburn, *The Overthrow of Colonial Slavery, 1776–1848* (London, 1988), 293–330, 419–472.

13. Ryan Hanley, "The Shadow of Colonial Slavery at Peterloo," *Caliban: French Journal of English Studies* 65/66 (2021): 73–85.

14. *The Times*, October 4, 1816; *Morning Chronicle*, October 4, 1816; *London Courier and Evening Gazette*, July 10, 1817; *Morning Herald*, July 10, 1817; *The Sun*, July 10, 1817; *Abridgment of the Minutes of the Evidence: Taken Before a Committee of the Whole House, to Whom It Was Referred to Consider of the Slave-Trade, 1790* (London, 1791), 55; *The Axe Laid to the Root*, 2:13.

15. *Forlorn Hope*, October 4, 1817, 1:15–16; October 11, 1817, 2:35–36; *The Axe*, 1:3.

16. *The Axe*, 1:5.

17. On slavery as a "predicament," see Vincent Brown, "Social Death and Political Life in the Study of Slavery," *American Historical Review* 114:5 (2009): 1231–1249; *The Axe*, 1:7.

CHAPTER 1. A Troublesome Woman

1. *Barbarity to a Female Slave! Authentic Particulars of the Inhuman Cruelty of Jacobus Overeem to America, his Female Slave* (London: John Fairburn, [1818]). I have collaged details from this engraving deliberately out of place to destabilize, rather than reproduce, the original pornographic depiction of an enslaved woman's suffering, a strategy inspired by Saidiya Hartman's article "Venus in Two Acts," *Small Axe*, 12:2 (2008) and her book *Wayward Lives, Beautiful Experiments: Intimate Histories of Social Upheaval* (New York, 2019).

2. Marisa Fuentes, *Dispossessed Lives: Enslaved Women, Violence, and the Archive* (Philadelphia, 2016), 127; Saidiya Hartman, "Venus in Two Acts," 3.

3. See, inter alia, contributions in special issues of *History of the Present* 6:2 (2016) and *Social Text* 33:4 (2015); Fuentes, *Dispossessed Lives*, 140; Brenda E. Stevenson, *What Sorrows Labour in My Parent's Breast? A History of the Enslaved Black Family* (Lanham, 2023); see also Tiya Miles, *All That She Carried: The Journey of Ashley's Sack, a Black Family Keepsake* (New York, 2021); DoVeanna S. Fulton,

Speaking Power: Black Feminist Orality in Women's Narratives of Slavery (Albany, 2006).

4. *The Axe*, 1:13.

5. On using Robert's accounts to explore Rosanna's and Amy's experiences, see Nadine Hunt, "Remembering Africans in Diaspora: Robert Wedderburn's 'Freedom Narrative,'" in Olatunje Ojo and Nadine Hunt, eds., *Slavery in Africa and the Caribbean: A History of Enslavement and Identity Since the 18th Century* (London, 2012), 175–198.

6. On poisoning, see Diana Paton, "Witchcraft, Poison, Law, and Atlantic Slavery," *William and Mary Quarterly* 69:2 (2012): 235–264; John Savage, "'Black Magic' and White Terror: Slave Poisoning and Colonial Society in Early 19th Century Martinique," *Journal of Social History* 40 (2007): 635–662.

7. *Horrors*, 4. Unless otherwise noted, all references to the text of *The Horrors of Slavery* are to the original 1824 edition.

8. *Horrors*, 4; "Charles James Sholto Douglas," Legacies of British Slavery Database (hereafter LBS), www.ucl.ac.uk/lbs/person/view/2146650635 (accessed August 18, 2023); *Horrors*, 7.

9. Sasha Turner, *Contested Bodies: Pregnancy, Childbearing, and Slavery in Jamaica* (Philadelphia, 2017), 182–210; Edward Long, *History of Jamaica*, 2 vols. (London, 1774), 2:276.

10. *Horrors*, 10. Ann Laura Stoler, "Tense and Tender Ties: The Politics of Comparison in North American History and (Post) Colonial Studies," *Journal of American History* 88:3 (2001): 829–865.

11. *Horrors*, 6, 7, 22.

12. *Horrors*, 7.

13. *Horrors*, 8.

14. *Horrors*, 7.

15. "Diary for 1759," August 31, 1759, OSB MSS 176, 169, Thistlewood Papers, Beinecke Library, Yale University. See also Trevor Burnard, *Mastery, Tyranny, and Desire: Thomas Thistlewood and His Slaves in the Anglo-Jamaican World* (Chapel Hill, 2009), 238; Elizabeth A. Dolan, "Following a Ghost: 'A Certain Mulatto Woman Slave Named Phibbah,'" *Journal of Literature and Trauma Studies* 2:1/2 (2013): 63–86; Burnard, *Mastery, Tyranny, and Desire*, 228–233; "Diary for 1760," August 29, 1760, OSB MSS 176, 80, Thistlewood Papers.

16. *Horrors*, 15, 22.

17. Matthew Lewis, *Journal of a West India Proprietor, Kept During a Residence in the Island of Jamaica* (London, 1834), 179.

18. "St Thomas in the East: Baptisms, Marriages, Burials 1708–1821, vol. 1," February 6, 1748, 89, Jamaica Archives, Spanish Town, Jamaica; *Horrors*, 22.

19. "Westmoreland Parish Baptism, marr., burial index (v. 1-2) 1739–1871," 39, Jamaica Archives, Spanish Town, Jamaica; *Horrors*, 7.

20. Fernanda Bretones Lane, "Free to Bury Their Dead: Baptism and the Meanings of Freedom in the Eighteenth-Century Caribbean," *Slavery & Abolition* 42:3 (2021): 449–465; Travis Glasson, "'Baptism Doth Not Bestow Freedom': Missionary Anglicanism, Slavery, and the Yorke-Talbot Opinion, 1701–30," *William and Mary Quarterly* 67:2 (2010): 279–318; Daniel Livesay, *Children of Uncertain Fortune: Mixed-Race Jamaicans in Britain and the Atlantic Family, 1733–1833* (Williamsburg, 2018), 20–89.

21. *Horrors*, 9.

22. *The Axe*, 1:3; *Horrors*, 9; Robert Wedderburn, *An Address to the Right Honourable Lord Brougham and Vaux, Chancellor of Great Britain, by the Descendent of a Negro; Suggesting an Equitable Plan for the Emancipation of the Slaves* (London, 1831), 3; Hunt, "Remembering Africans in Diaspora," 180; *Horrors*, 15.

23. *Horrors*, 13–14; for Charles Boswell, see "Charles Boswell, ????-1796," LBS, www.ucl.ac.uk/lbs/person/view/2146666939; and "Jamaica Almanac 1779," repr. in Jamaican Family Search, http://www.jamaicanfamilysearch.com/Members/1/1779alo3.htm (accessed August 18, 2023).

24. *The Axe*, 2:13; *Address to Lord Brougham and Vaux*, 3.

25. *Horrors*, 8; "Westmoreland, Copy Register: Baptisms Marriages Burials Vol. 1, 1739–1825," 114, Jamaica Archives, Spanish Town, Jamaica.

CHAPTER 2. Obeah Witch

1. Myles Ogborn, *The Freedom of Speech: Talk and Slavery in the Anglo-Caribbean World* (Oxford: Oxford University Press, 2019), 1–34; Diana Paton, "Gender, Language, Violence and Slavery: Insult in Jamaica, 1800–1838," *Gender & History* 18:2 (2006): 246–265; Julius Scott, *The Common Wind: Afro-American Currents in the Age of the Haitian Revolution* (London, 2018), 38–76; Lynn Thomas, "Historicising Agency," *Gender & History* 28:2 (2016): 324–339; Walter Johnson, "On Agency," *Journal of Social History* 37:1 (2003): 113–124; Sidney Mintz, "Slave Life on Caribbean Sugar Plantations: Some Unanswered Questions," in Stephan Palmié, ed., *Slave Cultures and the Cultures of Slavery* (Knoxville, 1995), 12–22.

2. *Horrors*, 10; *The Axe*, 2:30.

3. *Abridgment of the Minutes of the Evidence* [. . .] *Slave-Trade, 1791* (London, 1791), 130; Stevenson, *What Sorrows*, 229.

4. *Horrors*, 10.

5. Trevor Burnard, "Slaves and Slavery in Kingston, 1770–1815," *International Review of Social History* 65 (2020): 58–65; John Luffman, *A Brief Account*

of the Island of Antigua (London, 1789), 139–140; Simon Newman, "Hidden in Plain Sight: Escaped Slaves in Late Eighteenth- and Early Nineteenth-Century Jamaica," *William and Mary Quarterly* (2018): 48, https://oieahc.wm.edu/digital-projects/oi-reader/simon-p-newman-hidden-in-plain-sight/ (accessed June 28, 2023).

6. *Horrors*, 10; "Joseph Payne," LBS, www.ucl.ac.uk/lbs/person/view/2146 663019 (accessed August 21, 2023); Winnifred Brown-Glaude, *Higglers in Kingston: Women's Informal Work in Jamaica* (Nashville, 2011), 39–90; Ernst Pijning, "'Can She Be a Woman?' Gender and Contraband in the Revolutionary Atlantic," in Douglas Catterall and Jodi Campbell, eds., *Women in Port: Gendering Communities, Economies, and Social Networks in Atlantic Port Cities, 1500–1800* (Leiden, 2012), 215–250; Newman, "Hidden in Plain Sight"; *Royal Gazette of Jamaica*, June 26, 1779.

7. *Horrors*, 10; Nuala Zahediah, "Defying Mercantilism: Illicit Trade, Trust, and the Jamaican Sephardim, 1660–1730," *Historical Journal* 61:1 (2018): 77–79; Wim Klooster, "Inter-Imperial Smuggling in the Americas, 1600–1800," in Bernard Bailyn and Patricia Denault, eds., *Soundings in Atlantic History* (Cambridge, MA, 2009), 141–180; Trevor Burnard, *Jamaica in the Age of Revolutions* (Philadelphia, 2020), 37.

8. *Address to Lord Brougham and Vaux*, 13; *Horrors*, 11; see Jesse Cromwell, *The Smugglers' World: Illicit Trade and Atlantic Communities in Eighteenth-Century Venezuela* (Williamsburg, 2018), 239–270.

9. Robert spells it "Fort Homea," a mis-transliteration of "Fort Omoa," the Anglicized name for the Castillo de San Fernando de Omoa; *Horrors*, 11.

10. Benjamin Moseley, *A Treatise on Sugar* (London, 1799), 193; Vincent Brown, *The Reaper's Garden: Death and Power in the World of Atlantic Slavery* (Cambridge, MA, 2009), 149.

11. Brown, *Reaper's Garden*, 144–148; Ogborn, *Freedom of Speech*, 143–188; Bryan Edwards, *The History, Civil and Commercial, of the British Colonies in the West Indies* (London, 1798), 86.

12. Vincent Brown, *Tacky's Revolt: The Story of an Atlantic Slave War* (Cambridge, MA, 2020), 105–111; Diana Paton, *The Cultural Politics of Obeah: Religion, Colonialism and Modernity in the Caribbean World* (Cambridge, 2015), 17–42, quote on 41 (emphasis added).

13. Sasha Turner Bryson, "The Art of Power: Poison and Obeah Accusations and the Struggle for Dominance and Survival in Jamaican Slave Society," *Caribbean Studies* 41:2 (2013): 68–69; Randy Browne, *Surviving Slavery in the British Caribbean* (Philadelphia, 2017), 134.

14. See Turner Bryson, "The Art of Power"; *Horrors*, 11–12.

15. *Horrors*, 12; see Turner Bryson, "The Art of Power"; Randy Browne, "The 'Bad Business' of Obeah: Power, Authority, and the Politics of Slave Culture in

the British Caribbean," *William and Mary Quarterly* 68:3 (2011): 451–480; for an account of obeah at funerals, see *The Times*, November 23, 1787.

16. *Horrors*, 11.

17. *The Axe*, 1:13.

18. *The Address of the Rev. R. Wedderburn, To the Court of the King's Bench at Westminster, on Appearing to Receive Judgment for Blasphemy* (London, 1820), 4.

19. *Address to Lord Brougham and Vaux*, 4.

20. *Address to Lord Brougham and Vaux*, 3–4, 6; HO42/198, 196, November 10, 1819, TNA; *The Axe*, 4:54; *Address to Lord Brougham and Vaux*, 9.

21. *The Axe*, 1:4; *Horrors*, 6; *Address to Lord Brougham and Vaux*, 3; "Nabob," ADM 51/617, Admiralty: Captain's Logs, TNA; "Nabob: Storeship," ADM 36/7762, Admiralty: Royal Navy Ships' Musters, TNA.

22. *Public Advertiser*, January 27, 1779; *London Evening Post*, January 28, 1779; "Nabob: Storeship," ADM 36/7762, Admiralty: Royal Navy Ships' Musters, TNA; "Nabob (SS)," ADM 34/525, Navy Pay Office: Ships' Pay Books, TNA.

23. *Horrors*, 24.

24. Cited in David Worrall, *Radical Culture: Discourse, Resistance and Surveillance, 1790–1820* (London, 1992), 180.

25. *Horrors*, 24.

CHAPTER 3. The Skull Affixed to Temple Bar

1. Walter Thornbury, *Old and New London: A Narrative of Its History, Its People and Its Places*, 2 vols. (London, 1873), 1:29.

2. Alexander Wedderburn, *The Wedderburn Book, A History of the Wedderburns in the Counties of Berwick and Forfar*, 2 vols. (Private Circulation, 1896), 1:264–287.

3. *Horrors*, 5, 6.

4. Wedderburn, *Wedderburn Book*, 1:471, 505.

5. John W. Cairns, "After *Somerset*: The Scottish Experience," *Journal of Legal History* 33:3 (2012): 291. John Knight captained the *Phoenix* on two possible voyages where Joseph could have been transported to Jamaica: one arrived in 1765, after Rosanna had left John's house; and one arrived in 1760, one to two years before she stayed there. SlaveVoyages, voyage ID 17465; 17601, www.slavevoyages.org/voyage/database (accessed August 21, 2023).

6. *Edinburgh Advertiser*, July 3, 1772.

7. "Extract of Process: Joseph Knight against John Wedderburn of Ballindean Bart. 1774," CS235/K/2/2, ff. 9, 3, Court of Session: Unextracted processes, 1st arrangement, Innes-Mackenzie office, National Records of Scotland (hereafter, NRS).

8. "Memorial of John Wedderburn," CS235/K/2/2, 2, NRS.

9. "Extract of Process," CS235/K/2/2, ff. 3, 6–7, NRS; Cairns, "Knight, Joseph (b. c. 1753)," *Oxford Dictionary of National Biography* (hereafter, ODNB); Michael Bundock, *The Fortunes of Francis Barber: The True Story of the Jamaican Slave Who Became Samuel Johnson's Heir* (New Haven, 2015), 141.

10. "Extract of Process," CS235/K/2/2, ff. 11–12, 14, 27, NRS.

11. "Memorial for John Wedderburn," CS235/K/2/2, 8–9, NRS.

12. Cairns, "Knight, Joseph (b. c. 1753)"; David Dalrymple, *Decisions of the Lords of Council and Session, from 1766 to 1791* (Edinburgh, 1826), 776–780. For Dundas and slavery, see Stephen Mullen, "Henry Dundas: A 'Great Delayer' of the Abolition of the Transatlantic Slave Trade," *Scottish Historical Review* 100:2 (2021): 218–248; for Johnson and *Knight v. Wedderburn*, see Bundock, *Fortunes of Francis Barber*, 142–143.

13. *Truth Self-Supported*, 3–4. For Elizabeth's age, see "Holborn, British Lying-In Hospital Endell Street, London: Particulars of Patients," RG8/59, no. 18881, General Register Office: Registers of Births, Marriages and Deaths, TNA; "Robert Wedderburn and Elisth Ryan," November 5, 1781, P69/KAT2/A/01/Ms 7891/1, 331, St Katherine Cree, Register of Marriages, 1754–1785, LMA.

14. David Cressey, "The Fifth of November Remembered," in Roy Porter, ed., *Myths of the English* (Cambridge, 1992), 77; *The Times*, November 5, 1790.

15. *The Axe*, 4:71–72.

16. Adapted from "HMS Polyphemus," ADM34/602, Navy Board: Navy Pay Office: Ships' Pay Books, TNA.

17. "06 October 1819," HO42/196, 177, TNA.

18. "Holborn, British Lying-In Hospital," RG8/59, no. 18881, TNA.

19. Legacies of British Slavery Database, "James Wedderburn Colvile," www.ucl.ac.uk/lbs/person/view/2146643501 (accessed July 12, 2023).

20. *Horrors*, 23.

21. Livesay, *Children of Uncertain Fortune*, 20–89; Kate Gibson, *Illegitimacy, Family and Stigma in England, 1660–1834* (Oxford, 2022), 142–157; Amanda Goodrich, *Henry Redhead Yorke, Colonial Radical: Politics and Identity in the Atlantic World, 1772–1813* (London, 2019), 54–79.

CHAPTER 4. There Is a Day Coming

1. See Gibson, *Illegitimacy, Family and Stigma*, 141–176; Louise Falcini, "Accounting for Illegitimacy: Parish Politics and the Poor," in Peter Collinge and Louise Falcini, eds., *Providing for the Poor: The Old Poor Law, 1750–1834* (London, 2022), 25–52; Lisa Zunshine, *Bastards and Foundlings: Illegitimacy in Eighteenth-Century England* (Columbus, OH, 2005), 1–22.

2. *The Gorgon*, June 13, 1818, 28.

3. Hanley, "Shadow of Colonial Slavery"; Hanley, "Slavery and the Birth of Working-Class Racism," 103–123; Wood, *Slavery, Empathy and Pornography*, 141–180. James Forde, *The Early Haitian State and the Question of Political Legitimacy: American and British Representations of Haiti, 1804–1824* (Cham, 2020), 93–128.

4. See, inter alia, Cassandra Pybus, *Epic Journeys of Freedom: Runaway Slaves of the American Revolution and Their Global Quest for Liberty* (Boston, 2007), ch. 5–7; Stephen Braidwood, *Black Poor and White Philanthropists: London's Black and the Foundation of the Sierra Leone Settlement, 1786–1791* (Liverpool, 1994), 129–180; Hanley, *Beyond Slavery and Abolition*, 171–202; Ottobah Cugoano, *Thoughts and Sentiments on the Evil and Wicked Traffic of the slavery and Commerce of the Human Species* (London: [n.p.], 1787), 140.

5. Peter Fryer, *Staying Power: The History of Black People in Britain* (London, 1983, repr. 2010), 75; *Truth Self-Supported*, 4; *General Evening Post*, September 9, 1786; Hanley, *Beyond Slavery and Abolition*, 198, 181.

6. John Oldfield, *Popular Politics and British Anti-Slavery* (London, 1998), 41–70; *Address to Lord Brougham and Vaux*, 11; Cynthia S. Hamilton, "Hercules Subdued: The Visual Rhetoric of the Kneeling Slave," *Slavery & Abolition* 34:4 (2014): 631–665; Mary Guyatt, "The Wedgwood Slave Medallion: Values in Eighteenth-Century Design," *Journal of Design History* 13:2 (2000): 93–105; Thomas Clarkson, *The History of the Rise, Progress, & Accomplishment of the Abolition of the African Slave-Trade*, 2 vols. (London: Longman and Hurst, 1808), 2:191–192.

7. See Samuel Rowe, "'Universal Jubilee': Social Property and 1790s Radicalism," *Studies in Romanticism* 60:3 (2021): 307–329; Gareth Steadman Jones, "An End to Poverty: The French Revolution and the Promise of a World Beyond Want," *Historical Research* 78:200 (2005): 193–207; "Elizabeth Wedderburn, 15 February 1797," 2676/22, St Botolph Aldgate Parish Records, Pauper Examination Books, Guildhall Library, London; "Register of Baptisms, Marriages and Burials, 1538–1812," P69/KAT2/A/001/MS07890/001, St Katherine Cree: City of London, LMA.

8. See Tim Hitchcock, *Down and Out in Eighteenth-Century London* (London, 2004), 125–150; Nicholas Rogers, "Vagrancy, Impressment and the Regulation of Labour in Eighteenth-Century Britain," *Slavery & Abolition* 15:2 (1994): 102–113; "Robert Wedderburn, 03 October 1795," Middlesex Sessions of the Peace: Court in Session, MJ/SP/1795/10/034, LMA; "House of Correction Gaol Delivery List," Middlesex Sessions of the Peace: Court in Session, MJ/SP/1795/10/007, LMA.

9. "Elizabeth Wedderburn, 15 February 1797," 2676/22, Guildhall Library, London; "Elizabeth Weatherburn, Orders of Removal, 16 Jan 1819," P91/LEN/1312, London Poor Law Registers, LMA.

10. Mary's previous surname is imputed in the baptism record for her daugh-

ter (Robert's stepdaughter) Mary-Ann Durham. Robert and Mary's children were named Hope, Lydia, and Jacob. At his admission to Dorchester Gaol on May 16, 1820, Robert noted that he had six children, which tallies with the account here—three by Elizabeth and three by Mary. "Holborn St Giles in the Fields, Register of Baptisms, 1816," DL/T/036, Item 024, LMA; "Holborn St Giles in the Fields, Register of Baptisms, 1822," DL/T/036, Item 042, LMA; "Dorchester Prison Admission," NG/PR1/D2/1, 111, Dorset History Centre; *The Star*, October 30, 1809; "Register of Baptisms," DL/T/036, Item 024, LMA; "A Few Lines for a Double-Faced Politician," HO42/202, 73, TNA; "Register of Baptisms," DL/T/036, Item 042, LMA.

11. John Bohstedt, *The Politics of Provisions: Food Riots, Moral Economy, and Market Transition in England, c. 1550–1850* (Farnham, 2010), 206–240. As Robert recalled in 1824, "I was at that time . . . in extreme distress; the quartern loaf was then 1s. 10 ½ d., I was out of work, and my wife was lying in," *Horrors*, 23; "Register of Baptisms," DL/T/036, Item 024, LMA.

12. *Kent's Directory for 1803* (London: R. and H. Causton, 1803), 211; *Horrors*, 22, 15–16.

13. *Truth Self-Supported*, 5.

14. The publication date is an estimate, provided by Iain McCalman, the preeminent scholar of Wedderburn's ultraradical years in London. Wedderburn, *The Horrors of Slavery and Other Writings*, ed. Iain McCalman (Princeton, 1991), 9.

15. *Truth Self-Supported*, 5–6; see, for example, McCalman's excellent studies in his edition of Wedderburn, *Horrors of Slavery and Other Writings*, 1–40; McCalman, "Anti-Slavery and Ultra-Radicalism in Early Nineteenth-Century England: The Case of Robert Wedderburn," *Slavery & Abolition* 7:2 (1986): 99–117.

16. *Truth Self-Supported*, 12.

17. *Truth Self-Supported*, 12–13.

18. *Truth Self-Supported*, 7, 8.

19. *Truth Self-Supported*, 10–11.

20. *Truth Self Supported*, 2.

21. *The Star*, October 30, 1809; *Westminster Journal and Old British Spy*, November 4, 1809.

CHAPTER 5. The Press Is My Engine of Destruction

1. *National Register*, October 24, 1813; Anon., *The Tailors and their Cabbage: being a particular account of the cabbage extraordinary, made by forty-five tailors, in the employ of Mr. John Mabberley* (London: John Fairburn, 1813).

2. *Kentish Weekly Chronicle*, October 22, 1813; *National Register*, October 24, 1813.

3. Peter Linebaugh, *The London Hanged: Crime and Civil Society in the Eighteenth Century* (London, 1991), 245-248; *Caledonian Mercury*, November 1, 1813; *National Register*, October 24, 1813.

4. Peter King, "Gleaners, Farmers and the Failure of Legal Sanctions in England, 1750-1850," *Past & Present* 125 (1989): 116-150; Peter D'Sena, "Perquisites and Casual Labour on the London Wharfside in the Eighteenth Century," *London Journal* 14:2 (1989): 130-147; *The Public Ledger*, October 23, 1813; "Tailors' 'Cabbage'" merited an entry in John Timbs, *Things Not Generally Known: A Book for Old and Young* (London: David Bogue, 1856), 143.

5. *National Register*, October 24, 1813.

6. Francis Grose, *A Classical Dictionary of the Vulgar Tongue* (London, 1785), 65; Christina Parolin, *Radical Spaces: Venues of Popular Politics in London, c. 1790-c. 1845* (Canberra, 2010), 105-146; Herzog, *Poisoning the Minds*, 59-62; McCalman, "Anti-Slavery and Ultra-Radicalism," 104.

7. Malcolm Chase, "'The Real Rights of Man': Thomas Spence, Paine, and Chartism," *Miranda* 13 (2016): 1-13; McCalman, *Radical Underworld*, 113-127.

8. Thomas Spence, *The Important Trial of Thomas Spence* (London, 1803), 4 (emphasis in original).

9. Thomas Spence, *The Reign of Felicity* (London: Thomas Spence, 1796); Spence, *Important Trial*, 15; Mathilde Cazzola, "'All Shall Be Happy by Land and Sea': Thomas Spence as an Atlantic Thinker," *Atlantic Studies* 15:4 (2018): 436; *The Axe*, 1:5. See also Mathilda Cazzola, *The Political Thought of Thomas Spence: Beyond Poverty and Empire* (London, 2021), 128-170; Ajmal Waqif, "Cato Street and the Spencean Politics of Transnational Insurrection," in Jason McElligott and Martin Conboy, eds., *The Cato Street Conspiracy: Plotting, Counter-intelligence and the Revolutionary Tradition in Britain and Ireland* (Manchester, 2020), 101-117; Malcolm Chase, *The People's Farm: English Radical Agrarianism, 1775-1840* (Oxford, 1988), 41-69.

10. Allen Davenport, *The Life, Writings, and Principles of Thomas Spence* (London: Wakelin, [n.d.]), 5; McCalman, *Radical Underworld*, 100; "15 January 1817," HO42/158, 229, TNA.

11. Tony Ward, "The Corn Laws and English Wheat Prices, 1815-1846," *Atlantic Economic Journal* 32:3 (2004): 245-255; J. R. Wordie, "Perceptions and Reality: The Effects of the Corn Laws and Their Repeal in England, 1815-1906," in J. R. Wordie, ed., *Agriculture and Politics in England, 1815-1939* (Houndmills, 2000), 33-69; Vic Gatrell, *Conspiracy on Cato Street: A Tale of Liberty and Revolution in Regency London* (Cambridge, 2022), 186-216.

12. "13 November 1817," HO40/8, 113-114, TNA; "31 January 1818," HO 42/158, 172, TNA.

NOTES TO PAGES 98–112

13. "13 November [1817]," HO40/7/3, 236, TNA; *Address of the Rev. R. Wedderburn*, 13.
14. *Forlorn Hope*, 1:15, 16.
15. *Forlorn Hope*, 2:35–37.
16. *The Axe*, 1:12; 3:33.
17. See Shelby Johnson, "'The Fate of St. Domingo Awaits You': Robert Wedderburn's Unfinished Revolution," *Eighteenth Century* 61:3 (2020): 373–390; Thomas Spence, *The Rights of Infants* (London, 1797); *Forlorn Hope*, 1:1.
18. Eric Pencek, "Intolerable Anonymity: Robert Wedderburn and the Discourse of Ultra-Radicalism," *Nineteenth Century Contexts* 37:1 (2015): 61; see also Peter Linebaugh, "A Little Jubilee? The Literacy of Robert Wedderburn in 1817," in John Rule and Robert Malcolmson, eds., *Protest and Survival: The Historical Experience*, Essays for E. P. Thompson (London, 1993), 174–220.
19. David Brion Davis, "Impact of the French and Haitian Revolutions," in David Geggus, ed., *The Impact of the Haitian Revolution in the Atlantic World* (Columbia, SC, 2001), 3–9; Robin Blackburn, *The American Crucible: Slavery, Emancipation and Human Rights* (London, 2011), ch. 9.
20. *The Axe*, 1:12.
21. The most influential reading of Robert as a "revolutionary firebrand" is Marcus Rediker and Peter Linebaugh, *The Many-Headed Hydra: Sailors, Slaves, Commoners, and the Hidden History of the Revolutionary Atlantic* (London, 2000), 295–334.
22. *The Axe*, 2:22.
23. *The Axe*, 1:13–14.
24. *The Axe*, 2:24, 31.
25. *The Axe*, 1:11; *Address to Lord Brougham and Vaux*, 6; *The Axe*, 1:12; 4:52–60; 6:84–96.
26. *The Axe*, 2:26, 28; 2:29–30.
27. *The Axe*, 4:53; 1:12; 4:53.
28. "31 January 1818," HO40/8/5, 166, TNA.

CHAPTER 6. Notorious Firebrand

1. Malcolm Chase, "Thistlewood, Arthur (*bap.* 1774, *d.* 1820)," ODNB.
2. *Commercial Chronicle*, May 23, 1818; McCalman, *Radical Underworld*, 130–132.
3. *Morning Advertiser*, June 9, 1818; "2 November 1818," HO42/182, TNA, cited in McCalman, *Radical Underworld*, 131; *The Star*, September 22, 1818; "A Few Plain Questions for an Apostate," HO42/202, 73, TNA; "A Few Lines for a Double-Faced Politician," HO42/202, 6, TNA.

4. "10 August 1819," HO42/191, repr. in Wedderburn, *Horrors* (ed. McCalman), 116; *The Champion*, June 16, 1821.

5. "Deposition of Joseph Wood," TS11/45/167, Treasury Solicitor's Papers, TNA; "Vengence Awaits the Guilty," HO42/192, 119, TNA; "[11 October 1819]" HO42/196, 175, TNA; "13 October 1819," HO42/196, cited in Wedderburn, *Horrors of Slavery* (ed. McCalman), 120; *The Statesman*, June 30, 1819; *Morning Herald*, June 30, 1819; "10 August 1819," HO42/191, 61, TNA.

6. "8 August 1819," HO42/191, 193, TNA.

7. "10 August 1819," HO42/191, TNA; "9 August 1819," HO42/195, TNA, both repr. in Wedderburn, *Horrors of Slavery* (ed. McCalman), 114–117.

8. "Testimony of J. Brown," TS11/45/167, TNA.

9. "Henry Addington to Prince Regent, 12 August 1819," 152M/C/1819/OH/57, Addington Papers, Devon Heritage Centre, Exeter; "Case Respecting the Legality of a Meeting for Debate at Hopkins Street Chapel," HO42/191, 403, TNA; *The Star*, August 19, 1819; *Commercial Chronicle*, September 23, 1819; *Morning Chronicle*, October 1, 1819.

10. See Robert Poole, *Peterloo, the English Uprising* (Oxford, 2019), 318–350.

11. Poole, *Peterloo*, 351–384; Malcolm Chase, *1820: Disorder and Stability in the United Kingdom* (Manchester, 2013), 44–69.

12. See, for example, "Rev R. Wedderburn, V.D.M." [pseud. George Cannon?], *Cast-Iron Parsons, or, Hints to the Public and the Legislature, on Political Economy* (London, [1820]); "04 August 1819," HO42/191, 127, TNA.

13. "8 November 1819," HO42/198, 337, TNA.

14. "10 November 1819," HO42/198, 196, TNA.

15. "10 November 1819," HO42/198, 196, TNA.

16. "Examination of William Plush," TS11/45/167, TNA; *The Trial of the Rev. Robt. Wedderburn (A Dissenting Minister of the Unitarian Persuasion) for Blasphemy* (London, 1820), 5.

17. "Newgate Prison Calendar, 1820," HO77/27, Criminal Department, TNA.

18. *Commercial Chronicle*, November 2, 1819; *The Examiner*, November 7, 1819; "5 August 1819," HO41/191, 150–151, TNA.

19. Gatrell, *Conspiracy on Cato Street*, 3–26.

20. "18 Oct. 1819," HO42/197, 11, 14, TNA, cited in McCalman, *Radical Underworld*, 136; "01 August 1819," HO41/191, 267, TNA; "10 November 1819," HO42/198, 196, TNA.

21. Hanley, "Cato Street and the Caribbean," in McElligott and Conboy, eds., *The Cato Street Conspiracy*, 81–100; Gatrell, *Conspiracy on Cato Street*, 321–340.

22. George Theodore Wilkinson, *An Authentic History of the Cato Street Conspiracy* (London, 1820), 71; Gatrell, *Conspiracy on Cato Street*, 167–185.

23. *The Edinburgh Magazine and Miscellany*, 85 (1820): 477.
24. Davenport, *The Life and Literary Pursuits of Allen Davenport*, ed. Malcolm Chase ([1845] London, 1994), 17, 70.

CHAPTER 7. Inside

1. "Robert Wedderburn to [George Cannon?], 02 February 1820," TS11/45/167, TNA.
2. "Handbill: R. Wedderburn, Tailor, &c.," TS11/45/167, TNA.
3. Samuel Johnson, *A Dictionary of the English Language* (London, 1755), s.v. "destitution," https://johnsonsdictionaryonline.com/1755/destitution_ns (accessed August 23, 2023).
4. *A Short Account of the Refuge for the Destitute, Hackney Road and Hoxton* (London, 1818), 5.
5. *Report of the Society for the Suppression of Mendicity* (London, 1819), 21; John Thomas Smith, *Vagabondiana: or, Anecdotes of Mendicant Wanderers through the Streets of London* (London, 1817), 33–34; Oskar Cox Jensen, "Joseph Johnson's Hat, or, The Storm on Tower Hill," *Studies in Romanticism* 58:4 (2019): 545–569; William Hone, *A Slap at Slop and the Bridge Street Gang* (London, 1820), 1; Charles Matthews, *Othello, the Moor of Fleet Street* ([London, 1833] Tübingen, 1993); McCalman, "Anti-Slavery and Ultra-Radicalism," 104.
6. *Report of the Society for the Suppression of Mendicity*, 41.
7. See Iain McCalman, "Cannon, George [pseud. Erasmus Perkins] (1789–1854)," *ODNB*; Iain McCalman, "Unrespectable Radicalism: Infidels and Pornography in Early Nineteenth-Century London," *Past & Present* 104 (1984): 74–110; Philip W. Martin, "Carlile, Richard (1790–1843)," *ODNB*.
8. *Trial of the Rev. Robt. Wedderburn*, 3, 4.
9. *Trial of the Rev. Robt. Wedderburn*, 20, 8.
10. *Address of the Rev. R. Wedderburn* [. . .] *on Appearing to Receive Judgment for Blasphemy*, 4, 11, 13. The tract advertised to the court was the *Critical, Historical and Admonitory Letter*.
11. "Dorchester Prison Admission and Discharge Records, 1782–1901," NG/PR1/D2/1, 111, Dorset History Centre.
12. Erasmus Perkins [George Cannon], *A Few Hints Relative to the Texture of Mind and the Manufacture of Conscience* (London, 1820); *The Republican*, May 19, 1820, 112; On Jane Carlile, see Angela Keane, "Richard Carlile's Working Women: Selling Books, Politics, Sex and the *Republican*," *Literature and History* 15:2 (2006): 20–33.
13. Wedderburn [George Cannon?], *Cast-Iron Parsons*, 5–8; *To the Reformers*

of Great Britain, June 24, 1821, 13 (this sui generis text is available as part of a bundle of unregistered Carlile publications, digitized from Yale University Library's special collections, https://catalog.hathitrust.org/Record/009832663 [accessed August 17, 2023]); *Cast-Iron Parsons*, 3. Regarding *High-Heel'd Shoes*, Carlile wrote in June 1821: "Now I think it fitting publicly to state that the pamphlet which has been published in Mr. Wedderburn's name is not of his writing, but has been got up on his behalf by a friend" (*To the Reformers of Great Britain*, June 24, 1821, 13). See R. Wedderburn [George Cannon?], *High-Heel'd Shoes for Dwarfs in Holiness* (London, 1821); R. Wedderburn [George Cannon?], *Cast-Iron Parsons, or, Hints to the Public and the Legislature on Political Economy* (London, 1820); Robert Wedderburn [George Cannon?], *A Critical, Historical, and Admonitory Letter to the Right Reverend Father in God, His Grace the Lord Archbishop of Canterbury* (London, 1820). Carlile and/or Cannon probably also collaborated on Robert Wedderburn [George Cannon? Richard Carlile?], *A Letter Addressed to Solomon Herchell* (London, 1819), repr. in HO42/198, 197–200, TNA.

14. *The Republican*, March 3, 1822, 554; *The Republican*, May 26, 1820, 158; *The Republican*, May 26, 1820, 158.

15. *The Republican*, September 8, 1820, 40; *Cast-Iron Parsons*, 6; *The Republican*, March 1, 1822, 265. An incomplete list of subscribers is reproduced in "Rev. R. Wedderburn, V.D.M." [George Cannon], *High-Heel'd Shoes for Dwarfs in Holiness* (London: George Cannon, 1821). For the subscription, see *To the Reformers of Great Britain*, June 24, 1821, 12–14; *The Republican*, September 15, 1820, 108; October 20, 1820, 364–367; *The Republican*, March 3, 1822, 554; *The Republican*, May 7, 1822, 178.

16. Hanley, *Beyond Slavery and Abolition*, 220–223; Stephen Tomkins, *William Wilberforce: A Biography* (Oxford, 2007), 54–55.

17. *The Republican*, July 5, 1822, 178; *Horrors*, 3; McCalman, introduction to Wedderburn, *Horrors of Slavery* (ed. McCalman), 1; "Holborn St Giles in the Fields, Register of Baptisms, 1822," DL/T/036, Item 042, LMA.

18. *Horrors*, 4.

CHAPTER 8. Outside

1. Carlile cited in Colette Colligan, *The Traffic in Obscenity from Byron to Beardsley: Sexuality and Exoticism in Nineteenth-Century British Print Culture* (Houndmills, 2006), 46; see Deana Heath, *Purifying Empire: Obscenity and the Politics of Moral Regulation in Britain, India and Australia* (Cambridge, 2010), 35–64.

2. For Mitford, see Colligan, *Traffic in Obscenity*, 44; McCalman, *Radical Underworld*, 166–167; *Gentleman's Magazine* 51 (December 1831): 647–648. Inciden-

tally, about two weeks earlier, Benbow had himself been convicted of publishing obscenity on an indictment initiated by Wilberforce's colleagues in the Society for the Suppression of Vice. *Trewman's Exeter Flying Post*, February 18, 1823.

3. *Morning Herald*, February 28, 1823; John Wight, *Mornings at Bow Street* (London: Charles Baldwyn, 1824), 150–153.

4. John Thomas Smith, *Vagabondiana: Or Anecdotes of Mendicant Wanderers Through the Streets of London* (London, 1817); Pierce Egan, *Life in London: Or, the Day and Night Scenes of Jerry Hawthorn Esq. and his Elegant Friend Corinthian Tom* (London, 1821), 286.

5. *The Republican*, February 20, 1824.

6. *Bell's Life in London*, February 1, 1824.

7. Sue Thomas has explored this sequence of letters in more detail in Sue Thomas, *Telling West Indian Lives: Life Narrative and the Reform of Plantation Slavery Cultures, 1804–1834* (New York, 2014), 105–117; *Bell's Life in London*, February 8, 1824.

8. *Bell's Life in London*, February 15, 1824.

9. *Bell's Life in London*, February 29, 1824.

10. *Bell's Life in London*, March 21, 1824.

11. *Bell's Life in London*, March 28, 1824.

12. "Registration of Printing Press, 6 May 1824," MR/L/P.1824/012, LMA; one example of Dugdale's output during this period is John Mitford, *The Private Life of Lord Byron, Comprising his Voluptuous Amours, Secret Intrigues and Close Connection with Various Ladies of Rank and Fame* (London, 1828); *Horrors*, 24.

13. For the "march of intellect," see Brian Maidment, "Caricature and Social Change 1820–1840: The March of Intellect Revisited," in Victoria Morgan and Clare Williams, eds., *Shaping Belief: Culture, Politics and Religion in Nineteenth-Century Writing* (Liverpool, 2008), 149–170.

14. "11 March 1828," HO64/11, 86, TNA; *The Lion*, March 21, 1828, 359; "n.d. [April 1828]," HO64/11, 94–95; 89, TNA.

15. "n.d. [April 1828]," HO64/11, 83, TNA; "11 March 1828," HO64/11, 86, TNA; *London Courier and Evening Gazette*, August 12, 1829.

16. *The Lion*, March 28, 1828, 395.

17. HO64/11, f. 89, TNA.

18. "James Mott, Mary Ann Barrand, Theft, housebreaking," December 4, 1828, t18281204-217, Old Bailey Online, www.oldbaileyonline.org/browse.jsp?id=t18281204-217&div=t18281204-217 (accessed August 23, 2023); *Address to Lord Brougham and Vaux*, 15–16; "Sessions of the Peace," September 15, 1830, CLA/047/LJ/03/364, City of London Sessions, LMA; "Minute Book (fair)," CLA/047/LJ/06/009, 249, City of London Sessions, TNA.

NOTES TO PAGES 157–169

19. For reports of Robert's speech, see, inter alia, *London Courier and Evening Gazette*, November 5, 1830; *The Sun*, November 5, 1830; *Morning Advertiser*, November 5, 1830; *Weekly Times*, November 7, 1830; *Lancaster Gazette*, November 13, 1830; *Sheffield Independent*, November 13, 1830.

20. Quotes from *Morning Advertiser*, November 5, 1830.

21. For prostitution and moral reform, see Maria Isabel Romero Ruiz, *The London Lock Hospital in the Nineteenth Century: Gender, Sexuality and Social Reform* (Oxford, 2014), 25–56; Tony Henderson, *Disorderly Women in Eighteenth-Century London: Prostitution and Control in the Metropolis, 1730–1830* (London, 1999), 141–165.

CHAPTER 9. Outsider

1. *London Courier and Evening Gazette*, November 5, 1830; *The Sun*, November 5, 1830; *Morning Advertiser*, November 5, 1830.

2. "Robert Wedderburn to Francis Place, 22 March 1831," Add. MS.27, 808, f. 322, Place Papers, British Library, repr. in Wedderburn, *Horrors of Slavery* (ed. McCalman), 78.

3. *The Anti-Slavery Monthly Reporter* 13:3 (June 1830): 254, 255, 256, 272.

4. Michael Lobban, "Brougham, Henry Peter, first Baron Brougham and Vaux (1778–1868)," ODNB. For reform and the antislavery movement in the early 1830s, see Seymour Drescher, *Abolition: A History of Slavery and Antislavery* (Cambridge, 2009), 245–266; Blackburn, *The Overthrow of Colonial Slavery*, 436–455.

5. "Robert Wedderburn to Francis Place, 22 March 1831," Add. MS.27, 808, f. 322, British Library; Hanley, *Beyond Slavery and Abolition*, 220–236. This publication is reproduced in Ryan Hanley, "A Radical Change of Heart: Robert Wedderburn's Last Word on Slavery," *Slavery & Abolition* 37:2 (2016): 423–445.

6. *Address to Lord Brougham and Vaux*, 7, 4, 7, 5.

7. *Address to Lord Brougham and Vaux*, 9–10.

8. *Address to Lord Brougham and Vaux*, 13.

9. *Address to Lord Brougham and Vaux*, 4, 7, 10, 8, 6. On challenging histories of agency, see Johnson, "On Agency," 113–124; Mintz, "Slave Life on Caribbean Sugar Plantations," 12–22; Browne, *Surviving Slavery*, 157–189.

10. See, for example, *The Condition of the West India Slave Contrasted with that of the Infant Slave in our English Factories* (London, [1833?]); Samuel Roberts, *A Cry from the Chimneys; or an Integral Part of the Total Abolition of Slavery Throughout the World* (London, 1837).

11. *The Lion*, February 1, 1828, 145; Hanley, "Slavery and the Birth of Working-Class Racism," 120–122.

12. William St Clair, *The Reading Nation in the Romantic Period* (Cambridge,

2004), 320. In 1834, Ascham went on to cater to a "low" radical readership by publishing a cheap, unauthorized edition of Percy Shelley's *Queen Mab* that was wildly successful among Chartists.

13. For details of the case, see, inter alia, *Morning Chronicle*, February 13, 1832; *Morning Post*, February 13, 1832; *The News*, February 13, 1832; *Freeman's Journal*, February 15, 1832; *Morning Advertiser*, February 21, 1832; *Morning Chronicle*, February 21, 1832; *Bell's New Weekly Messenger*, February 26, 1832.

14. "Daily Reports from Metropolitan Police Offices," February 11, 1832, HO62/9, no. 1278, TNA; testimony quotations from *The News*, February 13, 1832; *Freeman's Journal*, February 15, 1832.

15. Testimony quotations from *Morning Advertiser*, February 21, 1832.

16. Testimony quotations from *Morning Advertiser*, February 21, 1832.

17. "Daily Reports from Metropolitan Police Offices," February 11, 1832, HO62/9, no. 1278. For conflicting reports of these two trials, compare *Morning Chronicle*, February 13, 1832; *Morning Post*, February 13, 1832; *The News*, February 13, 1832; *Freeman's Journal*, February 15, 1832; *Morning Advertiser*, February 21, 1832; *Morning Chronicle*, February 21, 1832; *Bell's New Weekly Messenger*, February 26, 1832. I have taken my preferred spelling of the names from the police records.

18. *Bell's New Weekly Messenger*, February 26, 1832.

19. *Morning Advertiser*, November 5, 1830. For the methodological issues surrounding using newspaper reports of criminal trials, see Simon Devereaux, "From Sessions to Newspaper? Criminal Trial Reporting, the Nature of Crime, and the London Press, 1770–1800," *London Journal* 32:1 (2007): 1–27; Peter King, "Newspaper Reporting and Attitudes to Crime and Justice in Late-Eighteenth- and Early-Nineteenth-Century London," *Continuity and Change* 22:1 (2007): 73–112.

20. "Daily Reports from Metropolitan Police Offices," February 20, 1832, HO62/9, no. 1285, TNA.

21. *Bell's New Weekly Messenger*, February 26, 1832.

22. "17 March 1834," HO64/19, 738, TNA; "Registers of Births, Marriages and Deaths," RG8/35, 55, General Register Office, TNA.

23. *Morning Herald*, February 28, 1823.

Epilogue

1. *The Times*, March 1, 1833; Jessica L. Allen, "Pringle's Pruning of Prince: The History of Mary Prince and the Question of Repetition," *Callaloo* 35:2 (2012): 509–519; Sue Thomas, "Pringle v. Cadell and Wood v. Pringle: The Libel Cases over *The History of Mary Prince*," *Journal of Commonwealth Studies* 40:1 (2005): 113–135. For a competing interpretation of Prince's relationship with her editors

as being more collaborative and supportive, see Juliet Shields, *Mary Prince, Slavery, and Print Culture in the Anglophone Atlantic World* (Cambridge, 2021).

2. E. P. Thompson, *The Making of the English Working Class* ([1963] London, 1968), 886; Caroline Bressey, "Race, Antiracism, and the Place of Blackness in the Making and Remaking of the English Working Class," in Antoinette Burton and Stephanie Fortado, eds., *Histories of a Radical Book: E. P. Thompson and the Making of the English Working Class* (New York, 2021), 71–84.

3. See Kennetta Hammond Perry, *London Is the Place for Me: Black Britons, Citizenship and the Politics of Race* (Oxford, 2015); Folarin Shyllon, *Black People in Britain, 1555–1833* (London, 1977), ix; Folarin Shyllon, *Black Slaves in Britain* (London, 1974). As late as 1993, Paul Gilroy complained of the "statist modalities of Marxist analysis that view modes of material production and political domination as exclusively *national* entities"; Paul Gilroy, *The Black Atlantic: Modernity and Double Consciousness* (London, 1993), 3–4.

4. James Walvin, *Black and White: The Negro in English Society* (London, 1973); Edward Scobie, *Black Britannia: A History of Blacks in Britain* (Chicago, 1972).

5. Rob Waters, "Thinking Black: Peter Fryer's *Staying Power* and the Politics of Writing Black British History in the 1980s," *History Workshop Journal* 82 (2016): 108; Peter Fryer, *Staying Power: The History of Black People in Britain* (London, 1984), 213, 220; Ron Ramdin, *The Making of the Black Working Class in Britain* ([1987] London, 2017), 33.

6. David Worrall, *Radical Culture: Discourse, Resistance and Surveillance, 1790–1820* (New York, 1992); McCalman, *Radical Underworld*, 50–72, 128–151; Iain Duncan McCalman, "A Radical Underworld in Early Nineteenth Century London: Thomas Evans, Robert Wedderburn, George Cannon and Their Circle, 1800–1835," PhD Thesis, Monash University, 1984; McCalman, "Anti-Slavery and Ultra-radicalism," 99–117.

7. McCalman, *Radical Underworld*, vii–x; Wedderburn, *Horrors of Slavery* (ed. McCalman), 1–40.

8. Linebaugh, "A Little Jubilee?," 174–220; Julius Sherrard Scott III, "The Common Wind: Currents of Afro-American Communication in the Era of the Haitian Revolution," PhD Thesis, Duke University, 1986; this thesis was eventually republished in 2018 as Scott, *The Common Wind*; Gilroy, *The Black Atlantic*, 12–13.

9. Peter Linebaugh and Marcus Rediker, *The Many-Headed Hydra: The Hidden History of the Revolutionary Atlantic* ([2000] London, 2012), 289; Sue Thomas, "Robert Wedderburn's Correspondent Miss Campbell," *Notes and Queries* 61:4 (2014): 510–514; Cazzola, *Political Thought of Thomas Spence*, 128–170.

10. Ben Pitcher, *The Politics of Multiculturalism: Race and Racism in Contem-

porary Britain (Houndmills, 2009), 39–74; Les Back et al., "New Labour's White Heart: Politics, Multiculturalism and the Return of Assimilation," *Political Quarterly* 73:4 (2002): 445–454; Nam-Kook Kim, "Deliberative Multiculturalism in New Labour's Britain," *Citizenship Studies* 15:1 (2011): 125–144.

11. On Equiano as "representative" of the enslaved experience, see Ryan Hanley, "The Equiano Effect: Representativeness and Early Black British Migrant Testimony," in Jennifer Craig-Norton, Christhard Hoffmann, and Tony Kushner, eds., *Migrant Britain: Histories and Historiographies, Essays in Honour of Colin Holmes* (London, 2018), 262–271.

12. Helen Thomas, *Romanticism and Slave Narratives* (Cambridge, 2000), 270–271; Alan Rice, *Radical Narratives of the Black Atlantic* (London, 2003), 11–12; Martin Hoyles, *The Axe Laid to the Root: The Story of Robert Wedderburn* (London, 2004); Maev Kennedy, "Slave Owner and Abolitionist Come Face to Face," *Guardian*, November 8, 2007, www.theguardian.com/artanddesign/2007/nov/08/art1 (accessed December 10, 2023).

13. Hanley, *Beyond Slavery and Abolition*, 203–239; Alan Rice, "Vagrant Presences: Lost Children, the Black Atlantic, and Northern Britain," *Zeitschrift für Anglistik und Amerikanistik* 65:2 (2017): 179–181; Michael Morris, *Scotland and the Caribbean, c. 1740–1833: Atlantic Archipelagos* (London, 2015), ch. 5; Hunt, "Remembering Africans in Diaspora"; Raphael Hoermann, "'A Very Hell of Horrors'? The Haitian Revolution and the Early Transatlantic Haitian Gothic," *Slavery & Abolition* 37:1 (2016): 183–205; Raphael Hoermann, "'Fermentation Will Be Universal': Intersections of Race and Class in Robert Wedderburn's Black Atlantic Discourse of Transatlantic Revolution," in Gretchen Gerzina, ed., *Britain's Black Past* (Liverpool, 2020), 295–314; Katey Castellano, "Provision Grounds Against the Plantation: Robert Wedderburn's *Axe Laid to the Root*," *Small Axe* 25:1 (2021): 15–27; Shelby Johnson, "'The Fate of St. Domingo Awaits You': Robert Wedderburn's Unfinished Revolution," *Eighteenth Century* 61:3 (2020): 373–390; see also Sam Plasencia, "Locating and Narrating Revolution: A Reflection on Method," *English Language Notes* 61:1 (2023): 110–113.

14. Joseph Albernaz, "Abolition, Black Ultraradicalism, and the Generation of the General Strike," *Critical Times* 5:3 (2022): 538–569; Chris Taylor, "The Plantation Road to Socialism," *Amerikastudien* 62:4 (2017): 551–565; Eric Pencek, "Intolerable Anonymity: Robert Wedderburn and the Discourse of Ultra-Radicalism," *Nineteenth-Century Contexts* 37:1 (2015): 61–77; Michael Morris, "Robert Wedderburn: Race, Religion and Revolution," *International Socialism* 132 (2011), http://isj.org.uk/robert-wedderburn-race-religion-and-revolution/ (accessed 8/30/2023).

ACKNOWLEDGMENTS

THIS BOOK STARTED OUT as a series of lectures at the Hutchins Center for African American History at Harvard University. I am extremely grateful to Henry Louis Gates, Jr., Abby Wolf, and the whole team there for the opportunity to share my research about Robert Wedderburn with such an extraordinary community of scholars. I am also truly grateful to Vincent Carretta, not only for his wonderful scholarship but also for all his help and guidance. In the United Kingdom, my first thanks must go to Caroline Bressey, for calming me down when I got stuck at the beginning of the writing process, for helping me to find my direction for the first part of the book in the idea of Robert "bearing witness," and for recommending Saidiya Hartman's *Wayward Lives, Beautiful Experiments*, which has changed my whole approach to writing history. When I was preparing this manuscript, I was lucky enough to hang out regularly with May Sumbwanyambe and share many meals, drinks, and fascinating conversations about Robert and his world. May was also kind enough to share some thoughts on draft sections of the manuscript as it was being written. So, too, was Michael Morris, whose insights have also helped

ACKNOWLEDGMENTS

immensely. I must also thank Jessie Kindig at Yale University Press for her keen attention to the manuscript and for that special kind of patience that only great editors possess. My final thanks, as ever, are reserved for my partner and teammate Jessica Moody.

INDEX

Page numbers in italic type indicate illustrations. Select individuals are referred to by first name in index subentries following the author's practice as noted in "A Note on Names."

Abbott, Chief Justice, 135–38
abolitionism: in Britain, 8, 103, 148–49, 162–69, 177–78; conventional understanding of, 8–9; enslaved and formerly enslaved people active in, 8, 189; gradualism in, 103, 148–49, 165, 178; legal cases and, 62–64; poverty alleviation linked to, 162–63, 167–69; Robert and, 4, 6, 8–10, 12–15, 77–78, 99–109, 114, 116, 120–21, 142, 150, 162–69, 177–78; Spence and, 95; the working class and, 9–11
Abolition of the Slave Trade Act (1807), 189
Addington, Henry, 110
African diaspora, 187–88
African Institution, 11
Amy (grandmother): and James, 40–41; Payne as master of, 41–44; reputation of, 41; Robert's upbringing by, 5, 35, 37, 39–40, 49, 53, 96, 107, 179, 193; slave experiences of, 14, 23–24; and smuggling, 43–44; and the Sunday market, 41–42; use of speech and language by, 39–41; violence experienced by, 44–45, 47–50, 135; and witchcraft, 45–49, 135
antislavery. *See* abolitionism
Anti-Slavery Society, 162–63
Archer Street chapel, 111
Ascham, John, 169, 212n12
Association for the Relief of the Manufacturing and Labouring Poor, 1–2, 97
atheism, 98, 134–35
Atkinson, Ann, 170–74
authority. *See* legitimacy; Wedderburn, Robert: anti-authoritarianism of
Axe Laid to the Root, The (periodical), 22–23, 100–109, 119, 122, 124, 165

INDEX

baptism, 26, 33
Barbados, 67, 188, 192
Barrand, Mary Ann, 157
Bell, Robert, 149–51
Bell's Life in London (newspaper), 148–54, 168
Benbow, William, 145, 210n2
Bethnal Green, 177
Bhabha, Homi, 190
Bible, 49, 100–101, 135–36, 162, 181
Black Atlantic, 33, 187–88, 190
Black British history, 182–85, 188
Blackburn, Isabella, 68
Black community: and abolitionism, 8–9; in London, 4–5, 76–77, 94, 133; popular attitudes toward, 80, 92, 134, 137–38, 145–48, 161, 169, 178; in postwar Britain, 183–85; scholarly interest in, 183–85, 187, 189. *See also* enslaved people; "mixed" families
Black Pantherism, 183
blasphemy, 121, 123, 135–37, 156
Blincoe, Robert, 168
Boswell, Charles, 22, 36, 150
Boswell, James, 63
Bow Street Runners, 123
Braverman, Suella, 196n8
British Nationality Act (1981), 185
Brougham, Henry, 162–65
Brown, Vincent, 45
Brown-Glaude, Winnifred, 42
Brunt, John Thomas, 125
Bryson, Sasha Turner, 47
Bullock, Sarah, 69
Bussa's Rebellion, 103

"cabbage" (leftovers from labor), 92–94

cabbage-net sellers, 82
Campbell (doctor), 35
Campbell (half-sister), 106
Cannon, George, 131, 134, 136–39
Carlile, Jane, 138, 141–42
Carlile, Richard, 117, 126, 134–35, 137–44, 154–56, 161, 168–69
Catholicism, 135, 163
Cato Street Conspiracy (1820), 123–27, 182
child labor, 155, 168–69
Christianity: linked to slavery, 120–21; obeah and, 45; Robert's attitude toward, 6, 10, 13–14, 34, 50, 83–86, 98, 119–21, 135, 138–39, 142, 154–55, 158. *See also* Catholicism; missionaries
Church Missionary Society, 120
Church of England. *See* Christianity
City of London Tavern, 1, 6, 7, 11, 149
Clarkson, Thomas, 77–78
Cleland, John, *Fanny Hill*, 170
Cobbett, William, 168
Cock tavern, Grafton Street, 6, 96
Colvile, Andrew (half-brother), 31, 57–58, 82–83, 85–86, 150–52, 192
Corn Law (1815), 97
Cressey, David, 65
Cruikshank (doctor), 28
Cruikshank, George, 146; "A Peep into the City of London Tavern," 7, 7, 147
Cruikshank, Robert, 146
Cuffay, William, 187
Cugoano, Ottobah, 76
Cupid (ship), 51

Davenport, Allen, *The Kings; or Legitimacy Unmasked*, 126

| 218 |

INDEX

Davidson, William, 124–27, 161, 187, 192
Demerara, 148, 188, 192
Dempsey, John, 133
destitution, 10, 70, 124, 132–34, 159–60, 177–79. *See also* poverty
Docklands Museum, London, 190
Dorchester Gaol, 137–44, 178
Douglas, Basilia, 25–28, 34–35
Douglas, Charles James Sholto, 13, 25, 27, 34–35, 43
Dugdale, William, 152, 155
Dundas, Henry, 63
Durham, Mary (second wife), 5, 81–82, 112, 131, 138, 141–43, 156–57, 203n10
Durham, Mary-Ann (stepdaughter), 81

Edgar, John, 155
Edinburgh Advertiser (newspaper), 59
Edwards, George, 112, 126–27
Egan, Pierce, *Life in London*, 146; "LOWEST LIFE in LONDON" (illustration), 147
enslaved people: in abolitionist movement, 8; childrearing practices among, 39–40; conditions of the working class likened to those of, 11–12, 74–75, 168–69; labor performed by, 24–25; legal rights of, 59–64; and obeah, 45–49; resistance and rebellion by, 9, 38, 46, 53–54, 75, 191; use of speech and language by, 38–39; violence against, 77. *See also* enslaved women
enslaved women: agency of, 30–37, 42, 182; labor performed by, 26; raped by masters, 27, 29, 31–33, 35; reputations of, within enslaved community, 39–40; and the Sunday market, 41–42; trust placed in, by masters and mistresses, 26, 42–44, 53; use of speech and language by, 38–39; violence against, 11–12, 19–22, 20, 36, 150. *See also* Amy (grandmother): slave experiences of; Rosanna (mother): slave experiences of
Equiano, Olaudah, 8–9, 181, 186, 188–90
Eustace, Chetwode, 112–14, 116
Evans, Janet, 111, 112
Evans, Thomas, 96, 110–12, 126

Fairburn, John, *Barbarity to a Female Slave!* 19–21, 20, 197n1
Fifth of November commemorations, 65–66
"Forlorn Hope," The, or a Call to the Supine (newspaper), 13, 98–102, 119, 183
free-and-easies, 94–95, 97, 108
Fryer, Peter, *Staying Power*, 185
Fuentes, Marisa, 21

Gilroy, Paul, 213n3; *The Black Atlantic*, 187
Giltspur Street compter, 158, 161–62, 167, 173
God, 84–87, 155
Gordon, Lloyd, 190
Gove, Michael, 189
government: criticisms/denunciations of, 10, 13–14, 74–75; political rights, 74; Robert's recommendations for, 105; suppression of

INDEX

government (*continued*)
  radicalism, 118–19, 123–26, 182. *See also* Home Office; spies/informers
Grey, Earl, 164
Grose, Francis, 94
Gunningham, John, 170, 172–76
Guy Fawkes Night, 65

Haitian Revolution (1791), 75, 102, 188, 192
Hanley, James, 111
Harris, William, 42
Hartman, Saidiya, 21
Heifer, Thomas, 51
Hibbert, George, 190
higglers, 42
Hill, John, 117
Holy Trinity, 84
homelessness, 78–79
Home Office, 6, 10, 108, 114, 116–19, 121, 126–27, 135, 154, 161–62, 177, 185–86
Hone, William, 75, 133
"honest poverty," 78, 80
Hooker, Richard, 132
Hopkins Street chapel, 112–14, 116, 119, 122, 124, 135, 154–55, 177, 185; handbill advertising debate at, 115
Howard, Paul, 190
Hunt, Nadine, 34

illegitimate children, 57, 59, 68–70, 73, 124–25
informers. *See* spies/informers
Ings, Thomas, 125
inheritance, critiques of, 69–70, 73–74, 95, 106

Institute for Race Relations, 183
Inveresk Lodge, 32, 67–68, 82–83

Jacobites, 56–58, 65
Jamaica: Robert's background in, 23–53, 191; Robert's writings on, 100–109, 124
James II, 56
Jea, John, 181
Jennison, Charles, 13, 98, 100, 102, 112
Jesus Christ, 10, 84–86, 121, 135
Johnson, Joseph, 133
Johnson, Samuel, 63, 132
Johnson, Shelby, 191

King, Boston, 181
Knight, John, 58–64, 167, 201n5
Knight, Joseph, 58–64, 167, 201n5
Knight v. Wedderburn, 62–64

land reform, 6, 95–97, 99
Lascelles, Edward, 2, 75
legitimacy: questioning of any authority's, 44–45, 95, 105–6, 126; questioning of government's, 13, 73–75, 125–26; questioning of slavery's, 14; religious/moral, 86–87
Lewis, Matthew "Monk," 31
Linebaugh, Peter, 187; *The Many-Headed Hydra* (with Marcus Rediker), 187–88
London Committee of the Society for Effecting the Abolition of the Slave Trade, 77
Long, Edward, 26
Luffman, John, 41

INDEX

Mansfield, Lord Chief Justice, 59
maroons, 50, 52
Marxism, 184
Mason, George, 170–71, 173–74
McCalman, Iain, 133, 142, 185–86;
    Radical Underworld, 185–86
McGee, Charles, 133
Medusa, The (periodical), 11
Mendicity Society. *See* Society for
    the Suppression of Mendicity
Methodism, 83, 120, 164
Middleton, Mary Ann, 169–76
missionaries, 120, 164
Mitford, Jack, 145, 146
"mixed" families, 80–81, 147
Morgan, Jennifer, 21
Morning Advertiser (newspaper), 158, 175
Morning Herald (newspaper), 145, 148
Morty, Robert, 51
Moseley, Benjamin, 45
Mulatto John (son of Phibbah and
    Thomas Thistlewood), 30
Mulberry Tree tavern, Moorfields,
    96, 97–98, 111
multiculturalism, 188–89

Nabob (ship), 51, 64
Napoleonic Wars (1803–1815), 1,
    90–91, 96, 118
National Front, 183, 184
New Cross massacre (1981), 185
New Labour, 188–89

obeah, 45–49
O'Connell, Daniel, 162–63
Ogilvy, Margaret, 59

Othello, the Moor of Fleet Street (light
    opera), 133
Overseers of the Poor, 173
Owen, Robert, 1–3, 6, 7, 13, 97

Paine, Thomas, 148
Paton, Diana, 46
Payne, Joseph, 41–44
Pegg, John, 77
Pencek, Eric, 102
Peterloo massacre (1819), 118, 182
Phibbah (favorite of Thomas
    Thistlewood), 29–30, 125
Phoenix (ship), 58
Pitt, William, 166
poisoning, 24, 31, 47
HMS *Polyphemus*, 66–67
pornography, 134, 144–45, 152, 169–70, 178
poverty: abolitionism linked to
    alleviation of, 162–63, 167–69;
    factors contributing to, 2–3, 97;
    "honest poverty," 78, 80; ideas
    for addressing, 1–3, 73–74; in
    London/Britain, 73, 78, 82,
    97; popular attitudes toward,
    145–47; Robert's experience of,
    5, 74–76, 78, 81–82, 131–33, 143,
    177; Robert's interest in, 6, 9. *See
    also* destitution; working class
Powell, Enoch, 183
press: credibility of, 174–76; and
    radicalism, 75, 98–109
Prince, Mary, 181–82
Pringle, Thomas, 182
property. *See* land reform
prostitution, 157–60, 173, 178
pubs, 6, 77, 87–88, 94–96

221

INDEX

race. *See* Black community: popular attitudes toward; "mixed" families
radicalism: anti-authoritarian, 84; anti-government, 74–75, 97–98, 110–27; antislavery, 12; and authorship, 102; backgrounds of some participants in, 124–26; government suppression of, 118–19, 123–26, 182; and outdoor rallies, 117–18; and the poverty issue, 3, 97; the press and, 75, 98–109; religious, 141–42; Robert and, 5–12, 23, 53, 55, 58, 73, 78, 84, 95–127, 134, 137, 144, 154–55, 161, 167–69, 177–78, 187–89, 191–92; Spence and, 94; transformations in, 144–45, 154, 161; working-class, 11, 75, 78, 96, 178
Ramdin, Ron, *Making of the Black Working Class in Britain*, 185
rape, 27, 29, 31–33, 35, 172, 175–76
Redhead-Yorke, Henry, 69
Rediker, Marcus, *The Many-Headed Hydra* (with Peter Linebaugh), 187–88
Refuge for the Destitute, 132
religion. *See* atheism; Catholicism; Christianity
Republican, The (newspaper), 134, 138, 142
Rosanna (mother): the Douglases as master and mistress of, 13, 25–28, 34–35; health of, 35; James and, 27–35, 82–83, 150–51; labor performed by, 26, 30–31; as mother of Robert, 4, 5, 11, 13–14, 22, 31, 96, 107, 179, 193; resistance to enslavement, 30–36, 53; slave experiences of, 12–14, 22–37, 47, 58; succession of owners of, 35–36; violence experienced by, 12, 22, 36, 150
Rose, William, 170–76
Royal Gazette of Jamaica (newspaper), 42
Royal Navy, 5, 51, 53, 66, 124, 125
Ryan, Elizabeth (first wife), 5, 65–67, 75–76, 78–81

Saint Domingue, 125. *See also* Haitian Revolution
Sancho, Ignatius, 181, 189
Scobie, Edward, 184
Scotland, 32, 59–64, 67–68, 191
sedition, 14, 48–49, 116–17, 122, 135. *See also* treason
Seven Years' War (1756–1763), 43
Shyllon, Folarin, 183, 184
Sierra Leone, 76
Six Acts (1819), 118–19
Slave Registry Bill, 12
slavery. *See* abolitionism; enslaved people; enslaved women
Slavery & Abolition (journal), 186
Smallwood, Stephanie, 21
Smith, John, 148
smuggling, 42–43
Society for the Mitigation and Gradual Abolition of Slavery, 103, 162
Society for the Relief of the Black Poor, 76
Society for the Suppression of Mendicity, 124, 133–34
Society for the Suppression of Vice, 141
Somerset v. Stewart, 59

INDEX

Spence, Thomas, 6, 94–96, 100, 101, 126; *The Reign of Felicity*, 95; *The Rights of Infants*, 101
Spenceans, 95–112, 117–18, 122–24, 126, 185
spies/informers, 6, 10, 52, 97–98, 108, 110–14, 116, 121, 126, 154–55, 177, 185
Stevenson, Brenda, 39–40
Stuart, Charles Edward (Bonnie Prince Charlie), 56
Sunday market (Kingston, Jamaica), 41–42

Tacky's War (1760–1761), 46, 53
tailors, 90–94, 133
"Talkee" Amy. *See* Amy (grandmother)
Taylor, Robert, 156, 177
Temple Bar, London, 55, 57–58, 192
Thistlewood, Arthur, 110, 118, 122, 124–27, 192
Thistlewood, Thomas, 29–30, 125
Thistlewood, William, 125
Thompson, Anne, 60–61, 64
Thompson, E. P., *The Making of the English Working Class*, 182–83, 185
Tidd, Richard, 125
treason, 56, 110, 122. *See also* sedition
Trotter, Esther, 32, 34, 47

Unitarianism, 84, 119, 136

violence: against enslaved women, 11–12, 19–22, 20, 36, 44–45, 47–50, 77, 150; Robert's advocacy of insurrectionary, 96, 103–4, 108–9, 113, 116, 121–24, 165

Walvin, James, 184
Watson, James, 110, 122
Wedderburn, Elizabeth (daughter), 67
Wedderburn, Hope (daughter), 157, 204n10
Wedderburn, Jacob (son), 157, 204n10
Wedderburn, James, Jr. (brother), 32–35, 37, 83, 163
Wedderburn, James, Sr. (father): and Amy, 40–41; father of, 56–57; as father of Robert, 4, 13, 40, 68–70, 82–83, 86, 150–52, 164, 192; medical practice of, 27, 30, 125; name changed by, 68; rapes of enslaved women by, 27, 29, 31–33; and Rosanna, 27–35, 82–83, 150–51
Wedderburn, John, Jr. (uncle), 27, 34, 56, 58
Wedderburn, John, Sr. (grandfather), 55–58, 65, 68
Wedderburn, Lydia (daughter), 157, 204n10
Wedderburn, Maria (daughter), 78
Wedderburn, Peter (uncle), 62, 64
Wedderburn, Robert: anti-authoritarianism of, 5, 14, 44, 49–50, 81, 83–85, 88, 121, 192; antislavery activities of, 4, 6, 8–10, 12–15, 77–78, 99–109, 114, 116, 120–21, 142, 150, 162–69, 177–78; assault charge against, 169–77; baptism of, 26; birth/parents of, 4, 5, 11, 13–14, 34; blasphemy charges against, 121, 123, 136–37; brothel-keeping charge against, 157–60; and the causes and cures of poverty, 1, 3–4; children of, 67, 78–79, 81, 204n10; death of, 177,

INDEX

Wedderburn, Robert (*continued*) 182; and family relations, 10, 57–58, 68–70, 82–83, 85–86, 105; fights joined by, 4, 87–88, 114; freedom for, 34–35, 37, 51–52; homelessness of, 78–79; images of, 7, 7, 147, 152, 153, 190; imprisonments of, 137–44, 161–62, 167, 178; injustices of slavery condemned by, 13–14, 24, 34, 44–45, 54; literacy/illiteracy of, 5, 65, 94, 98, 102, 108, 139, 144, 181; marriages and family life of, 5, 65–67, 75–76, 78–82, 131, 141–43, 156–57, 204n10; memories of violence against his mother and grandmother, 12, 22, 36, 44–45, 49–50, 77; migration to Britain, 50–53, 57, 64–65; naval service of, 66; occupation as a tailor, 4, 5, 65, 75, 79, 82, 91–93, 131–33; oratory of, 5, 6, 7, 10, 100; physical appearance of, 4, 147, 156; poverty experienced by, 5, 74–76, 78, 81–82, 131–33, 143, 177; publications of, 6, 13–14, 22–24, 54, 83–87, 98–109, 138–40, 144–45, 150–52, 164–66, 169, 191; and radicalism, 5–12, 23, 53, 55, 58, 73, 78, 84, 95–127, 134, 137, 144, 154–55, 161, 167–69, 177–78, 187–89, 191–92; raised by grandmother (Amy), 5, 35, 37, 39–40, 49, 53, 193; rebellious character of, 5, 15, 24, 31, 34, 57–58, 96, 154, 179; and religion, 6, 10, 13–14, 34, 50, 83–88, 98, 119–21, 135–36, 138–39, 142–43, 154–55, 158; reputation of, 6–9, 154, 161, 169, 172–75, 179, 182, 190, 192; scholarship on, 181–92; sedition charges brought against, 14, 48–49, 116–17; Spence's influence on, 94–96, 100–101; teenage years of, 5, 50–53; working class advocacy of, 6, 78, 81

Wedderburn, Robert, works by: *An Address to Lord Brougham and Vaux* [. . .] *Suggesting an Equitable Plan for the Emancipation of the Slaves*, 164–66, 169, 178, 191; *Cast-Iron Parsons* (attributed, possibly by Cannon), 138–40; *High-Heel'd Shoes for Dwarfs in Holiness* (attributed, possibly by Cannon), 139–40, 209n13; *The Horrors of Slavery*, 23–24, 142, 152, 153, 157; *The Horrors of Slavery and Other Writings*, 186; *The Truth Self-Supported*, 84–87, 89, 100, 119. See also *Axe Laid to the Root, The* (periodical); "*Forlorn Hope," The, or a Call to the Supine* (newspaper)

Wedderburn, Robert (nephew), 37, 163

Wedderburn, Robert (son), 67

Wedderburn and Company, 82

Wedderburn Book, The (genealogy), 57

Wedgwood, Josiah, "Am I Not a Man and a Brother?" cameo, 77–78

Wellington, Arthur Wellesley, Lord, 118

Wheatley, Phillis, 181

White Lion tavern, Wyatt Street, 122, 124

White's Alley chapel, 154–56, 168

| 224 |

INDEX

Wight, John, 145–47
Wilberforce, William, 141–43, 154, 162, 164, 168–69
Willcock, Alexander, 39
William of Orange, 65
Williams, Eric, 196n8
Wilmot, John, *The Amatory Adventures of John Wilmot, Earl of Rochester*, 170
witches, 45–49, 135, 137
women: and obeah/witchcraft, 45–49; and prostitution, 157–60, 173; revolutionary role of, 106–7; Robert influenced by, 5, 14, 23–24, 39–40, 53–54, 106–7, 152, 193; work done by, 80, 82, 156. *See also* enslaved women
working class: and abolitionism, 9–11; conditions of the enslaved likened to those of, 11–12, 74–75, 168–69; and Fifth of November commemorations, 65–66; middle class's anxieties about, 147; and radical politics, 11, 75, 78, 96, 178; reform movement concerning, 6, 11, 78, 95–96; Robert's advocacy for, 6, 78, 81, 184; societal changes harmful to, 2, 97; work conditions for, 92–94. *See also* poverty
Worrall, David, *Radical Culture*, 185